PERFORMANCE AND MOTIVATION STRATEGIES FOR TODAY'S WORKFORCE

PERFORMANCE AND MOTIVATION STRATEGIES FOR TODAY'S WORKFORCE

A Guide to Expectancy
Theory Applications

THAD B. GREEN

QUORUM BOOKS
Westport, Connecticut · London

Library of Congress Cataloging-in-Publication Data

Green, Thad B.
    Performance and motivation strategies for today's workforce : a
guide to expectancy theory applications / Thad B. Green.
      p.   cm.
    Includes bibliographical references and index.
    ISBN 0–89930–678–0 (alk. paper)
    1. Employee motivation. I. Title.
HF5549.5.M63G75   1992
658.3'14—dc20   91–48121

British Library Cataloguing in Publication Data is available.

Library of Congress Catalog Card Number: 91–48121
ISBN: 0–89930–678–0

First published in 1992

Quorum Books, 88 Post Road West, Westport, CT 06881
An imprint of Greenwood Publishing Group, Inc.

Printed in the United States of America

The paper used in this book complies with the
Permanent Paper Standard issued by the National
Information Standards Organization (Z39.48–1984).

10 9 8 7 6 5 4 3 2 1

Contents

Preface

In 1980, at the age of thirty-seven and with a file cabinet full of scholarly publications, I quit a job as a university professor to start a business, with the goal of becoming an after-tax, cash-in-hand millionaire in one year—and did. The usual way: Right time, right place, right idea. A few good decisions, and a lot of good people. But there was one factor that was out of the ordinary. Employee motivation. That was the key to reaching my financial goal.

In 1986, when burnout and boredom converged, I retired and for three years did all the things you never do when working around the clock. Then the urge to write hit. Not the scholarly, academic stuff I had written as a management professor, but practical things to help managers. So, here I am with such a book. It draws heavily on my experiences as a management professor, management researcher, management trainer, management consultant, and finally and more important, as a management practitioner heading up my own company and motivating employees by using a theory of motivation seldom applied in the business world.

In the early writing stages, I was hoping the book would have considerable impact on organizations. A foolish notion, it seemed, until I started having individual meetings with top-level executives in major corporations to get their reactions to the book. I want to thank the following executives, who were kind enough to share their time with me, who were willing to give a thoughtful, honest appraisal of the book, and who were very encouraging in terms of the impact the book could have on organizations:

Barry Anderson
Vice President Human Resources
Lanier Worldwide

William J. Barkley, Jr.
Vice President Human Resources
AT&T

Leo Benatar
Chairman and President
Engraph, Inc.

Bryant Byrd
Vice President Human Resources
    and Communications
GTE Mobile Communications

William Caldwell
Vice President Human Resources
Equifax Inc.

Donald L. Howard
Vice President Human Resources
National Data Corporation

David F. McDaniel
U.S. Managing Director
Hay Group, Inc.

Don McKenna
Vice President Human Resources
Home Depot

F. L. Minix
Chairman of the Board
Crawford & Company

David W. Reynolds
Senior Vice President
Georgia-Pacific Corporation

Dr. Homer Rice
Director of Athletics
Georgia Tech

Michael Walters
Vice President Human Resources
The Coca-Cola Company

Maurice W. Worth
Sr. Vice President Personnel
Delta Air Lines, Inc.

Other business professionals also have reacted to the book in its various stages of development to help shape it. I want to thank the following people for their contributions:

Dr. David A. Brookmire
Vice President Human Resources
Digital Communications Associates

Kenneth G. Byers, Jr.
President
Byers Engineering Company

David Connell
Southern Company College
Southern Company

Rod Cook
Executive Vice President Human Resources
Bank South

Gerald Cox
Vice President Human Resources
Crawford & Company

Jerome J. Cushing
Manager of Program Support
IBM

Wayne T. Dahlke
Senior Vice President Marketing
Georgia Power Company

Beverly J. Freeman
Vice President Human Resources
Coca-Cola USA

Walt Gansser
Executive Assistant to the VP-HR
Coca-Cola USA

A. L. Gay, Jr.
President
The Georgia Marble Company

Paul Graves
Director, Staffing and Equal Opportunity
The Coca-Cola Company

Dr. Merwyn A. Hayes
President
HR Consulting

David L. Holton
Senior Vice President
Wachovia Bank

Anita C. Hope
Manager, Home Office Training & Development
Life of Georgia

Jim Kirby
Vice President Human Resources
Southern Company

Denise Larrata
Internal Consultant
AT&T

Andy Logue
Vice President Human Resources
Lithonia Lighting, A Division of
    National Service Industries

Marty McCommon
Manager, Leadership Development
Delta Air Lines, Inc.

Bernadette V. McGlade
Associate Director of Athletics
Georgia Tech

Dr. Dorothea Mayhan
Director of Training and Development
Lockheed

Ricardo Moncada
Division Human Resource Manager
Weyerhaeuser Paper Company

James D. Moore
Director BellSouth Management Institute
BellSouth

Robert T. Peterson
District Manager
Management Education and Training
AT&T

Ronald J. Remillard
Director, Training and Employee Development
Georgia-Pacific Corporation

Denny Schmidt
Asst. Vice President Training
Delta Air Lines, Inc.

Dr. Joe Simonet
Director of Training and Development
Coca-Cola USA

A. L. Sivewright
Management Consultant

Lynn Slavenski
Asst. Vice President HRD
Equifax Inc.

Dr. Morris S. Spier
Consulting Psychologist

John Steed
Management Training & Development
BellSouth

Kurt H. Sutton
President
Sutton & Associates

Dr. R. Roosevelt Thomas, Jr.
President and Founder
American Institute for Managing Diversity
Morehouse College

Chuck Tufano
Regional Manager
Georgia-Pacific Corporation

Michael B. Wilson
Executive Vice President
Georgia-Pacific Paper Sales, Inc.

Jim G. Wright
Vice President
Hay Group, Inc.

Thanks also go to Dr. Walter B. Newsom, who first introduced me
to the expectancy theory of motivation in 1978, when we were faculty
members together. Then there was Dr. John Harper, who taught me
so much about human behavior and, as my business partner, helped
make my early retirement possible. A special thanks goes to Lynda
Hart, who through a single courageous business decision changed my
life forever and helped make my writing career possible. To Dr. Jay T.
Knippen, my good friend for over twenty years, I want to express my
sincere appreciation for carefully reading the manuscript and suggesting changes that were important in the final shaping of the book.
I want to thank a family friend and three former professors because

they were instrumental in my getting a college education, and there-fore each contributed to making this book possible—Gus White, who was responsible for getting me a full athletic scholarship to play foot-ball at the University of Florida; Dr. John Wells, who inspired me there as an undergraduate; Dr. William Wilmot, who did the same for me as a graduate student; and Dr. H. R. Smith, who made it possible for me to obtain a Ph.D. at the University of Georgia.

Last but not least, I want to thank my family—my wife, Joyce, my daughters, Stacy and Shannon, and my son, Eslie, who always are supportive and make me feel special and loved. Thanks!

PERFORMANCE AND MOTIVATION STRATEGIES FOR TODAY'S WORKFORCE

1

The Expectancy Theory of Motivation

The diversity of today's workforce presents managers with a problem of considerable magnitude. Enormous differences among employees in every organization and work group mean that there is no "one best way" to deal with them. An approach that motivates some employees to perform well misses the mark with others. Employees have been telling us this for years, and now may be the time to listen. What we need are strategies for managing the individuality of each employee. A framework for such strategies, the expectancy theory of motivation, is presented here in chapter 1.

Fundamental to all the popular theories of motivation, including those of Abraham H. Maslow[1] and Frederick Herzberg,[2] is the notion that employees are motivated to perform better when offered something they want, something they believe will be satisfying. Yet many employees are not so motivated when faced with such opportunities. You know this from your own experience. How often have you seen employees offered something they wanted, only to discover they were not motivated to work harder and perform better? Most managers have seen this sequence all too often.

Offering employees something they believe will be satisfying is necessary, but not enough. Employees must believe they will get what they want. Employees are not motivated to perform better when managers focus on the "offering" and ignore the "believing."

Employees' confidence that they will get what they want involves three separate and distinct beliefs. The first is believing that they can perform well enough to get what is offered. The second is believing that they will get it if they perform well. The third is believing that what is offered will be satisfying. The popular theories of motivation deal only with the third belief.

MOTIVATING INDIVIDUALS TO PERFORM

Motivation and performance strategies that fail to address all three beliefs do not work, a finding that is stressed in the expectancy theory of motivation popularized by Victor H. Vroom.[3] That theory is reconceptualized here for clarity and applicability. Each of the three beliefs deals with what employees think will happen if they put out effort to perform. The first belief (B1) deals with the relationship between effort and performance, the second (B2) with the relationship between performance and outcomes, and the third (B3) with the relationship between outcomes and satisfaction. This is shown in the following diagram, which indicates that an employee's effort leads to some level of performance, the performance leads to certain outcomes, and the outcomes lead to some amount of satisfaction or dissatisfaction.

$$\underset{\text{Effort}}{} \xrightarrow{\text{B1}} \underset{\text{Performance}}{} \xrightarrow{\text{B2}} \underset{\text{Outcomes}}{} \xrightarrow{\text{B3}} \underset{\text{Satisfaction}}{}$$

More specifically, the first belief (B1) is the employee's belief about the likelihood (probability) that effort will lead to performance. There are other definitions for B1. One is that B1 is the employee's perception of how hard it will be to accomplish something. Another is that B1 is the expectation that effort will lead to success. It can be stated as the employee's belief about whether or not what is expected can be done. It also can be seen as the belief about the answer to the question, Can I do it? All these statements refer to the employee's belief about the relationship between effort and performance.

The second belief (B2) is the employee's belief about the likelihood (probability) that performance will lead to outcomes. B2 also can be stated in different ways. It is the employee's belief about the relationship between "what you do" and "what you get." It is the expectation that performance will lead to certain outcomes. It is the belief about outcomes following performance. It is the belief about the answer to the question, Will I get what I deserve? These statements all focus on the employee's belief about the relation between performance and outcomes.

The third belief (B3) is the employee's belief about how satisfying outcomes will be if and when they are received. B3 too can be stated in various ways. It is the employee's belief about how personally rewarding the outcomes will be. It is the expectation about how satisfying or gratifying the outcomes will be. It is the belief about how fulfilling or worthwhile they will be. It is the belief about how much value the outcomes will have in the future when they are received, rather than what their value is now. It is the belief about the answer to the question, Will I like it? All of these statements emphasize the relationship between outcomes and satisfaction.

Let's take a closer look at B1—the "can I do it" belief. Think of something you've wanted to do for a long time, but have put off because you're not really sure you can do it. Do you have something specific in mind? Now, how motivated are you? If you don't believe you can do something, it is hard to be motivated. The fact that you have been putting it off indicates that something is holding you back. Something has curtailed your motivation, and you have not been able to put out the effort necessary to get the job done. Does this mean something is wrong with you? Certainly not. When you don't believe you can do something, it is very difficult to be motivated to act. Let's look at an example.

Rob had been in sales all his life and had done well. He believed he could sell anything to anybody. When he was in his late forties, he took a new job, selling a different product in a different market. He was a "good old boy," and people had always bought from him because of it. Rob and his boss both learned quickly and painfully that his style of selling was not successful with the new market. His boss worked with him, and Rob worked hard, believing he could sell in the new market. As long as he believed he could do it, he was motivated and worked hard. Then one day he gave in to his frustration and said to himself, "I just can't do it." At this point, he lost his motivation. He stopped trying. The old saying "Can't never could" fits here. How often have you seen the "I can't do it" belief affect employees this way? How often has it affected you?

The discussion of B1 leads us to the first conclusion about motivation and performance. One condition for employees to be motivated to perform is this: They must believe that their effort will lead to performance (B1). Without confidence in themselves, they will not try as hard as they could. In fact, they may not try at all.

Now, take a closer look at B2—the "will I get it" belief. When employees see no chance that performance will lead to desired outcomes, they are not motivated. Why put out the effort to perform if you don't believe you will get what you want? Think of a similar situation that you are in now or might face. What outcomes do you want? Why don't you believe you will get them, even if you perform? How motivated are you in this situation? Why push yourself? Motivation doesn't come easily when you believe you will not get what you want even if you do a good job. Consider the following example.

Dick had learned the government training market well, having held various government training positions, before joining the company that employed Rob. But he had learned something else, too, something his new boss didn't realize at the time he hired Dick. Outcomes typically are not tied to performance in the government. Government employees often come to believe that even if you do a good job, you're not likely to get rewarded for it. By the same token, they often believe they'll get by even if they do a poor job. Dick made the transition from government to business exceptionally well in many ways, but he brought with him the belief that outcomes are not tied to performance. He just didn't believe he'd get what he wanted if he did a good job, and he did not believe he would suffer for poor performance. It showed. He believed he could handle the job, but his belief that performance didn't matter kept him from being motivated. How often have you seen this "I can't get what I want" belief affect your employees? How often has it affected you?

The second conclusion about motivation and performance evolves from this B2 discussion. Another condition for employees to be motivated to perform is this: They must believe that their performance will lead to expected outcomes (B2). If they think there is no chance of getting what they want, even if they perform well, they will have little, if any, motivation to do a good job. To be motivated, employees must believe they will get what they want if they perform well.

Let's take a closer look at B3—the "do I want it" belief. This is the belief about how satisfying the outcomes will be. How do employees view outcomes? First, they believe some will be satisfying while others will be dissatisfying. Second, different employees expect to receive different levels of satisfaction from the same outcomes.

The overall satisfaction employees expect from a set of outcomes is a critical factor in motivating them to perform. The positively valued outcomes in the set must outweigh the negatively valued ones for the employee to be motivated. If the positive outcomes are outweighed by negative ones, the employee will not be motivated.

The third conclusion about motivation and performance can now be stated. Another condition for employees to be motivated to perform is this: They must believe that the overall value of the outcomes will be satisfying rather than dissatisfying (B3).

The expectancy theory of motivation can be summarized as follows. Employees are motivated to perform only when all three of the following conditions are met:

1. The employee believes that effort will lead to performance (B1)
2. The employee believes that performance will lead to outcomes (B2)
3. The employee believes that the outcomes will lead to satisfaction (B3)

MORE THAN MOTIVATION

Motivated employees, however, do not necessarily perform well. The effort that results from motivation is not the only determinant of performance. Motivation and effort are required for performance, but alone do not guarantee it. What else is needed? First, employees must have the required skills. A motivated but unskilled employee cannot perform well. Second, the work environment must be supportive. A skilled employee who is motivated cannot perform well without the necessary resources (budget, time, information, manpower, equipment, tools, and supplies) and good working conditions.

To summarize, performance is a function of effort, skill, and environment, where effort is a function of motivation and where motivation is a function of three conditions, that is, of employee beliefs that effort will lead to performance (B1), performance will lead to outcomes (B2), and outcomes will lead to satisfaction (B3).

performance = f(effort, skill, environment)

effort = f(motivation)

motivation = f(B1, B2, B3)

Although employee skill and a supportive work environment are critical to employee performance, they also influence employee motivation. Skill and environment are partial determinants of the employee's B1 (belief about effort leading to performance), and B1 is one of the three determinants of motivation.

OTHER ISSUES

Several other issues are fundamental to understanding the expectancy theory of motivation. These issues include the questions of how you can give employees certain outcomes but only they can give themselves selected ones, why some outcomes are only instrumental in getting employees what they want, how the difficult task of tying outcomes to performance is easily accomplished for one category of outcomes, how events on the job have a major influence on the motivation and performance of employees, and how employee perception is more important than reality in determining motivation.

The outcomes resulting from employee performance come from two sources. One source is the employee's environment, from which come what are called extrinsic outcomes. As a manager, you have control over some of them but not others. Although you may be able to give the employee a pay raise, a reprimand, a pat on the back, etc., coworkers decide whether or not to accept new employees into the work group; customers register complaints and give compliments; and the organization provides health benefits and paid holidays, offers job security, and sometimes relocates or lays off employees.

The second source of outcomes is the employee himself. Some outcomes cannot be given to the employee by anyone else, but can be derived only from doing the work. Called intrinsic outcomes, they include the positive feelings associated with doing a good job, knowing you did your best, accomplishing something others couldn't do, achieving more than you thought you could, and just plain enjoying the work itself. Intrinsic outcomes also include the negative feelings associated with performing poorly, accomplishing little, and doing meaningless work.

Although some outcomes are satisfying because they have direct value to the employee (like praise and recognition), others are preferred because they lead to another outcome. That is, one outcome (first-level outcome) may be instrumental in the attainment of some other outcome (second-level outcome). For example, an employee may see a pay raise as an outcome for good performance. The pay raise will allow the employee to buy a new boat, car, or house. Knowing the satisfaction an employee will get from second-level outcomes, which you cannot directly offer, will help you better understand the employee's preference for first-level outcomes and therefore enable you to motivate the employee better.

A special point should be noted about the relationship between intrinsic outcomes and employee beliefs about the likelihood that outcomes will be tied to performance (B2). Because intrinsic outcomes are associated with doing the work itself, employees themselves control the administering of intrinsic outcomes. By choosing to perform, employees guarantee the receipt of intrinsic outcomes. Therefore, employees can be certain that intrinsic outcomes will always be tied to performance. If they choose to work, they get the outcomes. If they don't, they won't. This means you can perform the difficult task of tying certain outcomes to performance simply by assigning employees work that is intrinsically rewarding.

Another relationship influences the employee's motivation, too. Not only is the effort-performance-outcomes-satisfaction chain directly related to and determined by the employee's motivation, but the employee's motivation is also influenced in large part by what happens in the chain of events. This interaction works in three ways. First, B1: The employee gets feedback about whether or not the effort expended resulted in good performance. The feedback may maintain the currently held belief about effort leading to performance or may strengthen the belief or weaken it. Second, B2: Feedback also is obtained about whether or not outcomes resulted from performance as expected. Again, the feedback either maintains the current belief about performance leading to outcomes, strengthens it, or weakens it. Third, B3: When an outcome is received, the employee can determine whether it is as satisfying as anticipated. Based on this feedback, the employee's current belief about outcomes leading to satisfaction is either maintained, strengthened, or weakened.

As the B1, B2, and B3 of employees are either maintained or changed by what actually happens in the effort-performance-outcomes-satisfaction chain of events, employee motivation likewise is either maintained or changed. Change does occur. It may occur frequently and sometimes significantly. Employee B1s, B2s, and B3s, and therefore motivation, vary over time; the variation results from employee experiences and the feedback associated with those experiences. What it takes to motivate is different today from what it was yesterday and will be different tomorrow.

A word of caution is fitting here. B1, B2, and B3 are influenced not by what actually happens but instead by the employee's perception of what happens. A B3 example is the situation where an employee places less value on a sizable pay raise because of a mistaken perception that everyone received a large pay raise. A B1 example is the case where an employee does some work, gets no feedback, decides the performance wasn't good enough, and concludes "I can't do it" when in reality the performance was good. A B2 example is the case where the employee's boss may not communicate clearly what a good job the employee has done. As a result, the employee perceives criticism rather than praise and concludes that outcomes are not tied to performance. Perception is more important than reality. You can't simply assume that employees see reality the way you do. You have to find out what they are thinking.

SKILLS TO LEARN

So how do you do all this? What skills do you need? The expectancy theory of motivation requires that you have the skills to insure that employees believe their effort will lead to performance, believe their performance will lead to outcomes, and believe that outcomes will lead to satisfaction. When employees are not motivated, there is a deficiency in one or more of these three beliefs. Your goal as a manager is to be sure all three beliefs are strong. This book will help you develop the skills necessary to meet this goal.

Specifically, you will learn how to diagnose motivation problems and causes and how to select and implement appropriate solutions. The book is organized to focus first on diagnosing and solving effort-performance (B1) problems (chapters 2 and 3), then on diagnosing and solving performance-outcome (B2) problems (chapters 4 and 5), and finally on diagnosing and solving outcome-satisfaction (B3) problems (chapters 6 and 7). Chapter 8 shows you how to integrate and apply these simple, practical skills quickly and easily in one-on-one discussions with employees.

APPLICABILITY OF EXPECTANCY THEORY

Behavioral scientists generally agree that the expectancy theory of motivation "represents the most comprehensive, valid, and useful approach to understanding motivation."[4] However, understanding motivation is one thing. Being able to motivate people to perform is another. In this regard, expectancy theory generally has been regarded as "quite difficult to apply."[5] This is no longer true. The application model presented in this book convincingly demonstrates that applying expectancy theory to performance problems is simple and straightforward. The model has been developed and tested over a twelve-year period. It works. Hundreds of managers at all levels have been trained to use it. It works for them. You can make it work for you.

NOTES

1. Abraham H. Maslow, "A Theory of Human Motivation," *Psychological Review* 50 (July 1943): 370–96; Abraham H. Maslow, *Motivation and Personality*, 2d ed. (New York: Harper & Row, 1970); Abraham H. Maslow, *Eupsychian Management* (Homewood, Ill.: Irwin, 1965); and Abraham H. Maslow, *Toward a Psychology of Being*, 2d ed. (Princeton, N.J.: Van Nostrand Reinhold, 1968).

2. Frederick Herzberg, Bernard Mausner, and Barbara B. Snyderman, *The Motivation to Work* (New York: Wiley, 1959); Frederick Herzberg, *Work and the Nature of Man* (Cleveland: World, 1966); Frederick Herzberg, *The Managerial Choice*, 2d ed., rev. (Salt Lake City, Utah: Olympus, 1982); and Frederick Herzberg, "Workers' Needs: The Same around the World," *Industry Week*, September 21, 1987, pp. 29–32.

3. Victor H. Vroom, *Work and Motivation* (New York: Wiley, 1964).

4. David Nadler and Edward E. Lawler III, "Motivation: A Diagnostic Approach," in J. Richard Hackman, Edward E. Lawler III, and Lyman W. Porter, eds., *Perspectives on Behavior in Organizations*, 2d ed. (New York: McGraw-Hill, 1983), pp. 67–78.

5. Ricky W. Griffin, *Management*, 2d ed. (Boston: Houghton Mifflin, 1987), p. 401; and Arthur G. Bedeian, *Management*, 2d ed. (New York: Dryden Press, 1989), p. 404.

2

Diagnosing Effort-Performance Problems

Everyone experiences the uncomfortable feelings of inadequacy and lack of confidence at one time or another. Some people find themselves in jobs they simply cannot handle. Even when people are put into jobs that match their abilities, they may not have all the skills they need, particularly in positions involving a wide variety of tasks and rapid change. It also happens when employees are promoted or transferred, when jobs are redesigned, and when employees are asked to do something different from the usual or to do things in a different way. All these are occasions for employees to question their ability to get the job done. Nobody is good at everything; and everybody is asked, at one time or another, to do something he or she is not good at. When this happens, employees often conclude, "I can't do it." This is the belief that effort will not lead to performance (B1). In expectancy theory terminology, this is an effort-performance problem. When this kind of problem occurs, employee motivation suffers, as do effort and performance.

The widespread prevalence of effort-performance problems, where employees believe "I can't do it," generally is not recognized, and for good reason. Employees do not talk about it. They keep it to themselves. They even lie about it, saying, "Sure, I can do it," even when they don't believe they can. Why do people act this way? They often are afraid of the consequences of speaking out. Making others aware of a weakness tends to intensify our feelings of inadequacy. Beyond this lies the fear that people will reject us or take advantage of us because of the weakness, particularly when it comes to superiors. Employees sometimes do everything imaginable to hide weaknesses from the boss.

From the manager's perspective, what does this mean? Several things should be noted. One, every manager has employees whose motivation, effort, and performance suffer at times because of self-doubt. Two, employees tend to hide a problem, which may go unnoticed for a long time. Three, the impact can be costly and far-reaching. Motivation, effort, and performance suffer. Managers blame employees. Employees blame managers for throwing them into situations they are ill-prepared to handle. The work becomes stressful and less enjoyable. Manager-employee relationships become strained. Suddenly, things are out of hand. Why? Because the employee didn't say, "Look, I don't think I can do this," and because the manager wasn't aware there was a problem.

Effort-performance problems can be identified and solved quickly, and in many cases can be prevented all together, by applying the expectancy theory of motivation. You will learn numerous strategies in chapters 2 and 3 to diagnose and solve these problems quickly, easily, and effectively. The simplicity and power of expectancy theory will become evident.

In this chapter you will see that diagnosing effort-performance problems requires two skills, how to obtain the needed information and how to interpret it. Because these skills can be developed faster by starting with interpretation, this chapter will focus first on interpreting information and then on ways to obtain it. The next chapter will show how the diagnosis leads to solutions.

INTERPRETING B1 INFORMATION

As you interpret B1 information, you want to do two things. One is to diagnose the level of the employee's B1, that is, the extent to which the employee believes "I can do it." Does the employee believe "I'm certain I can do it" or "Maybe I can" or "I'm not sure" or "I know I can't" or what? When the level of the employee's B1 is something other than the "I can do it" belief, the second thing you want to do is to diagnose what is causing the employee to doubt that effort will lead to performance.

Diagnosing B1 Levels

An important kind of B1 information is what the employee tells you. Employees express their effort-performance beliefs (B1) in a variety of ways. Here are some examples. Can you interpret them? Look at each one and answer this question: Does the employee believe effort will lead to performance?

1. "I did this every day in my last job."
2. "I know I can do it. It matches my training perfectly."
3. "I can't do this. You're asking the impossible."
4. "I can't do that. Not until I understand what's required."
5. "I'll try, but my confidence really is down after I failed last time."
6. "I'm not sure. A budget this tight really makes it tough."

How did you do? The employees in responses 1 and 2 are saying, "Yes, I believe my effort will lead to performance," in one case because of work experience and the other because of training. Responses 3 and 4 can be interpreted as "I can't do it" beliefs, the first because of unrealistic performance requirements and the second because of a lack of understanding of performance requirements. The interpretation of responses 5 and 6 are the same—both employees are saying, "Maybe I can do it, but I'm not sure." The first is unsure because self-confidence has been shaken by a previous failure. The second is doubtful because management has provided a budget believed to provide inadequate resources to get the job done. "Maybe I can do it" beliefs are a signal that employees doubt that their efforts will lead to performance.

B1 can be viewed as the employee's belief about the "likelihood" that effort will lead to performance. You can think of likelihood as chance (like 50-50), odds (like 9 to 1), or probability (like .5 or .8). This idea of a range is important because an employee's B1 usually lies between the "Yes, I can" and "No, I can't" beliefs. To classify all of the in-between beliefs simply as "maybe" would be meaningless. We must know an employee's belief more precisely, though exactness is not necessary.

The way to get more precision is easy. You simply rate the effort-performance belief (B1) on a ten-point scale. A B1 rating of "10" should be given when you think the employee is certain that effort will lead to performance. You can award a "10" rating when the employee convincingly says something like "I can do it," "I'm sure I can," "I'm positive I can," "I'm certain I can," "I know I can," "Consider it done," "You can count on me," "I will do it," "No problem doing this," "No question about it," "I'll do it right away," etc.

Ratings of 7, 8, or 9 are given when you think the employee believes it is likely, but not certain, that effort will lead to performance. These ratings are appropriate when employees say things such as "I'm fairly certain I can," "I have a lot of confidence I can do this," "I feel really good about doing this," "My chances of doing this are very good," "The odds of accomplishing this are in my favor," "If things go well, I can do this," "I have a much better than even chance of being successful with this," "I can't guarantee it, but I'm almost certain I can," etc.

When you sense an employee is thinking "maybe I can," give a rating of 4, 5, or 6. These ratings fit when employees say "I have a 50-50 chance of doing this right," "I think the odds are even for accomplishing this," "Maybe I can," "I have a fair chance of getting it done," "The odds of being able to do this are in my favor, but only slightly," "I'm not real pessimistic about doing this, but I'm not very optimistic either," etc.

Ratings of 1, 2, or 3 are given when you think the employee believes it unlikely that effort will lead to performance. These "unlikely" ratings should be used when employees make comments like "I don't think I can do it," "It's possible I can do it, but not at all likely," "There is only a slim chance I can do it," "This is next to impossible to do," "The odds really are stacked against me," "I have about one chance in ten of doing this," etc.

Use the "0" rating when you think the employee believes it is impossible for effort to lead to performance. Rating B1 of "0" is justified when employees convincingly say things like "I can't do it," "There's no way I can do it," "It's impossible," "I couldn't do that in a million years," "I know I can't do it," "I'm certain I can't," "I'm positive I can't," "I could never do that," "No way," etc.

Can you use the B1 rating scale? Here are some examples of how employees might express their effort-performance beliefs (B1). Rate each statement to reflect the employee's belief about the likelihood that effort will lead to performance.

1. "There is no way I can increase sales 50 percent. Impossible. I can't do it."
2. "I can handle this. I'm absolutely certain I can."
3. "I believe I have a 50-50 chance of making this project successful."
4. "I'm not interested. I figure I have about one chance in ten to succeed."
5. "There is a slight chance I'd fail, but I'm almost certain I can do it."
6. "All things considered, my chances are a little better than even."
7. "I don't feel good about it. Success is possible, but not likely at all."

The interpretation of responses 1 through 4 is straightforward. In response 1, the employee is saying "no way, impossible, can't do it," clearly indicating the "I can't do it" belief. A rating of zero fits here. The "I can" and "absolutely certain" statements in response 2 clearly indicate that the employee believes with certainty that effort will lead to performance, making a B1 rating of 10 appropriate. When an employee says, "I have a 50-50 chance," as in response 3, the message really is, "Maybe I can." This response calls for a rating of 5 for B1. As in response 3, the employee in response 4 is telling us exactly what B1 is. With a "one chance in ten" statement, the employee is saying it is very "unlikely" that effort will lead to performance. A rating of 1 for B1 is appropriate here.

Responses 5 through 7 are reasonably specific, too, but more difficult to rate precisely. This is no cause for concern. Exactness isn't necessary and often isn't possible. You do the best you can with the information you have. Let's see how this works with the remaining responses. "Almost certain" that effort will lead to performance, as in response 5, means just that, not certain (not a rating of 10) but almost. Do you rate this B1 as a 9, an 8, or maybe a 7? It really does not matter. Any of the three is close enough. The "chances a little better than even" statement in response 6 suggests a B1 rating of 6 or maybe 7. Response 7 is a little tougher. "Possible, but not likely at all" certainly puts the B1 in the "unlikely" part of the rating scale, probably in the middle or lower part of it, for a rating of 1 or 2.

At this point you have diagnosed the B1 level for each of the seven employees presented. But what about the causes for the B1s with low-level ratings? Can you diagnose the causes for employees 1, 3, 4, 6, and 7? Only one of them gives enough information to identify the cause. Employee 1 says a sales increase of 50 percent is "impossible." An unrealistic performance requirement is causing this employee to believe "no way," "impossible," "I can't do it." More attention will be given to diagnosing causes later.

For more rating practice, go back to the earlier list of six employee responses. Rate each item, then come back here to check yourself. Remember, exactness is not necessary when you rate. Just make your best guess. When you finish rating each item, compare your ratings with the following discussion. How did you do? For response 1 the rating is high because of experience ("I did this every day"). This employee seems certain that effort will lead to performance. A B1 rating of 10 would be appropriate. In response 2, "I know I can" also suggests a B1 rating of 10. The "I can't, impossible" statements in response 3 indicate a B1 rating of 0. The same rating is indicated for response 4, again because of "I can't." Responses 5 and 6 are more difficult to rate with precision. Regarding response 5, it is clear that the employee's B1 is not in the "certain," "likely," or "impossible" parts of the B1 scale. A good guess would be that the employee is thinking, "Maybe I can," thus earning a rating somewhere in the 4 to 6 range. Response 6 is just as difficult to rate. This employee's B1 seems to be in the "maybe" range, or slightly higher, like a rating of 7.

Have you noticed the word "guess" several times? Are the B1 ratings a guessing game? That's right. You start with limited B1 information, like responses 5 and 6, and guess. Then you get more and more information and guess and guess again, until your final guess becomes a fairly accurate rating that can be substantiated reasonably well. This method is not a science, and you seldom know exactly what the employee's belief is. That's OK. Close is good enough.

As we continue interpreting B1 information using the B1 rating scale, let's add another dimension, B1 information related to specifically stated performance requirements. Take a minute to look at the following requirements and the matching employee responses. Rate the B1 for each employee.

1. Decrease cost 33 percent this month—"No way. That's impossible."
2. Finish the report by Friday—"No problem."
3. Meet the new sales quota—"I'm not sure. Maybe."
4. Close the deal by the 30th—"I can't guarantee it, but I'm fairly certain I can."
5. Ship the order by 5:00 P.M.—"The odds are in our favor but just barely."
6. Increase profit 25 percent this year—"That could happen, but it's next to impossible."

The "impossible" response of employee 1 clearly indicates an "I can't" belief, and a B1 rating of 0 is assigned. Employee 2 has responded with "I can do it." This is rated 10. This employee believes with certainty that effort will lead to performance. Response 3 with a "maybe" suggests a B1 rating in the 4 to 6 range. The response of employee 4 suggests a B1 with a high rating. The "I can't guarantee it" indicates the rating is not 10, but combined with the "I'm fairly certain" suggests a high B1 of 7 or 8. In response 5, the employee is fairly specific—"the odds are in our favor, but just barely"—indicating B1 is at the 6 or maybe 7 level. It's great when employees give specific B1 information. The "impossible" response of employee 6 would have a B1 rating of 0. "Next to impossible" would be a 1 or maybe 2.

How did you do? Can you diagnose employee B1 levels by interpreting things they say? That is, what is your B1 for diagnosing B1 levels? It should be fairly high, like a 7 or 8. If it is, great. If not, try rereading everything up to this point and concentrate on (1) understanding what you read, (2) thinking about situations as you are asked to do, and (3) practicing how to diagnose B1 levels where suggested. You'll do fine.

Diagnosing B1 Causes

Thus far you have been practicing only one of the two skills for diagnosing B1, namely, how to diagnose B1 levels. The other skill is how to diagnose B1 causes. This latter skill must be used when you find an employee's B1 level to be a problem. Diagnosing the cause or causes of the problem is central to selecting a solution and implementing it. For the remainder of this chapter, the emphasis will be diagnosing B1 causes as well as B1 levels.

There is another change in emphasis, too. Up to this point the focus has been on interpreting B1 information given verbally by the employee. Our attention turns now to interpreting B1 information obtained in other ways, by (1) observing employee behavior, (2) analyzing the skills the employee has in comparison to the skills required for the job, (3) analyzing actual performance levels compared to performance expectations, (4) analyzing the job for its impact on employee motivation, (5) analyzing resources available compared to those needed to do the job, (6) analyzing the impact of the organization on motivation and performance, (7) analyzing the way your management style influences your employees, and (8) analyzing the employee's B1 history. Let's look at some specific cases that demonstrate these ways of obtaining B1 information.

Case 2-1—Interpreting B1 Information Obtained by Observation. Perry worked for a management consulting firm as a project director. He had experience as a teacher and trainer in previous jobs, but his primary responsibility was managing large projects. Perry's manager asked him to conduct a one-day training program for a client. As Perry started preparing for the program, his manager noticed that Perry was putting out a moderate amount of effort but was wasting time, unable to concentrate on other work, busy but not getting much done, seeming anxious about the program, and frequently asking for feedback on his plans for the program. What was Perry's B1 for conducting the program?

Several things in Case 2-1 suggest Perry had a B1 in the middle range of the rating scale. He was putting out a moderate amount of effort, so his B1 was definitely not as low as a rating of 0 or 1, and probably not a 2 or 3. Yet he was not highly motivated. This indicates that he didn't feel certain that effort will lead to performance (a rating of 10), nor does his observed behavior indicate a B1 rating as high as 7, 8, or 9. A moderate amount of effort combined with the other observations of Perry are typical symptoms of a "maybe I can, but I'm not sure" B1—wasting some time, concentrating with difficulty, busy but not getting much done, seeming anxious, and frequently asking for feedback. A B1 rating of about 5, maybe a 4 or 6, would be a good guess.

Case 2-2—Interpreting B1 Information Obtained by Skills Analysis. Dewitt had been doing a great job in his sales support position. His sales manager started thinking of moving him into direct sales. After the manager assessed Dewitt's selling skills and considered Dewitt's own assessment, it became obvious that Dewitt's selling skills were not strong enough for the direct sales job. What was Dewitt's B1 for selling? What was it for sales support? What caused the low B1?

You see in Case 2-2 that Dewitt's performance in sales support was exceptional. His sales manager was thinking of putting Dewitt into sales right away to fill a pressing need. Luckily he decided to do a skills analysis first. He evaluated the selling skills Dewitt had and compared them with those required for the job. This showed, without doubt, Dewitt did not have two or three essential selling skills. He was smart and knew his capabilities. The sales manager guessed Dewitt's B1 for selling was somewhere at the "unlikely" level, a 1, 2, or 3 rating. He asked Dewitt and got a confirmation of this. Dewitt did not have the skills needed for direct selling. As long as he lacked the skills, he would believe "I can't sell," and therefore he would not be motivated if moved into the direct sales position. As far as sales support work was concerned, Dewitt was motivated. He did good work and he knew it. His B1 for his current sales support position was high, probably at the 9 or 10 level.

Case 2-3—Interpreting B1 Information Obtained by Performance Analysis. Robbie was a word processing (WP) operator/manager. As a WP operator, his skills were phenomenal. He could do anything and could produce more quality work than anybody. The standards he imposed on himself were higher than anyone would ever ask of him. As a WP manager, he expected nearly as much of everyone as he did of himself. What was Robbie's B1 as a WP operator? What was the B1 for WP operators with average skills that Robbie supervised? What caused any low B1s?

In Case 2-3, Robbie's B1 as a WP operator was a "perfect 10." You seldom see anyone with a higher B1. He could do anything and knew it. He did a great job meeting the high performance standards he set for himself. But what were the B1s for the WP operators he managed?

As a WP manager, Robbie established high performance requirements for each operator. Most of the people he hired were high performers like himself whose B1s were affected little by his high expectations. But operators with average skills had a problem. They invariably ended up concluding, "I can't do it." Robbie was a great trainer. He could and would help the operators develop skills to their fullest potential. Even so, it was difficult for average operators ever to perform as Robbie required. They had low B1s initially, maybe at the 4, 5, or 6 level, and even lower ones when they realized Robbie did indeed demand that everyone meet his stringent performance requirements. Performance requirements that were too high caused the B1s of the average operators to be low.

Case 2-4—Interpreting B1 Information Obtained by Job Analysis. Supervising trainers in a government-funded training program wasn't easy even though each supervisor was responsible for only three trainers. The trainers were providing eight hours of intensive training daily during the summer to high school youth who were economically disadvantaged and considered at high risk of becoming school dropouts and unemployed. An analysis of the job of the supervisors was revealing in terms of B1. The supervising part was well structured. There was a specific list of things to do, and each supervisor was trained well to do them. But supervisors also were responsible for unusual situations, like handling complaints by prominent politicians who were upset because a friend was not selected for training or because the training was not held in their district. Other demands included working with the media to prevent disruptions while videotaping a story on trainees for the evening news and working with a building manager to get a new training site when the air conditioning went out during hundred-degree temperatures. The number and variety of "unusual" things was staggering. It seemed the supervisors never handled the same situation twice. That's how unstructured a major part of their job was. How would you rate the B1 for most of the supervisors for the structured part of their job? What was it for the unstructured part? What do you think caused any low B1s?

For the structured part of the job described in Case 2-4, supervisors knew what to do (specific list of things) and how to do it (thorough training). As you would guess, B1s tended to be high, with ratings varying from 7 to 10. The situation was different for the unstructured part. Supervisors never knew what would happen next. They had no training for the unexpected and usually had to decide and act quickly without any guidance from their project manager. This was unnerving to some of the supervisors. The uncertainty about what would happen next caused them to question whether or not they could handle the unstructured part of their job. Most of the supervisors had B1s that would be rated 4 or lower for the unstructured tasks.

Case 2-5—Interpreting B1 Information Obtained by Resource Analysis. The job of the trainers referred to in Case 2-4 was structured. Trainers spent about thirty minutes "telling how" to do a specific skill, such as how to handle conflict with the boss. Another thirty minutes was for "showing how" to do the skill by having trainees view and discuss videotaped demonstration models. Finally, three hours was devoted to having each trainee "practice" the skill while being videotaped and receiving feedback from the trainer and other trainees. Video equipment that worked was essential to the success of the trainers. A few trainers saw themselves as the "fix-it" type who could repair just about anything. What was their B1 for effectively conducting the training programs? What was it for trainers who had no "fix-it" experience or aptitude? What would it be for trainers if additional resources, namely backup equipment, were made available? What caused any low B1s?

You would guess that the trainers in Case 2-5 who saw themselves as "handy" with equipment would have high B1s. They would have reason to believe they could handle most equipment problems. But this group of trainers was in the minority. You would expect trainers with no mechanical experience and aptitude to be fearful of equipment failures and believe they couldn't handle such trouble. If adequate resources in the form of backup equipment were made available, you would expect more B1s to be high.

Case 2-6—Interpreting B1 Information Obtained by Organization Analysis. A project management company was growing fast. Hiring and training hourly employees was not a problem, but hiring and training managers was. The labor market had a shortage of qualified managers. Employees in the company with the technical skills needed by project managers had no management experience. Both promoting from within and hiring managers from outside left the company weak at the project manager level. This problem was magnified because the rapid growth was accompanied by little or no training for the managers. How would you size up the B1 of the project managers in light of the staffing problem?

As you might guess, most of the project managers did not have high B1s. Without the necessary experience or training, what else could be expected? When they became project managers, they normally had B1s of about 5. After being in their positions for a while, the B1 for some went up dramatically, for others it hit bottom, and for a few there was only a slight change. The changes in B1s were directly related to performance. The B1 for high performers went up, for low performers it went down, and for the so-so performer it changed only a little. Whatever happened, happened. The rapid growth in the organization created a situation that was not conducive to assuring a high B1 for all of the project managers.

Case 2-7—Interpreting B1 Information Obtained by Manager Analysis. Mary worked in word processing for Robbie, the WP manager mentioned in Case 2-3. Mary had excellent WP skills and worked hard to be even better. But Robbie was the ultimate perfectionist. Good was never good enough. Something was always wrong. Robbie wanted everything perfect. What was Mary's B1? If it was low, what was the cause?

Mary was a victim of a perfectionist manager. Robbie wanted his staff to be perfect, "too." His way of achieving this was to help his staff learn new ways to perform better. He pushed them constantly. If they didn't do the work "right" according to his perfectionist standards, he had them do it over again. And again. This happened frequently. After facing Robbie's "it's never good enough" management style day after day, Mary concluded exactly what you would expect—"no matter how much I try, I can't do what Robbie expects." Mary's

B1 gradually declined until it was practically 0 and, of course, her motivation went with it.

Case 2-8—Interpreting B1 Information Obtained by Analyzing B1 History. Rita was a genius at handling accounting, financial, insurance, investment, and legal matters. She could do any and all of this. If something new came up, she knew she could learn how to do it, and she did. As the company grew, she needed a staff to help with the work. She had hired and trained numerous part-time and full-time employees, but there were problems and high turnover. Consider Rita's B1 in light of her past experience. Focus on her B1 for managing people separately from her B1 for technical work.

Case 2-8 suggests that Rita's history in managing people would leave her with a low B1. From the beginning as a manager, she had problems. She knew her management style needed to be different, but she did not have a lot of flexibility in her style. Consequently, her B1 for managing was very low. A rating at the 0, 1, or 2 level would accurately describe it. Rita's B1 for doing the technical work, however, was different. It was clearly high. She could do anything, and she knew it. Her B1 was probably a 9 or 10. Thus we can infer that it was not Rita's B1 for technical work but rather her B1 for managing people that led to her motivation problem.

The discussion of these eight cases has focused on diagnosing B1 levels and B1 causes. Compare your diagnosis with the following summary of B1 causes: Case 2-1—Not enough information to identify the cause. Case 2-2—Dewitt had "inadequate skills" for the sales position. Case 2-3—Robbie set "performance requirements too high" for his word processing operators. Case 2-4—The supervisors had "inadequate job structure" for a major part of their job. Case 2-5—Trainers had "inadequate resources" when there was no backup video equipment. Case 2-6—This was a "B1-inhibiting organization" in the sense that it did an inadequate job of hiring and training project managers. Case 2-7—Robbie had a "B1-inhibiting management style" as he imposed his need for perfection on his word processing operators. Case 2-8—Rita had a "history of failure" as a manager. An additional cause of a low B1 is "employee misperception," namely the misperception that skills, job structure, and resources are inadequate and the misperception that performance requirements are too high.

Our discussion so far has focused on diagnosing an employee's B1 level and the corresponding causes. You can see from these methods that doing so is easy. The key is to obtain the right information, and how to obtain it is the topic of the remainder of this chapter.

Before you read on, take some time to review. Make sure you can use the B1 rating scale and can identify B1 causes. For an exercise, determine what your own B1 is for doing this. Your B1 should be reasonably high. If it isn't a 7 or higher, reread the last few pages until you feel confident not only that you understand the method, but also that you can teach someone else how to do it. When you feel this way, you will have a high B1. Then continue reading the chapter to learn how to obtain B1 information.

OBTAINING B1 INFORMATION

The first and most important step in motivating employees to perform well is getting the right information. Getting it is the trick. Once you have it, the interpretation is relatively easy, as you saw in the previous section. Keep in mind that you want to accomplish two things. One is to diagnose the B1 level of employees. The other is to diagnose B1 causes when B1 levels are a problem. So, how do you get the information?

There are nine ways to obtain B1 information: communication, observation, skills analysis, performance analysis, job analysis, resource analysis, organization analysis, manager analysis, and B1 history analysis. You'll use most of them regularly, though some more than others. Although it is not necessary to use all of these ways, it is better to use more than one. Start by getting one piece of B1 information, interpret it by making your best guess about it, then get more information and guess again. Continue this "guess and guess again" process until you have an accurate diagnosis. Each method will reveal slightly different information. The more ways you use, the better your understanding of the employee's B1 will be.

Communication

Communicating with employees generally is the best way to get started. This means going directly to the source when you want to know what employees are thinking. Most employees will tell you their effort-performance beliefs (B1) if you give them a chance. It is surprising how much information you can get when you stop talking, ask a few questions, and really listen. That's the key. But this is where many managers screw up. They ask the wrong questions, or none at all. And they ask questions in the wrong way, making employees uncomfortable, defensive, or angry. Even when good questions are asked, failure to listen comes into play. Some simple but effective ways of asking and listening can make a real difference for you.

Three types of questions are essential: open, direct, and clarifying questions. Open questions are designed to "open the door" for a wide range of responses by encouraging and allowing employees to say whatever is on their minds. You should always begin with one or more of these open questions to set the stage for a successful discussion with employees. Start by asking, "How are things going?" or "How is your work coming along?" Follow up with other open questions that address your concerns more specifically. For example, you might ask, "What is your reaction to the new production quotas?" or, "How do you feel about the new project?" These questions will help you determine the employees' B1 level. When you think you have a good picture of that level, you can pursue the causes with other questions. Ask questions like, "What has happened to make you feel this way?" Open questions like this allow employees to tell you their perception of the situation and to explain why they perceive it that way. When asked in the effort-performance context, open questions normally will yield the B1 information you want and need.

Remember, if an employee has a low B1, you are asking for a confession of a weakness—"I can't do it"—to the boss. The intent of the open question is to create a situation where the employee feels free, and safe, to disclose this kind of sensitive information. The right open question will accomplish this, and you will be flooded with invaluable B1 information. You may be surprised how much your employees will reveal when given the chance.

A few standard open questions have proven to be successful over the years in obtaining B1 information. Use them verbatim, or change the wording so they feel right to you. In either case, they will work.

To Diagnose B1 Level

—"How's your work coming along?"
—"How are things going?"
—"Now that we've gone over this, what do you think?"
—"What do you think about our performance standards?"
—"How can I help you get ready for this?"
—"How do you feel about tackling this new assignment?"

To Diagnose B1 Causes

—"What's causing you to have doubts?"
—"What's behind the way you feel?"
—"What's making you question yourself?"
—"What's happened to cause this?"

Next, you can use the second type of question, the direct question, to address specific issues the employee did not elaborate on. Direct questions are designed to direct employees to respond to specific issues. They leave little room for them to respond with whatever is on their mind. For example, you might ask, "Have you ever done this before?" or, "Do you want me to explain this again?" or, "Can you handle this assignment?"

You can see that direct questions get right to the point. As a result, they can make employees feel uncomfortable, especially if asked without first creating the appropriate environment. Remember not to skip the first step of asking a few open questions. Besides, without the open questions, (1) you would not know which direct questions would be most helpful to your diagnosis, (2) you might not get all the B1 information you need, (3) employees may become frustrated because you didn't make it easy for them to tell you everything they wanted to say, and (4) you lose some credibility. Using open questions followed by direct questions works best.

Several direct questions that have become standard over the years are listed at the end of this paragraph. Although direct questions often call for yes/no answers, they tend to have the same effect as open questions. Employees generally go beyond the "yes" or "no" to tell you what they are thinking. You can use most of these questions verbatim, but vary the wording as you feel necessary.

To Diagnose B1 Level

—"Is everything OK?"

—"Are things going all right?"

—"Anything wrong?"

—"Any problems?"

—"Can you handle this?"

—"Nervous about doing this?"

—"Can you meet these standards?"

—"Are you worried about doing a good job?"

—"Do you want me to explain this again?"

—"Do you want me to work with you on it?"

—"Are you ready to get started?"

—"Do you need any special preparation for this?"

—"Do you think you can handle this new assignment?"

—"Do you feel (un)comfortable with this new assignment?"

To Diagnose B1 Causes

—"Do you understand what to do?"

—"Do you know how to do it?"

—"Have we prepared you?"

—"Do you have the skills?"

—"Have you been trained for this?"

—"Have you done this before?"

—"Do you have any experience?"

—"Do you think our standards are reasonable?"

—"Have you had trouble doing this before?"

—"Have we laid this out well enough for you?"

—"Have we given you enough structure?"

—"Are your resources adequate?"

—"Are we giving you enough time?"

—"Do you need anyone else to help you on this?"

—"Do you have all the equipment and supplies you need?"

With the information employees give you in answering the open and direct questions, you will be able to come to some helpful conclusions regarding B1 levels and causes. However, to ensure the accuracy of the information and your interpretation of it, it is necessary to be prepared to use a third kind of question. Clarifying questions are designed to get employees to clarify something they have said or implied earlier. The same questions can be used to obtain information for diagnosing both B1 level or B1 causes. Here are several standard clarifying questions. They all work. Give them a try.

—"Could you give me an example?"

—"Can you tell me exactly what happened?"

—"Can you tell me more?"

—"Would you run that by me again?"

—"Can you help me understand that better?"

—"Can you be more specific?"

—"I don't understand." (Same effect as a question.)

With the answers to all your questions, you should be able to make a fairly accurate B1 diagnosis.

But let's not forget that asking questions is only part of the process. You will recall that listening is the other part, and listening is much more than passively keeping your ears open. Effective listening is an active process, and there are four active-listening techniques that are easy to use, yet invaluable for getting B1 information. The techniques are restating, summarizing, responding to nonverbal messages, and responding to feelings.

Restating is periodically repeating, in your own words, something of importance that the employee has just told you. Some typical examples of B1 restatements are as follows:

To Diagnose B1 Level

—"What you're saying is that with about one more week of training you can handle the job on your own."

—"Sounds like you're confident you can handle this."

—"You've mentioned a couple of times that you're a little uncomfortable about doing this."

—"So you've done something similar to this and think you'll catch on to it quickly."

To Diagnose B1 Causes

—"Basically the job is more technical than you expected, and you don't think you can learn all the technical stuff."

—"The main problem, then, is the confusion about what we're expecting you to do."

—"So you think we're expecting too much from you."

—"You're saying that the budget doesn't allow for the staffing needed to get the job done."

—"Sounds like your self-confidence has been pretty low since you were part of the big layoff at the last place you worked."

But why restate? It seems so trivial, but you can be the judge. Restating accomplishes the following: lets employees know you are listening; shows you understand what they said; allows employees to correct any inaccuracies in your restatement; permits them to complete any incompleteness in your restatement; encourages them to give you more information about the issue you restated; and makes employees feel good to know you are listening, understanding, and making it easy for them to talk. It makes sense. Doing something as simple as restating what an employee says can benefit both of you.

Another listening technique is summarizing, which means restating two or more major things that have been discussed. When used during a B1 diagnosis, summarizing usually includes only things the employee has told you, not anything you have said. Remember, you're only asking questions and listening, not giving information. Always summarize at the end of the conversation, but one or more prior and shorter summaries may be helpful if the conversation is long or if the employee is giving a lot of information. In any case, the final summary should include a statement of your understanding of the employee's B1. Here are some examples of common B1 summaries.

To Diagnose B1 Level

—"I'm hearing you say three things—you feel certain you can handle this, you see no reason that you can't complete it on time, and you'd like to get started on it tomorrow."

—"OK, you're discouraged about having to learn to operate the new equipment on your own, you don't think you'll ever be able to learn it, and you're about ready to give up."

To Diagnose B1 Causes

—"Let me summarize what I think you're saying. First, you think we're expecting too much too soon from everybody, including yourself. Second, you'd like a chance to explain what's going on in the field that makes you and the others feel this way."

—"If I understand you correctly, you're saying you did this in your last job, but it's been a while and you're not sure you can operate the newer equipment."

—"You're making three main points. One, you're uncertain about taking on more responsibility. Two, this happened in your last job and you couldn't handle it. Three, you'd rather pass up the promotion than have it happen again."

All of the reasons for restating apply to summarizing. In addition, the summary that concludes the discussion has the benefit of pulling the essence of the conversation together to give a feeling of closure to both you and the employee. Closure is important, whether you have concluded the employee has a B1 problem or not. You don't want the time spent to be viewed as a nice conversation that led nowhere, especially to no conclusion or action.

Responding to nonverbal messages is the third way to listen in an active rather than a passive way. This technique calls for you to say something when you pick up a nonverbal cue from an employee. Most managers tend to see the nonverbal, think about what it may mean, and store it away for later use. It is better to respond to a nonverbal message. You do so in basically the same way you restate a verbal message. Simply state what you think the employee has told you with the nonverbal message. You might say, "You're frowning, and I'm wondering if I might have confused you." Or, "Your smile seems to be saying you're fairly certain you can handle this." Nonverbal messages normally convey information about B1 levels, not B1 causes. But when you respond to them, the employee may go beyond telling you about their B1 level and also talk about causes behind it. Here are some examples of responding to nonverbal messages.

—"I know you said you could handle this, but the tone of your voice sounds like you're not too confident about it."

—"Judging from the look on your face, you seem worried about meeting the deadline."

—"You're saying you feel fairly confident you can do it, but that smile seems to be saying you're absolutely certain."

—"You seem nervous about making the presentation next week."

—"You've looked down-and-out ever since you started on the new project."

—"You say you can handle the assignment, but the frown on your forehead and the shaking of your head 'no' lead me to believe you might have some doubt."

The advantage of responding to nonverbal messages is that it lets employees know not only that you are listening, but also that you are sensitive to other things they are projecting. Employees will confirm or correct what you have said, and they usually will go on to give information you otherwise would not have gotten. All this makes employees feel good about themselves and very good about you. Both of you come out ahead when you use this simple technique.

The fourth active-listening technique is responding to feelings. This simply means saying something to acknowledge the employee's feelings, nothing more. There is no need to evaluate or judge their feelings. Simply let them know you recognize the feelings they have. In your response it is best to (1) name the feeling you think you see and (2) name the thing that seems to be causing it, as shown in the first three examples following this paragraph. Notice in the fourth example that the response can be in the form of a question. The fifth example shows how you can name the feeling, while omitting the cause when you're unsure of it. Although an employee's feelings may show B1 levels, it is hard to pick up B1 causes directly from such feelings. However, your response to the feelings likely will open the door for the employee to tell you much more.

1. "Looks like you're frustrated about not being able to get your work done on time."

2. "You seem pleased with how fast you're catching on to the new system."

3. "Sounds like you're upset about ranking last in production for the month."

4. "Are you hurt that we've helped everybody but you catch up on the backlog of work?"

5. "It seems like you've really been encouraged for the past several days."

Why respond to feelings? First, your response lets employees know you are aware of their feelings. Second, it helps diffuse the damaging effects of feelings like anger, hate, or vengefulness. Third, it allows and encourages employees to talk freely about their feelings and what is behind them. Fourth, it makes employees feel better about themselves and about you. Fifth, you will find yourself with a great deal more information about the cause of the employee's feelings, about the employee's effort-performance belief (B1), and about the extent to which these feelings are affecting the employee. All this enables you to help employees deal with B1 problems.

Let's quickly summarize where we are. The focus thus far has been on the first of nine ways to obtain B1 information, namely, communicating with employees. Overall, this is the best way to find out about an employee's B1. The emphasis has been on how to do this by asking three kinds of questions and using four active-listening techniques. Asking and listening are easy. You should be able to do both readily.

Though it may take a while to feel comfortable asking questions and listening actively, you should have a reasonably high B1 if you understand what you have read in this chapter. The hardest part may be containing your desire to talk. But remember, you cannot determine the effort-performance beliefs (B1) of your employees if you don't let them talk, and they will not have a chance if you do all the talking.

Most managers have the tendency to quit here, happy with the information obtained from the employee. The problem is that you may not have enough information. Don't make this mistake. The consequences of quitting early can be very costly! Sure, you save a little time and can take action faster when you only get a little information. But these positives are minimal compared to the negatives associated with making a wrong B1 diagnosis. The employee's motivation, effort, and performance get worse, and you spend a lot of time dealing with the resulting problems. All this occurs because too little information was obtained. So, what do you do? You get B1 information from several sources. In addition to communicating with the employee via "asking and listening," there are eight other ways to obtain B1 information, as summarized earlier. There are four important things to remember about these methods. One, they are easy to use. Two, they require little time. Three, they all work. Four, they will work for you.

All this can be seen by looking at a situation that happened not long ago to a friend named Mindy. Once you know her story, you will be able to see clearly the importance of the many techniques for obtaining B1 information.

Case 2-9: Obtaining Information from Several Sources. Mindy was hired to fill a key sales position in a leading firm in the service industry. After one month on the job, her sales manager had obtained quite a bit of B1 information about her from several sources: (1) communication—"I can do it" was Mindy's continual verbal message; (2) observation—she was very enthusiastic about her work; (3) skills analysis—according to employment interviews and discussions with previous employers, Mindy seemed to have the skills required for the job; (4) performance analysis—as in the first few months she was not expected to close sales, her performance could be judged only on progress, which seemed fine relative to her performance requirements, her sales goals, which were realistic; (5) job analysis—this sales job was far more structured than most, with a well-defined market, a standard product/service, and a specific approach to selling that had been used successfully for years; (6) resource analysis—Mindy had a sales support staff and all the necessary financial resources; (7) organization analysis—the organization supported her performance with a lot of training and coaching, and the organization culture was performance oriented; (8) manager analysis—her sales manager was very supportive and encouraging and helped her in every possible way whenever she asked, which she was willing to do; and (9) B1 history analysis—a thorough check showed that Mindy had an outstanding sales record in her previous jobs. How do you interpret each piece of information? What is your overall conclusion about Mindy's B1 to sell?

The sales manager's interpretation of every piece of information in Case 2-9 was "high B1." There was no sign of a problem, at least not from the information he had. It was the information he didn't have that told the story. Mindy had a low B1. It resulted in a costly and painful situation. You'll see this unravel in the discussion that follows.

First, let's look at more information about Case 2-9. Mindy was given a long time to produce. She never did. The cost to the firm was in salary and benefits and especially in lost business. Mindy suffered more. Having a job she could not handle was agonizing, and getting fired was traumatic. The bottom line is this: When a manager doesn't identify and solve a motivation problem, everyone loses. How could the problem have been solved had it been identified earlier? Probably by moving her into sales support, customer service, or some other position that was a better match for her skills. But this was not an option by the time an accurate diagnosis was made. Too many performance problems had developed. Unfortunately, this story illustrates the damaging consequences when a manager fails to deal effectively with motivation problems.

Case 2-9 illustrates another point that cannot be stressed too much. Mindy's sales manager did not handle the problem well because he didn't know there was one, until it was too late. The failure was caused by a lack of the right information, which made it impossible to diagnose accurately Mindy's B1 problem.

Getting the right information takes only a little more time, doesn't cost much more, and seldom causes a long delay. The negatives, which are minimal, are far outweighed by the positive—an accurate assessment of the employee's B1 and, therefore, a chance to improve it.

There are two things to keep in mind about the nine ways to get B1 information. First, if an employee has done the same work before, and has done it the same way and under the same circumstances, and has done it well, you have no reason to suspect a B1 problem. However, seldom is everything the same. When the work is even slightly different, or the way of doing it has changed in some small way, or the circumstances surrounding the work are different, be alert to a B1 problem. Second, the information you obtain can sometimes be misleading. Case 2-9 is a good example. The sales manager's communication with Mindy eventually revealed how she hated the industry she came from, didn't want to go back to it, and was terribly afraid that if she lost her current job she would have no place to go and no way to meet her financial obligations. This fear caused her deliberately to disguise her "I can't do it" belief by always saying, "I can do it." That is, she repeatedly lied to protect herself. This is not uncommon. Employees have many reasons for not being willing to say, "I can't do it." Something interesting in Mindy's past also accounted for the need to disguise her low B1. We will look at this when B1 history is discussed later in the chapter.

Observation

Observing an employee often is a good method of obtaining B1 information. Though you're not likely to get conclusive information this way, observing can provide a vital piece of the puzzle. Don't forget. Every bit of information counts in the "guess and guess again" approach to diagnosing B1. Any one piece can be the key.

Observation, like communication, may sound easy. It's only common sense, right? The problem for many managers is not knowing what to observe. What do you look for? The answer is, anything that suggests employees are either "sure" or "unsure" about whether or not they can do the work. Here is a list of several things to observe: (1) performance—poor performance suggests a low B1, good performance a high B1; (2) progress—little progress suggests a low B1, good progress a high B1; (3) amount of effort—too little or too much effort suggests a low B1, effort as needed a high B1; (4) kind of effort—effort that is not directed suggests a low B1, well-directed effort a high B1; (5) concentration—poor concentration suggests a low B1, good concentration a high B1; (6) use of time—poor use of time suggests a low B1, time used well a high B1; (7) anxiety—high anxiety suggests a low B1, low anxiety a high B1; (8) requests for help—requesting too much or too little suggests a low B1, making requests as normal a high B1; and (9) confidence—showing a lack of confidence suggests a low B1, appearing confident a high B1. When you make these observations, be sure to notice not only how the employee is now, but also whether there has been any change over time.

The most obvious thing to observe is the employee's performance. Is it good? Is it poor? Is it better or worse than last week, last month, or last year? If performance is good, you have no reason to suspect a B1 problem. If it is poor, you know something is wrong, but poor performance doesn't necessarily point to a B1 problem. If the employee has performed well in the past doing the same work in the same way under the same circumstances, you would expect the B1 to be OK and would look to something else as the cause of poor performance. If the employee is doing something new or doing the same thing in a different way or under different circumstances, B1 may be a problem. But you have to get more information to know.

If performance were the only thing to observe, you would have to wait days or even weeks in some cases to observe completed performance. This would cause a costly delay in detecting motivation and performance problems. Instead of waiting, you can observe several other things. Let's take a look at them.

The second thing you can observe is employee progress toward performance. Is it what you expected? Better? Worse? Good progress suggests an OK B1. Poor progress signals some kind of problem, and it could be B1. Observing employee progress can tell you a lot immediately, avoiding the need to wait for the completed performance, by which time it may be too late to act.

Next observe the employee's effort. This is a twofold observation. Make sure to notice not only the amount of effort but also the kind. Is the effort too much, too little, or about right? Is the kind of effort directed and focused toward the task, or is it misdirected?

If the amount seems about right for the job, a B1 problem is not suggested. However, if the employee is putting out too little effort, it may be because "I've given up." In this case, a B1 problem is indicated. But be careful here. The appearance of too little effort sometimes can be explained by a high B1. The employee may feel certain that effort will lead to performance, and lead to it easily. Only a little effort is put out because "I don't need to work hard, at least not yet." On the other hand, when an employee's B1 is low, but not at the "I give up" level, the response may be to put out more effort than is needed under normal conditions. Extra effort sometimes is a reaction to a B1 that is "low, but not too low," because the situation represents a challenge.

Observing the kind of effort is important because employees respond in two very different ways when they have a low B1. One is to give up and reduce the amount of effort they put out. The other is to put out effort, but the wrong kind, a misdirected effort. When you observe, ask yourself, Is the effort well planned and focused? Does it have direction? If so, B1 is probably fine. If not, B1 may well be a problem. Is the effort misdirected? Is the employee putting too much effort into the wrong things and too little in the right places? Remember, this was one of the things the sales manager observed in Mindy. It took him a while to realize she was working hard on things she could do well (i.e., had a high B1 for) and avoiding those she didn't believe she could do (i.e., low B1 things). She was researching and planning rather than prospecting and selling. The kind of effort she showed was misdirected.

The fifth thing you can observe to get B1 information is the employee's concentration. A B1 that is low, especially one so low that the employee has given up, often is accompanied by several "lack of concentration" behaviors that can be observed. What are they? Be alert to changes in employee behavior, such as shorter attention span, not listening as well, focusing on work for shorter periods, more breaks, and talking with others more. When an employee is able to concentrate as usual, a B1 problem is not suggested.

Sixth, you can observe how well employees use their time. When the amount of wasted time is about the same as usual, a B1 problem is not suggested. If there is more wasted time than usual, you may have an employee with a low B1. If there is a dramatic increase in wasted time, you may be seeing an "I've given up completely" employee.

The seventh thing you can observe is the employee's level of anxiety. Does the employee display tension? Frustration? Irritability? Nervousness? These and other manifestations of anxiety certainly can indicate that something is wrong. One possibility is that the employee is reacting to an "I can't do it" conclusion. High achievers who must do well on everything are the best candidates for feeling and showing increased anxiety when B1s are low.

The eighth thing that can be observed is the extent to which an employee comes to you and/or others for help, information, and feedback. An unusual increase may indicate a low B1. Going to others rather than to you may signal a low B1 that the employee doesn't want you to see. This is a common and normal reaction. An increase in requests for help, information, and feedback is a very common low B1 behavior. "Can you help me a minute on this," or "There are a few things I need to know about this," or "Would you look at this and tell me if I'm going in the right direction" are typical responses. This does not always mean the employee has a low B1, but it indicates the possibility of one. When you hear such requests, be suspicious and get more information. A dramatic decrease in coming to you and/or others may be an "I've given up" signal from the employee.

The ninth and final thing to observe is whether or not the employee appears confident. Does the employee look confused, unsure, uncertain, and lacking confidence? Or does the employee come across as knowing what to do and how to do it? Can you imagine a wimpy ten-year-old bench warmer with no confidence at all walking up to the batter's box against a big, experienced twelve-year-old pitcher? Compare this with a twelve-year-old all-star slugger with all the confidence in the world walking up to hit against a favorite pitcher. Observing the nonverbal behavior of each player paints a picture of each one's confidence level.

This list of nine things to observe is not a complete list. It's enough, certainly, to do several things: to convince you that observations can yield B1 information, to encourage you to observe more, to help you observe better, and to inspire you to open your eyes further, beyond this list, to see all that your employees are telling you.

What about the observations of Mindy in Case 2-9? The most prominent observation was the enthusiasm she showed for her work, as mentioned in the summary of information in Case 2-9. Such a high level of enthusiasm can be misleading. Enthusiasm can mistakenly get translated as "she's motivated" to perform. Once this conclusion is reached, others follow, such as there being no need to worry and no need to obtain more information. Employee enthusiasm can lull you to sleep and keep you from seeing a motivation problem until it's too late.

Let's revisit Case 2-1. It was used to illustrate how to interpret B1 information obtained by observation. Perry had been asked to prepare for and conduct a one-day training program, with two weeks to prepare. Using the list of "things to observe" as a guide for observing Perry during his first week of preparation, here is what you would have seen. He was only making a fair amount of progress and was putting more effort into it than really was necessary. His effort was not well directed, as he skipped from one thing to another without following a plan. His concentration was poor at times, good at others, but overall was no better than fair. He was wasting a good bit of time sitting, staring, and walking around as if he were confused. His nonverbal behaviors, especially facial expressions, suggested some anxiety, although not an extreme amount. He made more requests than usual for ideas, for where to find information, and for reactions to what he was doing. He was not the perfect picture of confidence. None of this is hard to see, if we know what we're looking for. The battle usually is won when you know what to observe. Now you do.

But remember, observations are by no means foolproof. However, when all your observations are added together and then combined with the information obtained in other ways, your chances of correctly diagnosing an employee's B1 are good.

Skills Analysis

A skills analysis is a comparison of the skills an employee has with the skills required for the job. This method of determining an employee's B1 is more difficult than it may seem at first. There are several problems.

The first is that, although you may accurately conclude that the employee has all the required skills, the employee's B1 may not be high. This happens when the employee believes the skill requirements are greater than they really are or when the employee simply is unsure about how well his or her skills measure up. In either case, the employee's conclusion, inaccurate as it may be, is, "I don't have the required skills." The employee's B1 may thus be lower than your skills analysis alone suggests.

The second problem also stems from a difference between your skills analysis and the employee's assessment of the situation. When you accurately conclude the employee has a skill deficiency, you cannot necessarily diagnose a low B1. Employees sometimes underestimate the skills required for the job, and at other times they overestimate the skills they possess. Either mistake, and certainly both of them together, can cause the employee to have a B1 that is higher than you would conclude using only a skills analysis.

You can deal with both problems in the same way. Don't reach a final B1 diagnosis based solely on information from your skills analysis. Instead, use the analysis as the basis to "guess and guess again." Make a tentative diagnosis to be confirmed or refuted in other ways, especially by communicating with the employee. Some questions you may find helpful are as follows.

Perception of Skills
—"What are the things you do best?"
—"What are you most comfortable (uncomfortable) doing?"
—"What are the things you'd most like to improve on?"
—"What kind of special training would benefit you most?"
—"What are your greatest strengths (weaknesses)?"
—"Do you believe you have the skills to do the job?"
—"Do you perform well when you work hard?"
Perception of Skills Required
—"What skills are necessary to do your job well?"
—"What else?"
—"What else?"

The third problem in doing a skills analysis is not being able to enumerate clearly all the skills required for certain jobs. Some jobs have skills that are more definable than others, especially those calling primarily for technical skills, like electronic assemblers, data entry operators, or operators of specialized equipment. It is more difficult to identify all the skills required in jobs that call for a wide range of skills, especially behavioral skills. The jobs of a manager or salesperson certainly fit this category. When you find it difficult to identify skill requirements, it will be difficult to complete a skills analysis. Because identifying the skills required for any job does take time and may not be much fun, most managers tend not to do it. Yet, for most jobs it is easy to do. Maybe now is the time to do it.

The fourth problem involves assessing the employee's skills. Not knowing all the skills to assess can be the first stumbling block. If you don't know all of them, it is impossible to make a complete assessment of the employee. Even when you know all of them, being able to assess each one accurately can be a challenge. The second stumbling block simply is forgetting to assess a skill you know is important or not getting around to it because of other demands on your time. Third, it is common to make the mistake of assuming the employee has a certain skill. For example, when employees have done a good job on a wide variety of assignments over a long period, it is natural to assume they can do most anything you ask of them.

The skills analysis of Mindy in Case 2-9 involved several of these difficulties. First, she overestimated her own selling skills. Second, she underestimated the skill requirements for the job. These estimates caused Mindy to have an unrealistically high B1 at the time she started to work. She portrayed a high B1, and that is what her sales manager diagnosed.

However, Mindy was not long in reevaluating the skills she possessed and the skills required for the job. When she did, her B1 dropped considerably. As mentioned earlier, she then covered up the low B1 quite well, and the sales manager's initial diagnosis of a high B1 continued to seem well founded, though it was wrong.

This high B1 diagnosis of Mindy seemed to be confirmed by a third factor. The initial skills analysis was far from complete. For example, it did not include an assessment of Mindy's ability to deal with buyer objections. Later it became painfully clear she was not skilled in identifying and overcoming objections. The buyers were different from those she had sold in the past. They intimidated her. For these and other reasons, she found it difficult to handle buyer objections. This came to light as the sales manager talked with her after sales calls and later from his discussions with a few prospects she had called on. But the original skills analysis overlooked the "overcoming objections" skill. It seemed only natural to assume she had this skill, because she had a successful record in sales. Wrong. She was selling a different product in a different way in a different market to a different kind of buyer. Looking back, failing to do a thorough skills analysis on Mindy seems foolish.

Thinking back to Case 2-2 illustrates another important point about skills analysis. In this case, Dewitt was doing a good job in a sales support position and his manager was planning to move him into direct sales. This type of move is similiar to making the exceptional production worker a production supervisor or making a sales manager out of the top salesman. The employee often does not have the skills required for the next-level position. It is much better, for everyone, if you discover this ahead of time rather than later. In the manager's desire to move Dewitt quickly into the new position, a thorough skills analysis almost didn't happen.

These examples of almost forgetting to do a skills analysis with Dewitt and hardly doing one at all with Mindy illustrate how easy it is to go wrong even when we know what is right. Trying to do too much too quickly makes all of us vulnerable to this mistake.

There is a right way to do a skills analysis. The company described in Case 2-4 and Case 2-5 is a good example. This company specialized in government-funded training programs. Each time work was begun on a new contract, from 10 to 160 trainers were hired and trained to work full-time for the duration of the contract. A skills analysis was used to near perfection in the hiring and training process. Several hundred applicants sometimes would respond to advertisements for trainers. The company had reached the point, after months of struggling, of knowing the exact skills required for trainers.

Instead of interviews, the applicants were put into a situation where they could be assessed on most of the required skills. Applicants were given one of the company's detailed trainer manuals, with time to read it and to prepare to conduct a short training session (fifteen to twenty minutes); each was assigned a time to return to conduct the session while being videotaped. A staff of three managers acted as the trainees and behaved in ways that tested not only the applicants' skills in conveying the material but also their skills in handling typical training room situations.

Self-selection went into effect. Applicants who believed "I can't do it" tended to select themselves out of the hiring process, leaving either before getting a trainer manual or before the scheduled time to demonstrate their skills. Some applicants who selected themselves out probably had the required skills but were afraid of being videotaped or just didn't like the idea of it, for whatever reasons. However, the majority of those who remained tended to have good skills and reasonably high BIs.

The videotapes of each applicant conducting a brief training session were evaluated by several staff members, often including key managers at the company's headquarters who were not present at the videotaping sessions. The reviewing of the videotapes made it possible to make a fairly accurate determination of who had the required skills. However, this was not the end of the process.

Applicants who seemed to have the required skills were offered an opportunity to attend sixty hours of train-the-trainer training, where they constantly practiced the required training skills while being videotaped and receiving feedback. Self-selection continued throughout the training as each person began to know whether or not he or she had the skills to be an effective trainer. At the end of the training, job offers were made. Those who accepted could perform and knew it. Each one had, without a doubt, a high B1. Under one contract, the company hired 160 trainers in a two-week period using this approach. One trainer was terminated for reasons unrelated to skill level. The other 159 performed well.

Although a skills analysis of this intensity is not always practical, it can be done for some jobs. Many corporations have used this "assessment center" approach for years to evaluate managerial skills. It has been used even longer to assess secretarial skills such as typing. There are many other jobs, especially those involving technical skills, where a skills analysis can be used on this same scale of intensity. Are there any in your organization? Certainly on a lesser scale, you can use skills analysis rather easily and effectively to evaluate the skills, and consequently the B1, of your current employees.

Performance Analysis

A performance analysis is a comparison of actual performance with required performance. This normally is a rather straightfoward way of obtaining B1 information. Simply measure the employee's performance. Then compare it with the performance requirements. However, doing this is not always easy. Neither is interpreting the results of this comparison and diagnosing the employee's B1. Let's see why.

Doing a performance analysis is easy when you know what the performance requirements are and when actual performance is readily measurable. As you know, this often is not the case, and doing a performance analysis can be a problem. Even when the analysis is successfully completed, interpreting the results can be tricky.

If the performance analysis clearly shows the employee is meeting or exceeding performance requirements, it usually is safe to conclude that the employee has a high B1. It is possible, however, that an employee performs well, yet concludes that "I can't do it." Several things can cause this mistake. It can happen if the employee does not know how to measure his or her own performance or does not know performance requirements. It also can happen if the employee is "yelled at" regardless of performance or if rewards are never given for performing well. In such circumstances, the employee's B1 likely will be lower than your performance analysis will indicate.

Suppose your performance analysis shows actual performance to be less than required? What is your B1 guess? Normally you would assume that the employee realizes performance is poor and therefore has a low B1. This assumption is safe when performance requirements are quantitative and actual performance is easily measured, as in some types of production work. When this is not the case, as in many jobs, employees do two common things that make this assumption questionable. Both are perception problems. One, some employees tend to overestimate their performance and in doing so conclude that their work is OK. Their B1 is higher than you might guess from the performance analysis. Second, some employees tend to underestimate performance requirements and conclude that their work is better than it is. As a result, the employee will have a B1 that is higher than it should be. This also means it is higher than performance analysis leads you to conclude.

What's wrong with a B1 that is higher than it should be? The problem is that the employee is motivated to perform only at their current level, believing that it is an OK level of performance, even though it does not meet the required performance level. As long as the employees overestimate performance and/or underestimate performance requirements, therefore believing "I can do it," they have no reason to change. That is, employees are motivated to perform poorly. You can identify this problem by finding out employee perceptions about both performance and performance requirements. Here are some questions you may find useful in doing this.

Perception of Performance

—"How is your work coming along?"

—"Are you pleased with how you're doing?"

—"Any problems getting the job done?"

—"Anything I can do to help?"

—"Are you satisfied with the results?"

Perception of Performance Requirements

—"What do you think about our requirements?"

—"Are our expectations clear?"

—"Do we require too much (little) of you?"

—"How do others feel about our expectations?"

Another factor to consider when actual performance is less than required was illustrated in Case 2-3. This was the situation where Robbie, the word processing operator/manager, imposed the unusually high performance requirements he had for himself as an operator on the WP operators he managed. Because these requirements were unrealistically high for operators of average ability, those operators developed low B1s rather quickly. Unrealistic performance requirements cause employees to have low B1s. When the performance analysis shows an employee is not meeting performance requirements and is a long way from doing so, it may well be caused by requirements that are unrealistic. Communicating with the employee can alert you to unrealistic performance requirements. The last four questions in the list preceding this paragraph can be used to obtain this kind of information.

Case 2-9 shows how clever and devious some employees can be when they anticipate their performance will not meet performance requirements. Mindy tried to disguise her low B1 by creating the illusion of good performance. When performance takes several months for completion, performance analysis focuses on progress toward performance. This was the situation with Mindy, who was not expected to make a sale during the first several months. Initially her progress seemed fine. Looking back on it, it should have been obvious to her sales manager that she was shifting focus from results to activity. She spent far too much time learning the product, preparing sales aids, researching the market, getting information on the buyer, and writing proposals and too little time on prospecting, making sales calls, and closing sales. What seemed like progress was not progress at all, but instead an attempt to cover up a low B1 by having performance redefined as "activity completion" rather than "results attained," thereby creating the illusion of performance. A performance analysis done properly allows you to see through this, to diagnose the low B1, and to take proper action.

You can readily see that diagnosing B1 by using performance analysis is not always easy. Be aware of where you are likely to go wrong. Always get information from other sources to confirm or refute any B1 "guess" based on performance analysis. Let communication with the employee be one of the other sources.

Job Analysis

Job analysis, in the context of B1, refers to analyzing an employee's job to determine the extent to which it is structured. A job is highly structured when several conditions are met. First, all tasks to be performed are clearly identified, that is, the employee does not have to handle unexpected tasks. Second, each task is clearly defined. Third, there is a specific way to perform each task. Fourth, the tasks are prioritized, that is, the order of importance of each task is known as well as any sequence required in performing them. Fifth, the end result upon completion of each task is clearly specified.

The more structure jobs have, the higher B1s tend to be. When there is little structure, employees often say "I can't do this" because "I don't know what to do or how to do it." Not knowing what will come up next and wondering whether they have the experience or training to handle it may cause employees to doubt their ability to perform. However, when jobs are highly structured, employees tend to have high B1s. They find it easier to believe "I can" when they know exactly what to do and how to do it. Not all employees like structure, but nevertheless structure does yield higher B1s.

It is simple to analyze a job and determine how much structure it has. Just look for the extent to which the five conditions mentioned earlier are met. Using job analysis is an excellent way of getting information that helps you make good guesses about employee B1 levels. But a job analysis does not take into account employee perceptions about the amount of structure the job has. For example, employees may perceive less structure than really exists and therefore have a lower B1 than you would expect from the job analysis. Finding out their perception comes from communicating with them, especially by asking questions and listening. Here are some questions that will help.

—"Is everything in your job pretty much spelled out?"
—"Are the 'what to do' and 'how to do it' clear?"
—"How much freedom do you have in your job?"
—"Do you have to deal with a lot of unexpected things?"
—"Are the end results expected from your work clear?"
—"How much routine do you have in your job?"
—"Do you see your job as having a lot of structure?"

What can be learned from Case 2-9 about the way job structure influences an employee's B1? Mindy's sales job had a lot of structure. The market was well defined, the product/service was standardized, and the sales approach was laid out well. It was not the most highly structured job, but for a sales position it was relatively structured. Mindy either did not fully recognize the structure or did not appreciate it. In her mind there was little structure to follow. The net effect was the same as if the job were unstructured. This further contributed to her growing doubt ("I don't think I can") and eventually a feeling of hopelessness ("I know I can't"). Case 2-9 illustrates that job structure alone does not determine an employee's B1. The employee's perception of the structure also is important. This means you must go beyond the job analysis to determine the employee's perception of structure.

Case 2-4 illustrates another point about the relationship between B1 and job structure. In this case, supervisors were well trained for the highly structured part of their job but not prepared at all for the unstructured part. For the first part they had high B1s, but for the latter their B1s were low. What was the effect of this on the overall B1 for the job? Their overall B1 tended to be weighted more heavily by the unstructured part of the job. Even though they spent less time on unstructured activities, the necessity of handling them properly gave them greater importance. It seems that a job with only a few unstructured tasks can have a significant carryover to the employee's overall B1 for the job, even though much of the job is highly structured.

Resource Analysis

A resource analysis is a comparison of the resources needed with the resources available to the employee. To do a resource analysis, make your best judgment about what resources employees need and compare that with the resources they have. In doing this, look at physical, human, information, and financial resources, as well as authority to do the job. Employees can do the job only if they have the right tools, equipment, supplies, or other physical resources. Certainly not having enough human resources or properly qualified ones can make it impossible to perform adequately. Not having the right information at the right time can cause failure. Having inadequate financial resources to acquire all the other needed resources also leaves employees with an inability to perform. Not having the necessary authority can make it impossible to do the job, too. So can too little time.

OK, so you do a resource analysis. You'll conclude that the employee either has or doesn't have the necessary resources. If you conclude that resources are adequate, what do you know about B1? Not much, actually. Just because employees have the necessary resources does not mean they have a high B1. Other things may be causing their B1 to be low. All you know is that inadequate resources should not be causing a B1 problem.

"Should not" is used because, first, managers tend to think employees have adequate resources and, second, employees tend to believe they don't. In the first case, manager bias may yield a resource analysis that concludes that resources are adequate when they are not, thus causing the manager to guess that an employee's B1 is higher than it is. In the second case, an employee may perceive resources as inadequate even though they are not, with the result being a B1 lower than it should be.

You know more if resources are inadequate. The level of an employee's B1 is directly related to the degree of inadequacy. If resources are grossly inadequate, to the point that the employee is unable to do the job, a low B1 is almost certain. Unless resources are grossly inadequate, your best bet is guessing that B1s are "not high." More information is needed for a more precise guess.

Whether the resource analysis concludes that resources are adequate or not, employee perceptions of adequacy must be considered. The most common problem is for employees to perceive inadequacy and therefore to have a lower B1 than you would guess. The best way to find out their perception is to ask. Here are some examples of the kinds of questions you can use.

—"Any way I can help you do a better job?"
—"What do you think about the resources you have?"
—"How do you judge the adequacy of your resources?"
—"How do your resources affect your performance?"
—"How would you like to change your mix of resources?"
—"What one new resource would you most like to have?"
—"What one resource would be easiest to give up?"

Organization Analysis

Now comes organization analysis as a way to obtain information to diagnose B1. What factors do you look for when doing this analysis? How do they affect an employee's B1?

One factor is training. Good training has a positive impact on an employee's B1, poor training a negative impact. Does your organization provide frequent, high-quality training to all employees? If not, you may have a lot of employees with B1 problems. If it does, high B1s are not guaranteed, but at least lack of training is not a major cause of B1 problems.

The second factor to consider is the organization's growth rate. Rapid growth often means pushing employees too hard and too fast without giving them the proper resources or training to do their jobs adequately. This contributes to B1 problems. Lower growth rates are less likely to produce low B1s.

The third factor to look at is technological change. Rapid changes in technology require employees to update their skills constantly. As this is difficult to do when things are changing fast, skills tend to lag behind requirements. When this happens, B1s fall. In companies with few changes in technology, skills are less likely to become outdated and B1s are less likely to fall.

The quality of new hires is the fourth factor to consider. If skilled employees are hired, there should be few B1 problems. But unqualified applicants often are employed. The hiring process may be the culprit. Those responsible for hiring in many organizations simply do a poor job. This is a common, though unnecessary, problem. Another culprit, sometimes, is a shortage of qualified people in the labor market. Unemployment rates may be low and available applicants untrained. Whatever the reason, if your organization hires workers who do not have the necessary skills, you will have employees with B1 problems.

The fifth factor is staffing levels. When an organization is understaffed, the tendency is to push up performance expectations for everyone, which in turn pushes down B1s as many employees conclude, "I can't do it." Also, employees are moved around from one job to another to cover for understaffing, and the B1 for some of these employees will go down as they are placed in unfamiliar jobs without the necessary skills. These problems are not as likely to occur when organizations maintain proper staffing levels.

Turnover is the sixth factor that affects the B1 of employees. There are two problems with high turnover. First, when there is high turnover, new employees with low B1s often replace those with high B1s. Second, when there is high turnover in jobs where the performance of one employee is dependent on another, the performance and therefore the B1 of longtime employees will drop as they find that new employees have fewer skills than the employees they replaced. When turnover is low, these two problems are less likely. However, turnover that is too low can contribute to B1 problems. This happens in bureaucratic corporations, unionized operations, and government organizations where incompetent employees with low B1s hang on year after year. This is a major problem many managers face.

The seventh consideration in organization analysis is available resources. Employees who do not have adequate facilities, equipment, supplies, manpower, information, budgets, etc., can and do easily conclude, "I can't do it." Every organization sees this to some extent. However, if it is a pervasive problem in your organization, low B1s can be expected.

How does the corporation represented in Case 2-9 measure up in an organization analysis? The organization was training-oriented and provided Mindy with more than adequate training. The growth rate was stable, as was technological change. New hires were not a problem, staffing levels were appropriate, and turnover was low. Organizational factors were not contributing to B1 problems in this company and were not affecting Mindy's B1.

The company in Case 2-6 was a different story. This project management company was having B1 problems with project managers. There was little technological change, staffing levels were about right, and turnover was low. The good news ended there. The company was growing fast, very fast. The project managers were pushed hard to do too much too fast. The company was in a solid financial position, and project managers were given all of the resources they needed. However, because of the rapid growth, they received little training other than some coaching from their manager and an exchange of information with other project managers. A third factor, new hires, compounded the problems of the growth and training factors. The company had difficulty getting qualified project managers from both promoting from within and hiring from the outside. It is not surprising that inexperienced project managers who received little training in a rapidly growing organization had low B1s and therefore motivation problems. The organizational factors insured it. An organization analysis could have predicted it.

Organization analysis is simple and straightfoward. You will be able to handle it. Most of the factors in the analysis are things you face every day. Many of them have a direct impact on you. Some may be affecting your own B1.

Manager Analysis

Now comes the painful way to learn more about the B1 of your employees, namely, by analyzing the way you manage them. There are five things for you to analyze.

The first is the expectations you have for employees. Do you insist that everything must be perfect? Do you frequently send work back so that it can be improved? Is good never quite good enough? Do you continually insist on "doing it right"? If you have perfectionist tendencies, some of your employees have low B1s. They conclude, "No matter how hard I work or how well I perform, I can never please the boss. Why even try? I give up." High expectations can be fine. But if they are too high, employees will conclude, "I work my fingers to the bone and I can't produce what he wants. I can't do it. I'm not killing myself anymore." Sometimes pushing for more means getting less.

The second factor is the way you react to poor performance. When employees don't meet your expectations, what do you do? Criticize them? Make it clear you want no excuses? Demand more work and better work? Tell them, directly or indirectly, they are stupid or lazy? Make them feel guilty? Employees interpret these responses as "I don't measure up" or "I can't measure up," and with this comes a decline in their B1.

Maybe you are a more supportive manager. When work isn't what you want it to be, are you patient with employees? Do you listen to explanations of what happened? Are you understanding? Do you help them improve their work by showing them better ways to do things?

Do you let them know you have confidence they can do the work? Do you offer encouragement to overcome mistakes and do better work? Do you give support when they need it? If you respond these ways, your employees are likely to conclude, "If she keeps on helping and encouraging me, I'll soon be able to do this as well as anybody," and eventually to believe "I can." And you'll have fewer and fewer B1 problems.

The third factor is the way you react to good performance. Not giving positive reinforcement can leave employees thinking you are not pleased. They may interpret this to mean that their performance was not satisfactory and then conclude, "I can't do it." Saying nothing can cause low B1s. Giving positive reinforcement, on the other hand, clearly lets employees know their work is good. This makes it easy and natural for them to rightfully conclude, "I can do it."

The fourth consideration is job matching. Are you hiring employees who have skills that match the job? Are you assigning work to employees who have the skills needed to do the work? If so, your employees will have few B1 problems, because they have the needed skills. Or do you hire people based on chemistry, enthusiasm for the job, ability to get along with others, loyalty to you and the organization, and potential to contribute? Do you assign work on the basis of who is available, who has been getting off easy lately, and who is eager to do it? If so, you are putting some of your employees into situations they can't handle. They will have low B1s, and you will have problems.

The fifth thing to analyze is the amount of structure you provide to your employees. Do you give all of them freedom and independence to figure out the best way to get things done? Do you believe the less you interfere the better? Do you encourage and allow them to be creative? If so, there are some benefits from your methods. But many of your employees, if they are like most, want and need structure. They want you to tell them what to do and how to do it. They may not want you to tell them every detail, but they want more structure than you may think. When they don't get the structure, they are uncertain about whether or not they can do the work. That is, their B1s are not as high as you'd like them to be. Employees will have high B1s if you make it a point to clarify the end results you expect from them, if you give detailed directions and instructions, and if you outline specific ways to do things when they are uncertain how to do them.

Two of the five factors for manager analysis are vividly illustrated in the management style of Robbie, the word processing manager in Case 2-3 and Case 2-7. He imposed extremely high performance requirements on his WP operators, and he was the ultimate perfectionist. Robbie was very much aware of this. In fact, it was a source of great pride to him. However, he was not aware of the impact this attitude had on his employees. Even if he had been, it would have been difficult to change. Lowering one's expectations of others and, especially, becoming less of a perfectionist are not easy things to do. Nevertheless, recognizing the need to change is the first step in doing so.

Case 2-9 illustrates three of the five factors, one dramatically and two with an interesting twist. The biggest mistake Mindy's sales manager made centered on the job-matching factor. This has already been mentioned in the context of skills analysis. Because the manager's original skills analysis did not reflect some of Mindy's skill deficiencies, the manager placed her in a job that was a mismatch between the skills she had and the skills needed. This was the big mistake. Had this mistake not been made, none of the problems with Mindy would have happened. But she got the sales job, and her sales manager influenced her B1 in an unexpected way. Although he tended to be a perfectionist and held high expectations for himself, he did not impose these standards on Mindy. But here is the twist. Like many employees, Mindy wanted her supervisor's approval. To gain it, she tried to be more "perfect" than he expected and tried to sell more than he expected. She was expecting too much of herself and eventually concluded, "I can't do it." If you are a perfectionist with high expectations, you may influence the B1 of your employees negatively even if you don't directly impose your perfectionism and expectations on them. Consider this in your own manager analysis.

In addition to the five ways discussed for analyzing your managerial behavior, don't forget to evaluate yourself on the seven factors mentioned earlier for organization analysis. Each of the seven can be positive for the organization as a whole but not so for the unit for which you are responsible. Are you sure your employees, all of them, are getting the training they need? Are you managing the growth rate or rate of technological change in your unit to prevent B1 problems? Are you hiring qualified employees and keeping staffing levels where they should be? Are you keeping turnover at a desirable level? Are you giving your employees the resources they need to do the job? If not, you may be producing B1 problems in your employees that in turn create enough motivation, effort, and performance problems to keep you busy, really busy!

Analyzing the way you manage is not easy. It's hard to be objective, hard to see yourself the way others see you. And you stand alone in doing it. Employees seldom give managers feedback about the way they manage. When they do, the feedback understandably tends to be slanted for their own protection. What to do? You may have one or two employees who will level with you. Or a friend in another department may know, or can find out, how your employees see you. The five factors just discussed plus the seven borrowed from organization analysis are a guide to the kind of questions to ask. There's nothing to lose by asking, except that you may not like everything you hear. But there is a lot to gain.

B1 History Analysis

B1 history refers to the employee's past beliefs about the likelihood effort will lead to performance. Let's look at some of the ways these beliefs develop over time and how they influence an employee's current B1.

All employees have a history that affects their B1. It leaves them with both a general B1 and a B1 for each specific kind of work they have experienced. A general B1 (gB1) might be expressed as "I believe I can do just about anything" (gB1 = 8, 9, or 10) or "I just don't have any confidence in myself at all" (gB1 = 0, 1, or 2) or "I'm never quite sure if I can do things or not" (gB1 = 4, 5, or 6). Examples of a B1 for specific work they have experienced would be "I've been typing eighty-five words per minute for years so I know I can meet your sixty wpm standard" (B1 = 10) or "I took a course in computer programming once and I didn't learn anything except that I don't have the aptitude at all for it" (B1 = 0).

A close look at a large number of B1 histories suggests several things. The general B1 seems to be formed initially over several years during the employee's youth. If the general B1 is low, it tends not to improve much over time. Apparently it takes a very long line of repeated successes to erase a general feeling of "I can't." When an initial general B1 is high, however, it tends to go down over time as failures accumulate, as they invariably do. The amount and speed of the decrease is a function of the magnitude of the failures. One traumatic failure can cause a general B1 to decrease dramatically overnight.

A general B1 is influenced by many things. In youth, the influences come from personal life. In adulthood, both personal and work life influence it. The B1 history of many employees is filled with agonizing hurt. These negative experiences leave nagging self-doubts about what employees "can" and "can't" do. For some, the doubting seems to be only occasional, but for others it appears to be almost constant. A look at some B1 history may help you understand some of your employees better.

All that you read here comes from the actual B1 history of several hundred employees. It represents what seem to be the most common causes of general B1s that are low and the most common causes of those that are high. Although this account does not represent research findings in the strictest sense, it depicts reality for the hundreds who have told their stories.

In an employee's youth, many things cause the general B1 to be low. Some common causes are (1) many failures or few successes in school, relationships, sports, and other activities; (2) mental and/or physical abuse from parents; (3) mental and/or physical things that result in an "I'm not OK" feeling, like a learning disability or being overweight or ugly; (4) having critical parents who say things like, "You're stupid," or "You can't do that," or "Can't you ever do anything right?" or "Why can't you be like your brother or sister?"; (5) having parents who loved and accepted a brother or sister more; (6) having a brother or sister who had more successes with less effort and fewer failures; (7) having a parent who abandons the family, as when a parent leaves and seldom, if ever, is heard from again or when parents divorce and one severs the relationship with the child or when an alcoholic parent abandons the family emotionally; (8) being totally rejected by a girlfriend or boyfriend, as when the person chooses someone else or calls off marriage at the last minute; and (9) having a super-successful parent.

Equally impactful personal influences in youth can cause a general B1 to be high. The most commonly mentioned are (1) many successes and few failures in school, relationships, sports, and other activities; (2) having supportive parents who say things like, "Nice job," "You're OK," "I'm proud of you," or "You can accomplish anything you want to"; (3) having parents who are loving and accepting; and (4) having the ability to deal with failures in a positive way.

As adults, employees experience things in their personal lives that affect their general B1. Although most employees say a "successful personal life" has a positive influence on their general B1, they do not tend to isolate one thing as more important than another. However, they frequently point out the following specific factors as causing general B1s to decrease: (1) failure in marriage, especially if it happens more than once or if the spouse leaves for another person; (2) having poor relationships with children, with blaming and fighting rather than love and respect, or a child who leaves home and doesn't return for years; and (3) having problem children, with academic failures, drug addiction, and criminal activity.

The personal experiences in the life of adults that have a positive impact on their general B1 include (1) successful marriage, (2) good relationships with children, (3) children who are successful, and (4) good relationships with extended family and friends.

In looking at the impact of work experiences on an employee's general B1, there are no surprises. The factors that have a negative effect predictably are (1) having fewer successes than failures; (2) being passed over for promotions; (3) having traumatic failures, like making a costly mistake, blowing a major decision, losing a major power struggle, or performing poorly on something important; (4) being a victim of a lay-off; and (5) getting fired.

Likewise, the factors in the employees' work life that have a positive impact on their general B1s are not surprising: (1) no major failures; (2) one or more big, correct decisions; (3) one or more great perfor-mances; (4) more successes than failures; and (5) recognition for suc-cesses.

However, three things that come from B1 histories are real shockers. The first is how damaging a single failure, either personal or work-related, can be to an employee's general B1. It is appalling how fast, how much, and for how long a single failure can lower a person's gen-eral B1. This finding should inspire all of us as managers to help each of our employees not to fail. But what can you do with those who have already had damaging failures? Objectively speaking, the best advice may be "don't hire/do fire" these people. The compassionate side says "hire them/keep them." Some great motivation successes come with these people. There are two things to remember, however. One, the range of things you can assign them to do is limited. Two, you must be very supportive. If neither of these is a problem for you, give these employees a chance. They may work hard to prove something to you and to themselves.

The second shocker is the overwhelming number of employees who have a general B1 that is low. Many, many employees suffer from a nagging self-doubt. This situation seems to be the norm. And why not? Think of the number of chances everyone has to succeed or fail—thou-sands and thousands. Of course, everyone has failures, and plenty of them. In many group situations, the reward goes to one "winner," and all others are seen as "losers." Sooner or later, doubt starts to creep in. Most employees expect too much of themselves, more than they expect of others. When they don't measure up, they start to doubt them-selves. They never hear or read that failing is normal and expected, but it is. They have failures, but so what? The problem is that they think it's not OK, and they don't know how to deal with failure. They start to doubt, and never stop. What's the point? Many of your em-ployees probably have a general B1 problem.

The third shocker is how well most employees conceal this general lack of confidence in themselves. You heard in Case 2-9 how Mindy lied to her sales manager over and over, and very convincingly, about her B1. Most employees will go to this extreme to hide a general B1 that is low, too. Think about it. When is the last time you talked to your boss about your confidence level? Have you ever covered up a confidence problem? Are you aware of the general confidence prob-lems in your employees?

Looking at employees' general B1s is important, but doing so is a step away from where you need to be to motivate your employees. The real B1 issue is the B1 for the specific work they are doing or might be doing.

A B1 for specific work is influenced by an employee's general B1 as well as other factors. If employees have no experience with a certain kind of work, their B1s for it will be determined by their general B1s and by the circumstances surrounding the specific effort-performance relationship. Employees' general B1s will dominate their B1s for work they have never done. The general B1 will cause employees to say hastily, "I can't," when they can or, "I can," when they can't. Maybe this helps explain why so many employees are not motivated to do things they have never done before. If employees do make a thoughtful assessment of the effort-performance situation, they may say, "At first I didn't think I could handle this, but I see now I can" or, "There's more to this than I first thought, and I don't think I can do it."

When employees have experience with the specific work in question, their B1s will be influenced more by this experience, that is, by B1 history, and by the current circumstances of the work, and less by their general B1s. If an employee has done the specific work before and performed well and if the circumstances are perceived to be the same now, the employee will believe effort will lead to performance again. If the circumstances are different in a way that might prevent good performance, such as not enough time to perform or inadequate budget, B1 obviously will be lower even though there is a history of performing the same thing well. If the employee has a history of performing the same work poorly, you can expect the B1 to be low unless the circumstances are different now in a way that will facilitate performance.

Be careful when you look at employee B1 history for a specific kind of work. Find out if both the work and the circumstances then and now are identical, or nearly so. If they are, you can expect employee B1s to be similiar to the past. If either the work or circumstances are different, beware of two kinds of situations. Both concern cases where the employee forms an inaccurate B1 because of incomplete information.

The first type of situation is this: If employees have a high B1 based on past experience for a specific kind of work and if they see the present work and circumstances as the same when they really are not, the high B1s will drop quickly, and you will have a motivation problem on your hands. That is, the beginning B1 is higher than it would be if they had complete information. This was part of the problem with Mindy, as described earlier in Case 2-9. She at first saw selling as selling, no matter what was being sold or to whom it was sold. She started the job with a high B1, which dropped suddenly when she realized the work and circumstances were different.

There is a second type of situation. If employees have a low B1 for a specific kind of work based on prior experience and if they see the current work and circumstances as the same when they really are different in a way that would facilitate performance, these employees will resist doing the work because they believe they can't, though they probably could. Their B1 is lower than it would be if they had complete information.

As their manager, you can and should help prevent these situations. The biggest part of doing so is knowing it needs to be done. Talk with the employees to see if there are any differences in the work and circumstances now compared to the past. If there are, help the employees understand them and formulate a more accurate B1.

Now that you know that employee history can and does affect current B1, the question is how to learn this history. You may get some of it from people who know the employee. It could be anyone—a past or present coworker, a friend, a relative, a neighbor, or a casual acquaintance. These other people can be a valuable source of information. The problem is that you can't systematically get an employee's B1 history this way. Information comes from others in bits and pieces and from time to time, but not in a systematic way and not necessarily when you need it.

The best source of an employee's B1 history is the employee. You will not get this history in one sitting. It takes time, but you can get it. And you get a lot of it if you talk informally, and listen. That's when most employees discuss their personal life and work history. When the door is open for this kind of discussion, ask a few questions and listen a lot.

What questions do you ask? Ask the ones that have proven to be helpful in getting information about B1 history. Examples are shown following this paragraph. All of them are open questions that let employees go wherever they wish when responding. You control where the discussion goes by the questions you ask and the way you respond with active-listening techniques. Just ask and listen, and ask and listen.

—"What is the best (worst) thing that ever happened to you?"

—"What are the things you are best (worst) at doing?"

—"What is the biggest success (failure) you ever had?"

—"What do you remember best when you were young?"

—"Who has influenced you most? How?"

—"In what way did your parents have an influence on you?"

—"What personal (work) accomplishments are you proudest of?"

How does this method apply to Case 2-9? It was mentioned earlier that Mindy hated the industry she came from, did not want to go back, and was afraid she would have nowhere to go if she lost her job and would not be able to meet her financial obligations. This was pointed out as the primary reason she disguised her B1 problem by lying to her sales manager. This extraordinary fear strongly suggests that Mindy had a low general B1, that is, something in her B1 history contributed to her general feeling that she could not get another job. The sales manager's analysis of Mindy's B1 history did not reveal this early enough for any meaningful action to keep it from being a problem.

Case 2-8 focused on an employee's B1 history for a specific job. In this case Rita had had a less-than-successful experience as a manager, which left her with a low B1 for managing people. This case illustrates how easy it is to diagnose an employee's B1, if you know the relevant history. You can know; just ask. Ask, shut up, and listen.

SUMMARY

There you have it. You have learned how to interpret B1 information and nine ways to obtain it. Each way is helpful in diagnosing both B1 levels and causes. It is not necessary to use all nine ways to gather information in any given situation. However, it is best to use more than one to be sure you make an accurate diagnosis. Communication with employees generally is the best way to find out their beliefs about effort leading to performance (B1) and to determine what is causing any B1 problems that are identified.

What do you think? Can you diagnose the B1 of your employees? If you try, can you do it? What is your B1? You have learned a lot in this chapter. You should be able to say, "I understand the diagnostic techniques. I have seen them applied in numerous examples and cases. The discussion has been practical, detailed, and comprehensive. There has been a lot of repetition. I know how to do it. I can diagnose B1 levels and causes in my employees. I can do it. My B1 is high."

3

Solving Effort-Performance
Problems

Dealing with effort-performance problems, where employees are having doubts about being able to do the job ("I can't do it," or "I'm not sure I can do it") does not have to be difficult and frustrating. Nevertheless, for many managers, it often is. Whether managers carefully think through the problem or handle it on the spur of the moment, the result often is the same. Employees do not change much, and neither does their performance. It is not easy to influence employee beliefs. The approaches that seem sure to work often don't, the ones least expected to make a difference do, and sometimes problems that are ignored solve themselves.

The difficulty and frustration stem mainly from uncertainty about what to do. Effort-performance problems (B1) are different from technical, mechanical, and financial problems, where information is more likely to be black or white and solutions right or wrong. With employees, who knows what they are thinking, what they want, and how they will respond? Because of this uncertainty, managers tend to feel uncomfortable and at a disadvantage when trying to handle B1 problems. This often holds managers back, sometimes causing them to ignore the problem. When they do take action, it frequently is in the form of a pep talk with a "You can do it" theme or a heart-to-heart talk with the message, "If you can't do it, figure it out." Whatever the solution, it tends to be the manager's best guess about what to do. Solving B1 problems, however, does not have to be a guessing game. A variety of solutions are available, along with guidelines for when and how to use each one.

In this chapter you will learn how to select appropriate B1 solutions and implement them. Solutions are a natural and logical extension of causes. Once you know what is causing a B1 problem, as discussed in the preceding chapter, selecting solutions is easy. Implementing them is surprisingly simple, too, when you apply the concrete suggestions regarding each of the thirteen B1 solutions presented in this chapter: skill building, job design, employee transfer, termination of the employee, communication, creating opportunities for success, changing performance requirements, initiating structure, providing adequate resources, changing the organization, changing the manager (yourself), positive self-talk, and positive manager talk. This structured approach of first identifying B1 causes and then selecting matching solutions gives you a powerful and practical way to handle employees whose motivation, effort, and performance are suffering because they have concluded that "I can't do it" or "I'm not sure I can do it."

SKILL BUILDING

Many employees have inadequate skills; when they do, they usually know it. They say, "I don't have the skills," and then they conclude, "I can't do the job." For employees who are diagnosed as having low B1s because "I don't have the skills," the solution is to give them the skills they need. Skill building can be provided in various ways, most commonly through training, coaching, and work experience. Which of these three methods of skill building do you choose to solve a B1 problem?

Training here refers to classroom training offered by either your own organization or an outside training group. Here are some guidelines for deciding when to go with training. Training normally is used when the following conditions are met: when a lot of skills must be learned, when the skills are difficult to learn, when considerable training time is required, when it takes too long to learn the skills on the job, when it is not possible to do the training at work, and when you can give up the employee for the training.

Coaching is the management skill of (1) telling the employee how to do a skill, (2) showing the employee how to do it, (3) observing while the employee performs the skill, and (4) giving the employee feedback from the observed performance. The idea is to work with employees one-on-one until you feel confident they can do the skill on their own.

What about guidelines to know when to use coaching? The following circumstances suggest the use of coaching: when only a few skills must be learned, when only a few employees need skill building, when a good "coach" is available to do the coaching, when the employee cannot be away from the job long enough to attend classroom training, when classroom training is not available, when classroom training is too expensive, when learning from experience takes too long, and when learning from experience is too costly.

Work experience refers to learning on the job by having the employee do work that requires repeated use of the skills that the employee needs to develop. Work experience is "learning by doing." When should work experience be used to solve a B1 problem caused by inadequate skills? The following conditions suggest using work experience: when the skills can be learned from work experience, when trial-and-error learning is not too costly, and when other skill-building options are not available.

In a few cases work experience alone will provide an immediate solution to a B1 problem. However, work experience combined with coaching can be an effective B1 solution in the short run because coaching speeds up the skill-building process. Just as work experience alone normally is not an adequate solution, neither is training. Although training may improve the employee's B1, the certainty of knowing that effort leads to performance comes only from work experience.

To summarize, skill building is the B1 solution to use when the cause of a B1 problem is inadequate skills. Skill building solves B1 problems best when (1) training and work experience are combined; or (2) work experience and coaching are combined; or (3) training, work experience, and coaching all are used together.

JOB DESIGN

Managers often find that employees have been placed into jobs where there is a mismatch between the skills required and the skills the employee has. This commonly is discovered when doing a skills analysis, as discussed in chapter 2. Such a mismatch causes the employee to say, "I don't have the skills" and then to conclude, "I can't do the job." When this happens, the employee has a B1 problem caused by inadequate skills.

An alternative to skill building for solving this problem is job design. Rather than building the employee's skills to match those needed for the job, the idea is to redesign the job to make skills required match the skills the employee already has. This is not always an option. But when it is, changing the job may be a faster and easier solution than changing the employee's skills.

When do you go with the job design option rather than with skill building? Job design is suggested when the job can be redesigned, when the cost to redesign is minimal, when skill building is not practical, and when skill building is too costly.

Using job design to solve a B1 problem worked well for two entrepreneurs early in the start-up of a company in the service industry. Case 3-1 summarizes the results of their diagnosis of the problem using skills analysis. Analyze the case and decide how you would redesign the jobs of each entrepreneur. Then read how they successfully did it.

Case 3-1—Using Job Design to Solve B1 Problems. Preston was friendly and outgoing, with a typical salesman personality. He also was very creative and unusually intuitive and could read people and markets remarkably well. It made sense for Preston to be in charge of sales/marketing and product development. Tom was the logical, rational, systematic type. He was a loner with a bent toward perfectionism and a dogged determination to get the job done. Tom was in charge of all operations. After a few months in their respective roles, both Preston and Tom were doing well in parts of their jobs but not others. Preston was a genius at identifying market needs, but he was having trouble guiding the development of new products to adequately meet those needs. He also was a genius at developing overall marketing plans, packaging products and services, and pricing them for both optimum profitability and customer acceptance; but his direct sales efforts were not as successful as expected. Tom was very good at developing and implementing plans and great at developing a structure for employees that ensured high-quality delivery of services. Because he preferred working alone, he did not supervise employees closely enough. He spent only part of his time in direct sales, but he had phenomenal success making large sales to a small number of clients. Preston and Tom were becoming discouraged and losing motivation fast in the parts of their jobs they felt they could not handle. How would you redesign these two entrepreneur-partners' jobs to improve motivation and performance?

The redesign that took place with Preston and Tom was this: Preston became responsible for (1) deciding on new products and services to put on the market, (2) determining their pricing, (3) developing and implementing marketing plans, (4) hiring key employees, and (5) identifying existing and potential problems in the overall operation of the company. Preston was exceptionally strong at each of these. Tom became responsible for (1) developing new products and services and (2) direct sales. He continued to be responsible for the operations of the firm, but he did so by hiring an operations manager who interacted with the operations staff on a daily basis under Tom's close supervision. This redesign changed the jobs of both partners to match their skills rather than changing skills to match their jobs. Skill building simply was not practical for these entrepreneur-partners in a start-up firm, but redesigning their jobs was. This redesign worked well.

EMPLOYEE TRANSFER

A third option for solving B1 problems caused by inadequate skills is to transfer the employee into another position, either in your unit or somewhere else in the organization. Rather than changing the employee (via skill building) or changing the employee's job (via job design), the idea is to place the employee in another position that results in a better match between the skills required and the skills the employee has.

When should this option be used? The following conditions suggest transferring the employee: when skill building is not feasible and/or too costly and when job design is impractical and/or too costly.

Is solving a B1 problem by getting rid of the employee a cop-out? Suppose skill building and job design are not options, for whatever reasons. If you do nothing, the B1 problem doesn't simply continue. It worsens. The employee's motivation, effort, and performance deteriorate, and attitudinal and behavioral problems escalate. You lose. The employee loses. So does everyone else who is affected by the employee's performance and behavior. Doing nothing is not an option. A transfer can be a solution for everyone, and a big favor to the employee.

TERMINATION OF THE EMPLOYEE

What if removing the employee is your only option, but a transfer opportunity is not available? Suppose the employee does not have the necessary skills and you can do nothing about it because training, redesigning the job, or employee transfer are not possibilities. What do you do? Let the employee continue working even though motivation and performance are poor? Even though other workers are affected? Even though overall productivity is lowered? Even though the employee's feelings of helplessness and hopelessness are growing and a poor self-image is developing?

When skill building, job design, and transfer are not solutions available to you, termination is the preferred option to doing nothing. Everyone, including the employee, is better off in the long run. Sometimes doing nothing seems less painful than firing an employee, but doing nothing only seems less painful.

COMMUNICATION

Communication alone sometimes can solve an employee's B1 problem. This is possible when a low B1 results from employee misperceptions. The most common instances are the misperception of inadequate skills, misperception that performance requirements are too high, misperception of inadequate job structure, and misperception of inadequate resources. Communication also is a solution when a low B1 is caused by an employee history of failure. Let's explore each situation to see specifically how communication can solve B1 problems with these causes.

First, employees sometimes mistakenly perceive their skills to be inadequate. This happens for several reasons. It is important to understand each of these reasons and to be able to identify them in your employees. This enables you to know what to communicate to correct the misperception. Let's take a look at the reasons and the communication solution.

Some employees have a perception of inadequate skills because they overestimate the skill requirements for the job. Because of inaccurate and/or incomplete information, they are led to believe mistakenly that they need more skills and/or better skills than are required. This causes them to conclude, "I can't." The B1 solution is to clarify exactly what the skill requirements are for the job.

Other employees underestimate the skills they possess, in terms of both number and level of skills, thus resulting in a perception of inadequate skills and therefore a low B1. The B1 solution here is to communicate with employees to help them gain a more realistic understanding of their own skills. Emphasis should be placed on skills related to their specific job, but attention need not be confined exclusively to such a narrow focus. This broadened view will help prevent potential B1 problems in the future, as the employee is called upon to use additional skills.

Still other employees develop a perception of inadequate skills because they mistakenly believe they are not meeting performance requirements. This can happen because they (1) do not understand performance requirements, (2) do not know how to measure their own performance, or (3) are told their performance does not measure up. All of these are very common, especially the latter, where employees are criticized no matter what their performance or do not receive rewards that communicate that "you're doing a good job." The B1 solution for employees who think they are not meeting performance requirements, even though they are, is to communicate with them to (1) clarify what is required of them, (2) show them how to measure how well they are doing, and (3) tell them, in some appropriate way, that they are meeting performance expectations.

Second, employees sometimes have the misperception that performance requirements are too high. This results from a misunderstanding of what the requirements really are. It is the case where the employees would agree with the performance requirements, if only they had complete and accurate information. The solution is to communicate and to give more information to provide the necessary clarification.

Third, B1 problems stem from the misperception of inadequate job structure. Remember from chapter 2 that job structure includes five components: (1) identification of all tasks to be performed in the job, (2) a clear definition of each task, (3) a specified way of performing each, (4) the priority for performing each, and (5) the end result expected for each. Unfortunately, each component offers an opportunity for employees to have misperceptions. If employees do not clearly understand each component, they will perceive less job structure than actually exists. Perception problems of this type can be solved by communicating and providing clarification of the component(s) causing the employee to think mistakenly that there is inadequate job structure.

Fourth, employees may have the misperception that the resources available for the job are inadequate. When employees think they don't have enough time, information, money, staff, equipment, etc., they conclude, "I can't do it," even though they may have all the resources they need. How can employees have misperceptions about the resources available to them? There are at least two reasons; they may be (1) unaware of all resources that are available for a variety of reasons, such as a typing mistake in the budget, not knowing a shipment of materials arrived last week, or forgetting the computerized data base has the needed information and (2) ignorant of the best way to use and to stretch available resources. Again, communication is the solution. When employees think the resources to do the job are inadequate, communicate with them to be sure they know what resources they have and how to get the best mileage out of what exists.

Fifth, communication also can be a solution when B1 problems are caused by employee history of failure. This solution works well in one particular circumstance. When employees who have failed at a specific task or job in the past see a current task or job as being the same, even though it isn't, they will have a low B1. If by communicating with the employee you can show that the work is different, or the circumstances in which the work is to be performed are different, the employee's B1 will be improved.

CREATING OPPORTUNITIES FOR SUCCESS

Often, when employees think they can't do something, they don't try, or don't try very hard. This frequently occurs even when they have the needed skills. Not being willing to try may come from the employee's incorrect perception that "I don't have the skills." This misperception may result, as discussed earlier, from underestimating their own skills, overestimating the skills required, or both. Regardless of what is behind the incorrect perception, the conclusion they reach is, "I can't." That is, they have a low B1. Creating opportunities for these employees to succeed is one way to help them overcome the incorrect perception and therefore raise the level of their B1.

What does "creating opportunities for success" mean? First, it means designing work situations where employees will be willing to use skills they think they don't have. That is, the work situations must lead the employees to conclude, "I'll give it a try." One essential ingredient for this accomplishment is to make the work situations seem safe. That is, help the employee see that there are no adverse consequences for "giving it a try." Second, it means the work situations must take place in an environment that guarantees employee success. This is the heart of the "creating opportunities for success" concept.

How do you create opportunities for success? It's called "incremental doing." It's simple. Just have the employee do things in small increments. Be sure the employee knows how to do each increment before moving to the next one. You can use a four-step process to create opportunities for success for your employees and solve B1 problems caused by either (1) perception of inadequate skills or (2) employee history of failure.

The first step is to break the job down into small tasks that the employee will be able to do successfully. The tasks should be as big as possible yet small enough to insure that the employee can do them. Tasks that are too big can be a setback for the employee. Tasks that are too small can be boring and, even worse, will be interpreted as meaning, "the boss really thinks I'm stupid." Tasks that are either too big or too little can damage rather than improve the employee's B1.

The second step is to use coaching, as discussed earlier, to lead the employee to complete successfully each individual task. That is, (1) tell how to do the task, (2) show how to do it, then (3) let the employee do it while you observe, and (4) give the employee feedback regarding (a) everything done correctly (positive feedback) and (b) how to do anything differently and better (constructive feedback). Repeat this tell-show-do-feedback process for each task until the employee can do all tasks well.

Step three is to have the employee do the complete job, whenever possible, while you observe. Even though the employee has successfully performed all tasks separately, "putting it all together" for the first time normally is not easy. It is important for you to be there to observe, and to help if the employee has a problem. Give frequent positive reinforcement, but do not give a helping hand until the employee has made every possible effort. Helping too much too soon can diminish a B1 that is on the rise. The employee should be able to do the complete job, although it may go more slowly than either of you think it should. Be patient. Patience will pay off.

The fourth step is to have the employee do the complete job unsupervised. This is the final test. Can the employee do it alone or not? When the job is completed, evaluate the work carefully. Take care not to discourage the employee if everything is not perfect. Give corrective feedback as needed, but focus on giving a lot of positive feedback. If the employee's attempt to do the complete job is not satisfactory, coach on tasks that are a problem, then repeat step four until the essence of your feedback is "you can do it" and the employee believes "I can."

This simple and easy four-step process is one of the most-needed yet least-used B1 solutions. When it is not used, B1 problems not only go unsolved, they are intensified. This means motivation, effort, and performance will continue to decline. Case 3-2 illustrates this.

Case 3-2—Creating Opportunities for Success to Solve B1 Problems. Jay was forty-five years old when he walked into his new office and found a personal computer (PC) sitting on the desk. A fearful twinge came over him. Although he had taken computer courses in college and had used computers often in his work, he had never had his own PC. The departmental secretary gladly promised to teach him how to type his own work. Her first lesson went something like this. "Here's how you turn it on. And how to set a margin. And how to scroll. And edit, insert, move copy, save, search, and so on. If you need any more help, give me a call." She left, leaving Jay convinced he'd never learn. But he tried, half-heartedly. As he expected, he couldn't make the PC do much. He asked for more help. She gave him another rapid-fire lecture accompanied by an equally fast demonstration. More frustration set in, as well as a growing feeling of helplessness. "I can't do this," was Jay's overriding thought. "I've tried, and I can't do this," he said.

What is your diagnosis here? Specifically, what was Jay's B1 initially? What was it after he tried to use the computer? Jay's B1 in the beginning was low. It was lower after trying to use the PC. The secretary was helpful, but Jay was getting too much information too fast and it seemed very complicated.

What should have been done in view of Jay's low B1? Since he had never used a PC, his reluctance to do so now suggests that he was either underestimating his skills or overestimating the skills required, or both. Probably both. This is a situation that calls for creating opportunities for success. The four-step "incremental doing" process outlined above would be easy to apply here. Simply identify all of the tasks needed to type with the PC and start working on them one by one using the tell-show-do-feedback approach. This would help Jay overcome the B1 problem that is keeping him from being motivated to use his personal computer.

By following the "incremental doing" process, here's what happens. Employees engage in self-talk throughout the "doing" process. It goes something like this as they successfully complete each task (each opportunity for success).

—"I wasn't sure if I could do this first part or not, but, hey, I did it. Maybe I can do the next one, too."

—"I did it again. Maybe I can do all of the parts."

—"I'm pretty sure I'll be able to do it all. I'm really clicking."

—"I never thought I could do the whole thing, but I did. I can do this now, on my own. I can do it!"

Notice the incremental increases in B1. You can always expect this pattern. When opportunities for success are created, you lead employees from "I can't" to "I can." Doing so is not difficult. Yes, it takes a little time, but it's not hard to do. The return on your investment certainly makes it worthwhile.

CHANGING PERFORMANCE REQUIREMENTS

Some things are not as easy as they seem. When a B1 problem is caused by performance requirements that are too high, the obvious solution is to change the requirements. But what do you change them to? How do you go about doing it? Sometimes this is easier said than done. Let's first take a look at the consequences of doing it wrong. Then a proven way to implement this B1 solution will be outlined, and a case will demonstrate how this approach was used.

What are the consequences of changing performance requirements too much or too little? Lowering performance requirements below the capabilities of your employees is one kind of problem. Not only will this cause overall performance to decline, but employees will also interpret this to mean you don't have much confidence in them. This may cause B1s to go down rather than up. Employees also will question your ability as a manager, because you are mishandling this problem. Not lowering performance requirements enough is a second and entirely different kind of problem. Changing requirements too little doesn't help. The problem remains, and it causes employees to question your sensitivity to the problem and/or your ability to deal with it.

How do you change performance requirements? How do you go about it to get the desired effect, namely, higher employee B1 levels? The best way is to get employee involvement in the change process. Why? Because it's the employee's job. Because it's the employee's B1. And because the employee may know things about doing the job you don't know. Involving the employee is a four-step process. Case 3-3 demonstrates each step.

Case 3-3—Changing Performance Requirements to Solve B1 Problems. A technical skills training company had gotten a contract to train 300 new employees for the opening of a lawn mower manufacturing plant. The lawn mower company was one of the largest in the country and produced top-of-the-line mowers. Management's goal for the opening was to reach standard production levels by the end of the first six weeks of operation. This was not a training-oriented company, but management realized the need for preopening training for a workforce that was inexperienced. Eslie was in charge of the project for the training company. He wanted this to be a very successful training venture. His plan was to design a training program that would "tell" employees how to do the operations for their station on the assembly line, then "show" them how to do them, and finally have them "practice" each operation until their production rates during training were equivalent to those expected after six weeks. Eslie was ambitious. The "tell how" part was to be accompanied by first-rate printed materials. The "show how" part was to feature professionally produced videotape demonstration models of all assembly line operations. He had the approval and budget to do this, as well as the ability and determination to pull it off. Shannon worked for Eslie and was responsible for completing all training materials on this project. Her work was satisfactory until Eslie moved up the completion deadline by four weeks to match the revised plant opening schedule. Shannon's effort immediately became less than satisfactory. When Eslie talked with her, she said, "It's impossible to complete the materials on time. I'm so discouraged I can't concentrate enough to work on them."

The first step in changing performance requirements that are too high is to prepare to meet with the employee. There are several things to do here. Be sure that "high performance requirements" is causing the B1 problem, as you suspect. Think about the consequences of action and no action as a way of getting things into perspective. Identify any constraints you're faced with in changing the performance requirements. Plan out what you will say when you meet with the employee. Here is basically what the manager said to himself at this step.

Eslie: "Shannon is the best at designing this kind of training program, and she knows it. Her effort and progress were great until I moved the deadline up on her by four weeks. She definitely thinks it's impossible now. If she stays down about this much longer, the training materials will not be ready on time. Our client will be more than upset—and no training, no payment. The biggest constraint is time, not money. I don't know the best way to handle this. Maybe Shannon will have some ideas. I'll talk with her about her change in effort, confirm what's wrong, and ask her to think about what we can do to turn things around."

The second step is to ask for the employee's help. Begin by describing the B1 problem, as you see it, to the employee. Then ask for the employee's reaction to your diagnosis of a B1 problem caused by performance requirements being too high. Also, spend some time finding out how the problem is affecting the employee. Then, ask the employee to meet with you again to give you recommendations on changes in the performance requirements. Prepare the employee to do this by being sure the requirements and constraints are understood. Finally, set the day and time for the next meeting. The actual conversation between Eslie and Shannon went something like this:

Eslie: "I wanted us to talk again to see if together we can get this situation worked out. As I understand what you told me yesterday, your motivation dropped off when I told you last week that the finished product had to be completed by the end of next month. You said that basically you have given up because meeting the deadline was impossible. Is that pretty much the way you'd sum up the situation?"

Shannon: "That's it. Exactly."

Eslie: "How is all this affecting you?"

Shannon: "There's just no way I can do what you're asking. I'm really down about it. You know I'm not a quitter, but I'm about ready to throw in the towel over this."

Eslie: "Would you be willing to think this thing through carefully and meet with me again to tell me the best you can do on completing the job?"

Shannon: "Sure."

Eslie: "Do we need to talk about anything, like the requirements of the job or the constraints?"

Shannon: "I understand the design requirements. The main constraint is the completion deadline."

Eslie: "When can you be ready to meet and tell me what you think."

Shannon: "How about day after tomorrow, early, say at 7:30?"

Eslie: "Fine. See you then."

Step three is to reach agreement with the employee on changes in performance requirements. This can be done as follows. First, listen to the employee's recommendations, all of them, without interruption. Without any evaluation, restate what the employee tells you. Then present the changes you were thinking would be appropriate. Next, discuss the similarities and differences in what the two of you have presented. Negotiate the differences until both of you are in full agreement on exactly what changes will be made in the employee's performance requirements. Then, discuss and decide how the changes will be implemented. Finally, be sure the employee believes "I can do it," then get a commitment to meet the new performance requirements.

Eslie: "Well, Shannon, what do you think?"

Shannon: "I'm more hopeful now, if we can make a few changes that will save time and money and still give us an effective training program. I've based this on information from some of our client's middle managers and personnel director, the guys who really know what goes on in hiring, training, and managing the workers. Here's what I recommend. Almost all hires will be inexperienced, entry-level, uneducated employees with an average reading ability at a sixth or seventh grade level. I suggest we use simple but nicely printed handouts with few words and lots of pictures and diagrams of steps in assembly line operations. This reduces writing time and printing time and cost. Again, because of the type of workers, the managers tell me that slick videos that are professionally produced will not be received as well as tapes we could make ourselves using experienced supervisors demonstrating all of the assembly line operations. My suggestion is that we accept their advice on this. This not only will reduce video production time, but we can do it for about $40,000 less. I have a lot of production experience and feel comfortable with my time and cost estimates. What do you think? I know it's different from what you were expecting me to do."

Eslie: "So you're recommending two things, changing the format and length of our printed material and producing the videotapes yourself, using their supervisors to demonstrate everything."

Shannon: "That's it."

Eslie: "The best I could come up with was to increase the budget to give you more manpower to get the job done on time."

Shannon: "We can do it that way if you like."

Eslie: "Your suggestions are totally different from mine and much better. Let's go with your two changes. We can still have high-quality materials. They'll just be in a different format. I like it."

Shannon: "Thanks."

Eslie: "In implementing this, you'll personally direct the production of the videos?"

Shannon: "Yes, I will."

Eslie: "OK, let's go with the printed materials you're suggesting and produce the videos ourselves. And you're sure you can meet the new deadline this way?"

Shannon: "Yes, sir! I can do it."

Eslie: "Keep me informed, and let me know if I can help."

The fourth and final step is to monitor progress regarding the changed performance requirements to be sure they are having the desired effect. What is the desired effect? It is composed of three things. You want the employee's motivation, effort, and performance to improve. That's it. You simply need to keep an eye on these three things to know if the problem is solved.

In Case 3-3, Eslie can be pretty much assured the problem is solved. Shannon had a problem. Eslie let her come up with the solution. She believes she can meet the deadline. And she has said so—"Yes, sir. I can." Eslie only needs to watch Shannon's effort and performance to know for sure.

How did Case 3-3 actually turn out? Shannon pushed ahead with her suggestions and implemented them well. She met the time requirements and achieved the cost savings as predicted. The preopening training went well, the plant opened on time, and standard production levels were reached by the end of the second day rather than at the end of the sixth week as was management's goal. As they said, "The training saved us a lot of money." Why was all this possible? Who made it happen? It was Shannon's idea, and her skill, and her effort. But it was Eslie who made it all possible. He diagnosed a low B1, accurately diagnosed the cause, selected the right B1 solution (changing performance requirements), and effectively implemented it in a couple of short conversations with Shannon. Eslie turned a potentially disastrous situation around and retained an invaluable employee who was thinking of throwing in the towel. This process is so simple, yet so powerful. You can do it, too.

INITIATING STRUCTURE

An employee can be unsure that effort will lead to performance when there is a lack of clarity about any aspect of the job. That is, an employee will have a low B1 unless there is a clear understanding of (1) which tasks are to be performed, (2) all that each task involves, (3) the priority for doing each, (4) how each is to be performed, and (5) the desired end result upon task completion. When all this is clearly spelled out for a job, it is said that the job has structure.

When a B1 problem is caused by a lack of structure, the solution is to initiate structure. That is, you need to originate or create structure for the job. In other words, you need to spell out clearly each of the five things listed in the previous paragraph for the employee's job.

Structure gives clarity, which removes employee doubt that effort will lead to performance.

Although structure is a B1 solution, too much structure can be a problem. You may exchange a B1 problem for a B3 (outcome-satisfaction) problem. Some employees place great value on work that provides a degree of freedom and independence. Structure restricts this. It also makes the work routine and therefore boring, which may cause the employee's satisfaction in the work to decline, maybe causing a motivation problem and possibly pushing the employee to the point of quitting the job. When initiating structure, don't overdo it.

How do you end up with enough structure, yet not too much? How do you go about initiating structure to achieve the right amount? There is a proven five-step process for initiating structure. It is based on employee involvement. Why? Because the employee is closer to the job and knows how much structure currently exists, how much is needed, what kind is needed, and how best to get it. How do you work with the employee? Let's see. A "structure" for initiating structure will be presented and applied to Case 3-4. Case 3-4 is the same as Case 2-4 in chapter 2, which was used to illustrate how to obtain information using job analysis. Remember job analysis? It is the diagnostic technique that uncovers the need for more structure. Review Case 3-4 first. Then, each step in how to initiate structure will be discussed and the way each actually was applied to Case 3-4 will be described.

Case 3-4—Initiating Structure to Solve B1 Problems. Supervising trainers in a government-funded training program wasn't easy even though each supervisor was responsible for only three trainers. The trainers were providing eight hours of intensive training daily during the summer to high school youth who were economically disadvantaged and projected as at high risk for becoming school dropouts and unemployed. An analysis of the supervisor's job was revealing in terms of B1. The supervising part was well structured. There was a specific list of things to do and each supervisor was trained well to do them. But they also were responsible for unusual situations. It seemed the supervisors never handled the same situation twice. That's how unstructured a major part of their job was. What was the B1 for most of the supervisors for the structured part of their job? What was it for the unstructured part?

The first step in initiating structure is to do your homework. Think about the end results you expect from each unstructured part of the job. Then identify all the tasks that must be done to achieve those end results. Next consider how to do those tasks. Remember, do not view any of this as making final decisions, but instead simply as your preparation to work with employees to initiate structure.

Stacy was the project manager for the government-funded training program in Case 3-4. In trying to apply step one to the unstructured part of the jobs of the supervisors, she quickly realized she couldn't do it very well. She had ideas about end results for some of the unstructured parts of the job, but she didn't know all the unexpected things the supervisors faced that had no structure. Stacy did not panic because she knew who knew everything—the supervisors. Stacy called them together for a work session and had them identify all the unstructured parts of their job and arrange them in a hierarchy of importance, in terms of what they most needed help with.

Step two in initiating structure is to get the employee involved. Start by helping them understand what you mean by structure. Then lead them to see a need for more job structure. Next get a commitment from the employees to help create the structure. Ask the employees to come up with recommendations for more structure. Then prepare employees to do so. Finally, agree on a day and time for them to have the recommendations ready to present to you.

Stacy continued her work session with the supervisors by applying step two. She gave them a brief but detailed explanation of structure. Then she asked how more structure would be helpful to them. They saw numerous benefits immediately and were eager for more structure. She asked if they were willing to help create it, because they had experience with the situations and ideas about how to handle them. They said yes. She asked them to start working on their recommendations in the work session. They agreed on how to proceed, and they set a time later in the day to present the results of their work to Stacy.

The third step is to reach agreement with the employees on the additional structure. Do this by meeting with the employees and listening carefully to the recommendations they present. Listen to all they have to say before you say anything. Then summarize the essence of what the employees have recommended. Add any relevant information and ideas you have. Reach agreement on the structure.

At the designated time, Stacy met with the supervisors to carry out step three for each part of the job for which they had developed structure. Here is what happened. She listened to everything they had to say without interruption. Then she summarized from notes she had taken, getting clarification on several points. When she clearly understood their recommendations, she asked a few questions, mentioned some information they didn't have, and made a few minor suggestions. Based on her contributions, the supervisors usually recommended a few changes in the structure they had originally presented. Stacy normally didn't totally agree with the supervisors' finalized structure, but she endorsed it because it was good enough, it was theirs, and they were committed to using it. Although many managers have difficulty doing this, Stacy knew when to "leave well enough alone." Asking people to come up with solutions and then rejecting their solutions is a slap in the face not easily forgotten.

Step four is to develop an implementation plan for achieving the new structure. Begin by asking the employees for implementation suggestions. Listen to all suggestions without evaluating them. Then give your ideas. Discuss the ideas and agree on an implementation plan. Also, agree on who is to do what by what time in implementing the plan. Finally, agree to a follow-up plan to be sure everything gets done.

In Case 3-4, step four was applied as presented above. It was an easy step because implementation of the structure consisted simply of giving each supervisor a copy of the agreed upon structure and using it when the situations arose. The supervisors made a commitment to keep Stacy informed on how the structure worked, and she agreed to pass the results along to everyone on a timely basis. The work session ended on a positive note. The supervisors had some needed structure, it was their own, and they liked it. They appreciated having a project manager with enough confidence to let them develop it rather than imposing something on them that wouldn't have been as good.

The fifth step is to follow up. This includes monitoring to be sure the additional structure is having the desired effect, namely, to increase employee B1. This can be seen in employee motivation, effort, and performance. If all of the desired results are not found, meet with the employees to figure out why and to decide on other action to be taken.

Follow-up was easy for Stacy. She always stayed in close contact with her supervisors, and they were reporting the results when they used the new structure. She carefully watched her supervisors and used the diagnostic techniques in chapter 2 to identify changes in B1 levels. The result was more "I can" and less "I can't" by the supervisors. Stacy saw noticeable improvements in motivation, effort, and performance. Everyone felt the time, effort, and cost of initiating more structure was worthwhile. B1s for the remaining unstructured parts of the jobs of the supervisors were not high because of the uncertainty of what might happen, but this represented only a small part of the overall job. Consequently, B1s for the job as a whole increased to a rating at the 7-8-9 level.

Initiating structure is not complicated. You will be able to do it. The approach recommended here puts the burden on the employees to create the needed structure, but that is done under your direction. It works best this way, and you can make it work for you.

PROVIDING ADEQUATE RESOURCES

When diagnosing an employee's motivation problem, you may conclude that inadequate resources are making it impossible to do the job. What do you do? Do nothing, and observe how well the employee handles the situation? Or say, "Do the best you can," and hope for the best? Or what? When resources are inadequate, the only real solution is more resources. Only that will improve the employee's B1 and make it possible to get the job done. If resources are inadequate for the job, rather than a perception of inadequacy because the employee does not fully understand what resources are available or how to use them effectively, providing more resources is the only solution. When the employee has given up and said "I can't," nothing else will help. With the right pressure, the employee may give the appearance of believing "I can," but only for self-protection. The only real solution is more resources.

How do you know what additional resources are needed? Generally speaking, a good management philosophy is, "when in doubt, ask your employees." Why not? After all, they are closer to the situation than anybody else and likely know what is needed. When asking, remember that employees sometimes think they need more resources than really are necessary. Also remember that managers tend to think employees need less than is required. With this in mind, what do you do? Several things will help. Let's look at these in the context of Case 3-5 (discussed earlier as Case 2-5 in chapter 2).

Case 3-5—Providing Adequate Resources to Solve B1 Problems. The job of the trainers in the firm that conducted government-funded training programs was structured. Trainers spent about thirty minutes "telling how" to do a specific skill, such as how to handle conflict with the boss. Another thirty minutes was for "showing how" to do the skill by having trainees view and discuss videotaped demonstration models. Finally, three hours were devoted to having each trainee "practice" the skill while being videotaped and receiving feedback from the trainer and other trainees. Video equipment that worked was essential to the success of the trainers. A few trainers saw themselves as the "fix-it" type who could repair just about anything. What was their B1 for effectively conducting the training programs? What was it for trainers who had no "fix-it" experience or aptitude?

You may remember from the discussion of this case in chapter 2 that most trainers did not have the training, experience, or aptitude to handle video equipment problems. Their B1s as trainers suffered as a result. The question then was, "what to do?" Let's look at a proven way to solve this kind of B1 problem. It involves eight simple, easy-to-use steps.

The first, and often hardest, step is to get your mind right. Many managers react adversely to the thought that employees need additional resources. Managers say, "Why can't they work with what they have?" or "I don't have additional resources to give anybody" or "I can't get approval for anything else for this job." With this thinking comes an unwillingness truly to address the employees' problem of inadequate resources. A better beginning is simply to be openminded and say, "OK, maybe more resources are needed. If they are, I'll do whatever I can because if I don't, the job will not get done and that's trouble for everybody."

This step was not a problem for Joyce, one supervisor who faced the B1 problem in Case 3-5. As often happens, employee anxiety surfaced quite noticeably. Joyce checked things out, and the need for additional resources to deal with video equipment problems seemed real. She learned that it was a problem for trainers under other supervisors, too.

The second step is to decide what additional resources you think are needed. This is your chance to think and prepare to discuss the situation with the employee. Don't let this thinking lead to making a decision without employee input. Repeat, do not make this decision on your own and in isolation from employees who may have knowledge unavailable to you because they are closer to the situation.

Joyce thought through the situation and came up with two possibilities. Both were human resource solutions. One was to train supervisors to handle all the equipment problems. The other was to hire a person to take charge of all equipment matters, including maintenance and repair.

Step three is to ask the employees what additional resources are needed and why. As always, listen to all the employees have to say, asking questions and using active-listening techniques as necessary. Do not evaluate their ideas yet. Joyce did it basically this way:

Joyce: "How do you think we can best deal with the problem of trainers not being able to handle their video equipment problems?"

Trainer: What about a set of backup equipment?"

Joyce: "Do you mean a set for each trainer?"

Trainer: "I don't see that as necessary. One set for each group of three or four trainers who conduct training at each location should be adequate."

The fourth step is for you to add any ideas not mentioned by the employee. Do not focus on what you cannot do in the way of providing additional resources. Instead focus on sharing ideas that focus on how best to provide additional resources. Joyce applied this step as follows.

Joyce: "I thought of two possibilities—training supervisors to handle problems and hiring someone to handle everything related to the equipment, including maintenance and repair."

The fifth step is to evaluate the suggestions for what additional resources would best meet the needs of the situation. Get the employee to evaluate first, then add your thinking as appropriate. Joyce did it this way:

Joyce: "What do you think about these three options?"

Trainer: "You already have a tough job. And what do we do when you are not available? Hiring someone might not be easy or fast, and having one person to help three or four trainers occasionally could be expensive after a while. A set of backup equipment would be cheaper."

Joyce: "You're making some good arguments. My availability could be a problem. Over the long run, hiring another person would be prohibitively expensive."

Step six is to reach agreement as to what additional resources ideally would be made available. Let the employee give a final recommendation based on all the two of you have discussed. Negotiate additional needs as you feel appropriate.

Joyce: "OK, so what do you think we should do?"

Trainer: "I think backup equipment makes the most sense."

The seventh step is to figure out how to get the additional resources. This may be simple if you have access to the resources. It may take some work to come up with everything. If you can't come up with all that ideally is needed, discuss and reach agreement as to how the needs can be revised downward.

Joyce: "That reminds me. I've heard we have a few good sets of equipment in the warehouse from the last big project we did. If there isn't enough, I'll have to get approval to buy what we need. This is a big and important project, and the cost for backup equipment is not a significant item."

The eighth and final step is to make the additional resources available to the employee. This means taking whatever steps may be necessary and following through until the resources are in the hands of the employee when they are needed. This solution worked out well for Joyce and her trainers. She found the equipment she needed in the warehouse. It worked out well for her in another way. The project manager approved backup equipment to solve the same problem for other trainers and supervisors. With the warehouse inventory, only a few backup sets had to be purchased.

Why did the B1 problem among trainers get solved? Because one of the trainers had a good idea? Not really. Employees often have good solutions. This problem was solved because a good supervisor used a sound approach to find the right solution. She found it by using the simple, straightforward process outlined earlier. It worked for her. It will work for you, too.

CHANGING THE ORGANIZATION

Changing the organization, even a small part of it, is not a B1 solution unless you are in a position to make changes of the magnitude called for. Here is the situation. When organizational factors contribute to B1 problems, they often must be dealt with on an organizational-wide basis. This is a difficult, time-consuming, and costly matter. But if organizational factors are causing employees to have low B1s that reduce motivation, lower performance, and negatively impact profitability, then the difficulty, time, and cost of doing something about it become worthwhile. All things considered, this may be the most cost-effective way of improving performance, productivity, and profit. However, it is a solution that may have only limited feasibility for many managers.

What organizational factors contribute to B1 problems, and what can be done about them? The factors were discussed in chapter 2 in the section on "Organization Analysis" and are summarized as follows, along with appropriate action to take: (1) poor training—more/better training, (2) rapid growth—more/better training, (3) rapid technological change—more/better training, (4) hiring unqualified workers—improve the hiring process, (5) understaffing—build staffing levels, (6) high turnover—reduce turnover, and (7) inadequate resources—better resource management. Notice how the solutions are a natural and logical extension of the causes of B1 problems. Once you know the cause of the problem, picking the solution is easy. Implementation then becomes the key.

What can you do to change the organization? Probably more than you think and less than you'd like. Here are a few things that are possible. First, you can work toward changing the part of the organization under your responsibility. For each organizational factor that is negatively affecting the B1 of employees in your unit, do what you can to make the appropriate changes. This obviously is not an organization-wide solution, but it can give you and your employees some relief. That is, it can solve B1 problems among your employees. When you are successful, other managers may follow. Who knows? Your success may spread through the organization faster than you think.

Second, you can take a step toward changing the organization by directly influencing others to change. This includes helping them see the relationships between the organizational factors and worker motivation and between motivation and performance, productivity, and profit. Talk it up. It may make a difference, especially if your own unit is evidence that it works.

Being realistic, however, means admitting organization change is hard to come by. It is not in your best interest to focus too much on changing the whole organization. Change your own situation first. Make your own unit better and go from there. Then you'll probably have somewhere to go, most likely up. Then you can change more of the organization.

Case 3-6 revisits Case 2-6 from chapter 2 to illustrate how changing several organizational factors that have a crippling effect on employee B1s can improve individual motivation, effort, and performance and consequently enhance organizational performance. Read the case and think about what was causing the problem and what you would do to solve it.

Case 3-6—Changing the Organization to Solve B1 Problems. A project management company was growing fast. Hiring and training hourly employees was not a problem. Hiring and training managers was. The labor market had a shortage of qualified managers. Employees in the company with the technical skills needed by project managers had no management experience. Both promoting from within and hiring managers from outside left the company weak at the project manager level. This problem was magnified because the rapid growth was accompanied by little or no training for the managers. Having a growing business was great. Having staffing problems was not.

What were the main causes of the low B1s among project managers? Technological change was not a problem. The organization was not understaffed. Turnover was not a problem, nor were resources. The causes of the problem were (1) poor training, (2) rapid growth, and (3) hiring unqualified managers.

Improving hiring and training practices for project managers was the obvious solution. Implementation of the solution was not as clear. How did this company actually go about it? The first step was taken by the president. Bates saw the damaging effects of the problems and became very involved in dealing with them. This was important, always is, in making changes in the organization. Organizational change seldom takes place without the support of top management.

Three things were done to improve training, expensive things. Bates supported all of them. The first used the assessment center approach to identify a group of about fifteen employees who had the potential to become project managers. This group received extensive classroom training. They also were assigned to projects to give them the breadth and depth of experience needed as a project manager.

Second, current project managers also became a focus of training. They received special classroom training. Extensive structure was developed for their jobs as a way of training and guiding them to manage their projects using sound management practices. Work sessions were regularly conducted for project managers to share and learn from their own experiences. Project managers received closer supervision, primarily for the purpose of developing their skills. One benefit of the closer supervision was more coaching.

Third, new project managers spent weeks getting ready to take over a project. Extensive classroom training and a lot of coaching were initially emphasized. Then they went through an intensive job-rotation training program before being assigned to a project management position.

The financial commitment for these three training endeavors was substantial. It probably was the largest training commitment among companies its size in the country. It paid off, but it was not easy. It never is easy to change an organization. Individual managers can't bring about sweeping changes like Bates did in this project management firm, but you may be able to change your own unit. That's your responsibility. You're not responsible for the whole organization.

What about rapid growth as an organizational cause of B1 problems? There are two basic options here. One is to control the growth. The other is to hire and train to keep up with it. But in the project management company, there was only one option. Bates would not consider turning away business. The focus was to do whatever was necessary to keep up with the growth. Essentially that meant hiring and training people who could help the company keep the pace. The way training was handled to do this already has been described. The changed hiring practices are documented as follows.

Six things were done to hire better project managers. First, the positions were made more attractive financially. This made a difference. Second, some project managers were employed without being required to relocate. This widened the pool of interested applicants considerably and was not a problem for the company, as project managers spent most of their time at the project site rather than at the corporate office anyway. Third, executive recruiters were used to make a nationwide search for applicants. This too was effective, but it was expensive because the recruitment fees were considerable. The decision to incur this expense was a difficult one for Bates to make. Fourth, hiring criteria were identified and carefully thought out. Fifth, one hiring criterion that received special focus was the level of the B1, B2, and B3 of applicants; their employment history was examined in terms of these levels. Sixth, methods for assessing applicant skills were developed and used in order to base hiring decisions objectively on information that was more complete and accurate than that used in the past.

All six of these solutions for better hiring were expensive, very expensive in absolute dollars for a firm the size of this project management company. A significant cost was the amount of time devoted to the hiring process. It was costly and difficult, but it paid off. It would not have happened without the total commitment of the president. Without commitment from the top, making changes of this magnitude in an organization are not possible. Most managers simply have to do the best they can. As mentioned above, that usually is to concentrate first on changes you can make in your own unit rather than focusing on broader organizational changes. Take care of your own situation first, and see what happens. You may be surprised.

CHANGING THE MANAGER (YOURSELF)

When an employee's low B1 is caused by the way the manager manages, the solution is for the manager (you) to change. Why can't the employee change instead? It isn't the employee who is causing the problem. It is the manager. To eliminate the cause means either eliminating the manager or changing the way the manager manages. So what do you do? Maybe you can get by, but only for a while. That would mean placing the blame on employees, pressuring them until they quit or until you can justify firing them. But let's face it. Sooner or later this catches up with you. If you don't change, eventually you may have to go elsewhere or at best not go anywhere at all while others around you, even those below you, leave you behind. The issue here is bigger than simply changing yourself to solve the B1 problems of your employees.

This B1 solution, however, may not be as hard as it seems. Here's why. You don't really have to change yourself. You only need to change some behaviors, a few of the things you say and do. This is different and easier than changing your "self." Let's look at a few situations to see what this means and how you can change a few things. Specifically, attention will be given to five of the most common manager behaviors that lower employee B1s: (1) the perfectionist manager, (2) the manager who establishes performance requirements that are too high, (3) the manager who is critical rather than supportive, (4) the manager who hires employees for positions they don't have the skills for, and (5) the manager who does not give employees enough structure.

Perfectionist managers tend to cause B1 problems because they tell employees, "This isn't right," and "This isn't good enough," and "Do it again," until employees conclude, "I can't do anything right." Managers who are perfectionists may never be able to change the perfectionist part of themselves, but it is possible to change the way they work with employees. What can perfectionist managers do? How can they manage in a way that raises employee B1s rather than lowering them? It's a two-step process. First, initiate structure for your employees. That is, let them know up front exactly what you want them to do, how you want it done, and what the expected results are. Give them a lot of structure. The best way is to follow the guidelines suggested earlier in the chapter in the section on "Initiating Structure." Second, accept the responsibility for the structure you give them.

Accepting responsibility for the structure is the hard part for some managers. It involves three circumstances. First, what if the completed work complies with the structure you gave the employees, but the work isn't perfect because you didn't tell them everything you should have? What do you do? It's your fault, not theirs. Don't blame them, and don't accept their work and fix it yourself. They would interpret your fixing it to mean, "I did it wrong, and he figured he could fix it better than I could." This damages B1s. Instead, have the employees fix it, but accept the blame yourself. Say something like, "I made a mistake by not telling you a couple of things that needed to be done." When you do this, the employees' B1s are not lowered. Remembering that perfectionists tend to see what's wrong, not what's right, don't forget to praise the employees for doing the work in compliance with the structure you gave them. This is a B1 booster.

A second circumstance also requires the perfectionist manager to accept responsibility for structure. What if the completed work complies with the structure you provided, and it is as "perfect" as you had hoped? What do you do? You deserve a pat on the back for giving such good structure, but the credit should go to the employees for doing what you asked the way you asked. Give the credit, don't take it. This increases B1s. When you say, "You did a good job," employees will conclude, "I can do it."

The third circumstance arises when the completed work doesn't comply with the structure and therefore doesn't meet your expectations. What do you do? This is simple. Have the employees continue working until they do it right. Find out why they didn't do it right the first time. If they just didn't do it, nothing special needs to be said. If they didn't understand what you wanted, review your structure with them to leave no uncertainty about what they are to do and how they are to do it. If they understood what to do, but were unable to do it because they didn't have the skills or the resources or whatever, do what is necessary to equip them.

Let's move away from the perfectionist manager to the manager who negatively influences employee B1s because performance requirements are too high. How does this manager change? Just follow the process recommended earlier in the section on "Changing Performance Requirements." Remember, you don't have to change yourself, but only a small part of the way you manage. This will not be hard for you to do.

Managers who lower employee B1s by being critical rather than supportive can change, too. It starts with recognizing and then dealing with two of the main causes of manager criticism. The first cause is that employees are doing things their managers don't approve of. The second is that managers do not fully appreciate the value of being supportive rather than critical.

What can be done when you disapprove of employee performance and/or behavior? If certain things irritate you but do not affect the employees' performance, it may be best simply to overlook them. Why not, unless they affect your own performance? If the things affect employee performance, something must be done. But what? The first, and probably most common, reason employee performance and/or behavior does not meet the approval of managers is that employees do not know exactly what managers expect of them. The solution is simple. Let them know what you expect. Follow the process outlined earlier in the section on "initiating structure" to help employees know your performance expectations. In addition, you can spell out any behavioral expectations as well. This should provide the necessary clarification and enable capable employees to work and behave in ways that meet your approval.

The second reason employee performance and/or behavior does not meet with manager approval is that employees simply cannot do what they know should be done. That is, the employee may have inadequate skills, performance requirements may be too high, resources may be inadequate, and organizational factors may be preventing performance. Guidelines for dealing with these four causes have been presented earlier in this chapter.

The third reason employee performance and/or behavior does not meet manager approval is that employees think they can't do what they know should be done. That is, they are not motivated, because of low B1s resulting from perception of inadequate skills, perception that performance requirements are too high, perception of inadequate job structure, perception of inadequate resources, and a history of failure. The earlier section in this chapter on "Communication" describes how to deal with these perception problems.

Regarding the second cause of manager criticism, namely, that managers do not appreciate the value of being supportive rather than critical, what do you do? Being critical of employees does several things. It lowers B1s and therefore motivation, effort, and performance. It also is a B3 problem; criticism is an outcome employees do not like. Furthermore, it makes employees want to see you fail. Being supportive does the opposite. It raises B1s and B3s and consequently, raises motivation, effort, and performance. It also makes employees want to see you succeed. What more need be said? It pays to be more supportive and less critical.

Let's turn now to the manager who lowers employee B1s by hiring employees for positions requiring skills other than those the employees possess. Dealing with this is a matter of priority and focus. Once you make up your mind to do it, you can. However, in some situations matching employees to jobs is troublesome. One is when skill requirements for a particular job are difficult to enumerate. This is the case for higher-level jobs (corporate president, agency head), for jobs with a wide diversity of tasks (manager, entrepreneur), and jobs with ill-defined tasks (crisis manager, plant troubleshooter). Another situation where job matching is troublesome is when assessing employee skills is difficult. This is the case for management and sales jobs. Even though in some situations job matching is not easy, most jobs have identifiable skill requirements that can be readily assessed in employees. By identifying the skills required for each job and determining the extent to which a potential employee has those skills, you will achieve a better match between people and jobs. That is, employees will be hired and placed into jobs that they can handle. When they have the skills required, they can do the job. They will conclude, "I can do it," and B1 problems are prevented.

Then there are those managers who do not give employees enough structure and thereby cause B1 problems. Many good managers are like this. It is not their nature to initiate structure, so they don't. They probably could, but they don't think through everything in a detailed, logical, sequential way like others who are naturally good at creating structure. The battle is basically won, though, when you realize the need for more structure. Simply use the guidelines presented earlier in this chapter in the section on "Initiating Structure." These guidelines make it easy because the burden for creating the structure is placed on the employee, with you managing the process. You can do that.

Here we come to the end of the discussion of another solution to B1 problems, namely, changing the manager. Everything you need to change about the way you manage has not been mentioned here, although some of the most common practices that contribute to B1 problems have been discussed. Getting away from the details presented here, there are three broader points that ought to stay with you. One, managers sometimes behave in ways that lower the B1s of their employees. Two, the only way to solve the employees' B1 problem in this case is for you to change. Three, the best and easiest way to do this is to focus on changing your behaviors, not your "self," as has been emphasized and demonstrated throughout this section. This is a change you can make.

POSITIVE SELF-TALK

In addition to the eleven practical and proven solutions presented thus far to solve B1 problems, there are two others of perhaps even greater importance. Each deserves special attention. Both are important forms of "talk" that are critical, actually essential, in raising B1 levels and keeping them up. One is positive self-talk (PST). The other is positive manager talk (PMT). Their value should not, under any circumstances, be underestimated. All employees need this kind of "talk." They must have it. Otherwise they will not, indeed cannot, have B1s as high as you and they want them to be. What are PST and PMT? How do you use them?

Self-talk is what we say to ourselves. It can be either positive or negative. Positive self-talk is saying positive things about ourselves to ourselves. Negative self-talk is saying negative things about ourselves to ourselves. Employees control their own self-talk. Only they know how these conversations go, although sometimes they are not consciously aware of it.

The single most important way to deal with B1 problems is to have employees who use positive rather than negative self-talk. To understand why, consider the following six points. Collectively they spell out the necessity of showing your employees how to use positive self-talk and continually encouraging them to use it.

1. All employees talk to themselves.
2. The way they talk to themselves has a major influence on what they feel, say, and do. It even influences what they think they can do. That is, what your employees say to themselves has a major influence on their beliefs about effort leading to performance (B1). Self-talk inevitably leads employees to believe either "I can" or "I can't," depending on what they say to themselves.
3. All employees engage in negative self-talk to some extent. This contributes to occasional B1 problems.
4. Many employees are predominately negative, rather than positive, self-talkers. This continually contributes to B1 problems.
5. Positive self-talk is an essential part of every B1 solution because employees ultimately must talk to themselves positively and say, "I can."
6. Employees who use positive self-talk have fewer B1 problems. That is, positive self-talk not only solves B1 problems, it prevents them.

The bottom line is this. Positive self-talk is important! Very important. How do you get employees to use positive self-talk more often and negative self-talk less? Let's look first at negative self-talk and at some of the reasons why employees talk that way. Then a six-step process for positive self-talk that employees can use will be presented. Next, a simple approach for showing employees how to use the six-step process will be suggested. Finally, guidelines for reminding employees to use the process will be presented.

When employees use negative self-talk, what are they saying to themselves? Some of the most typical include the following.

—"I can't. . . . I didn't. . . . I knew I couldn't."
—"I'll fail. . . . I failed. . . . I knew I'd fail."
—"I'm not smart enough. . . . I'm stupid. . . . I'm really stupid."
—"Everybody is smarter than me."
—"Why can't I ever do anything right?"
—"Why am I the one who always screws up?"
—"I don't deserve anything."
—"I'm a failure."
—"I'm a bad person."
—"I'm not a worthwhile person."

Negative self-talk stems from several things. One is failing to interpret what happens and what it means. For example, an employee might say, "I missed the deadline and got chewed out; I'm really stupid." A more objective assessment of the situation would take the circumstances into account. As a result, the employee might say, "I missed the deadline because I underestimated how long it would take to do the work; next time I'll be more realistic and start sooner."

Another reason for negative self-talk is irrational beliefs. Employees talk negatively to themselves when they don't live up to strongly held but "impossible to live up to" beliefs such as the following.

—"I have to have the approval of my boss on everything."
—"I must be good at everything I do."
—"Everything has to work out the way I want."
—"I should succeed on everything."

A third reason for negative self-talk is that people sometimes project descriptors of behavior onto themselves. Some examples of this are:

—"I failed at this, therefore I am a failure."

—"That was a stupid thing I did, therefore I must be stupid."

—"What I said was thoughtless, therefore I am a thoughtless person."

—"I didn't make any worthwhile contributions in the meeting, therefore I must not be a worthwhile person."

What about positive self-talk? Rather than saying negative things and "putting ourselves down," we can talk positively and "lift ourselves up." There is a special way to do this. Following a few steps makes it simple. The "how-to" of positive self-talk includes six simple steps that are easy to use. These steps are shown following this paragraph and are accompanied by examples of self-talk that demonstrate each step. The self-talk is that of an employee with a history of failure who has not met his manager's expectations on a recently submitted report.

1. Objectively state the incident that is causing self-doubt: "Mr. Johnson said my report was not quite as good as he had expected."
2. Objectively interpret what the incident does not mean: "This doesn't mean the report was bad or that I can't write or that I will not meet his expectations in the future. Although I've had my share of failures in the past, this one incident definitely doesn't mean I'm a failure in this job."
3. Objectively state what the incident does mean: "This simply means the report was not as good as he had expected, and I need to do better next time."
4. Objectively account for the cause of the incident: "First of all, he didn't give me enough time to do a first-class job on it. But I have to confess that I didn't take the assignment as seriously as I should have. I got careless and left out one of the important issues, and I didn't polish the final draft as I usually do."
5. Identify positive steps to prevent a reoccurrence of the incident: "Next time Mr. Johnson gives me a report to do, I definitely will take it seriously and do my very best work. I'll find out exactly what his expectations are, and I'll meet them. I'll plan my time so that I can give him a polished final draft."
6. Make positive statements about yourself: "I usually know what Mr. Johnson wants and give it to him. Because of that, he probably expects more of me than he does from others. That's a compliment. After all, I am a good writer. My next report will meet his expectations. I can hear him saying, 'This is the best report I've ever seen.' I can't wait."

You can help solve, and can even prevent, B1 problems by showing your employees how to use the six steps that constitute the "how-to" of positive self-talk. How can you do this? Here are five steps you should follow:

1. Wait for an incident where you expect the employee to use negative self-talk.
2. Let the employee know you are aware of what happened and that it is normal to be discouraged.
3. Encourage the employee to view the incident objectively and positively, rather than subjectively and negatively.
4. Demonstrate how the six steps of positive self-talk can be applied.
5. Follow up to see if the employee understands and is using the process.

Let's see how this five-step process works. Case 3-7 describes a situation where the manager needs to encourage an employee to use self-talk. The cause of the B1 problem is the perception of inadequate resources, specifically, the perception of not having enough time to do the job right. Read the case and decide what you would say to carry out step four.

Case 3-7—Showing an Employee How to Use Positive Self-Talk When the Low B1 Is Caused by Inadequate Resources. Dale is new as a cost estimator. She has had good training and is making satisfactory progress. The hardest part of the job is giving customers accurate cost estimates because there are so many variations of the services offered. She made a mistake when giving a preliminary estimate over the phone to a pushy and demanding customer, but she discovered the error and was able to correct it in the final estimate mailed to him. Dale made the mistake because she did not have enough time to compute the preliminary estimate. At least, she didn't think she had enough time, as she tried to satisfy the customer by making the estimate quickly. When the customer got the estimate and saw that it was higher than the one given earlier by phone, he called Dale, complaining and criticizing her for the mistake. Now Dale is upset with herself for causing a problem. She said, "I don't know if I'll ever be able to handle this job when I'm under pressure." What would you say to her?

There are many "right" ways to show Dale how to use positive self-talk. The basic process is illustrated in the following dialogue. Case 3-7 represents an incident where you expect an employee to engage in negative self-talk (step 1). Letting the employee know you are aware of the situation (step 2) is as simple and straightforward as this:

—"Dale, since you are new here, I wanted to talk with you about Mr. Robertson's phone call this morning. You seem to be a little bit down about it."

Encouraging the employee to be objective and positive (step 3) also is simple and straightforward. Saying no more than the following can be satisfactory.

—"I hope you will look at this objectively and in a positive way."

The critical step of demonstrating how to apply the six-step process of positive self-talk (step 4) is easiest when one sentence is used for each of the six steps:

—"When this kind of thing happens, here's what I hope you will say to yourself: 'I overlooked a couple of things in the preliminary estimate, and Mr. Robertson got upset (step 1). This does not mean I am stupid or incompetent or anything like that (step 2). What it means is that I made a mistake in the preliminary estimate, but I caught and corrected it in the final estimate (step 3). I made the mistake by hurriedly and nervously making the estimate over the phone, because he was demanding to have it immediately rather than agreeing to wait for me to call him back shortly, as I normally do (step 4). To keep this from happening again, I will follow the usual procedure of calling the customer back with the estimate after I've taken the necessary time to come up with it (step 5). My next estimate will be right on the mark, and the customer will be pleased (step 6).' Dale, talking positively to yourself like this keeps you from doubting and questioning yourself anytime something goes wrong. Don't get discouraged. You're doing a good job."

Another way of showing employees how to use positive self-talk is to model it for them. Simply talk to employees as you want them to talk to themselves. Modelling is a more indirect approach than demonstrating the six steps. Either can work. You should choose the method you feel more comfortable using. Modelling is illustrated as follows, with an employee whose B1 is low because of inadequate skills.

—"Your work is still falling short of production goals (step 1). This doesn't mean you're going to get fired or anything like that (step 2). It only means you're not getting out enough units (step 3). The problem is that this is new to you and your skills are still developing (step 4). Keep working to learn the steps for everything, and that will take care of it (step 5). You're a hard worker, your quality is good, you're learning fast, and I know you can get your production up (step 6)."

How do you encourage employees to use positive self-talk continually? Frequent lectures aren't necessary or desirable. Perhaps the best way is to say something from time to time as a gentle reminder. Several ways of doing this are shown below. As usual, choose wording that feels comfortable to you.

—"Are you using positive self-talk?"
—"Remember, you don't have to be perfect."
—"You don't have to be good at everything."

—"Be objective as you interpret what happened."

—"Don't be too hard on yourself."

—"Think about everything that caused this."

—"Are you thinking positively?"

—"Are you talking positively to yourself?"

Whatever the cause of an employee's B1 problem, positive self-talk is an essential part of the solution. It is positive self-talk that leads the employee to conclude, "I can." You have seen how positive self-talk can be used when an employee's B1 is low because of (1) a recent history of failure (see example with the initial list of the six steps of positive self-talk), (2) perception of inadequate resources (see Case 3-7), and (3) inadequate skills (see the example of modelling positive self-talk). But remember, positive self-talk is applicable to each cause of B1 problems. Don't forget, positive self-talk not only is applicable to each cause, it is essential to treating all of them. Whichever B1 solution you use, the employee must eventually use positive self-talk to say, "I can."

The importance of positive self-talk as a way to prevent and solve B1 problems cannot be stressed enough. Employees who talk positively to themselves have fewer and shorter-lived B1 problems. Frequent and longer-lasting B1 problems are the result of negative self-talk. Positive self-talk can prevent B1 problems. It is a must for solving them.

POSITIVE MANAGER TALK

Whereas positive self-talk (PST) refers to what employees say to themselves to prevent and/or solve B1 problems, positive manager talk (PMT) refers to things you, the manager, say to employees. That is, in addition to showing employees how to engage in positive self-talk and encouraging them to do so, there is much you can do in the way of saying positive things that can help prevent and/or solve B1 problems among your employees.

Generalized statements of encouragement represent the most common, though not the most effective, kind of positive manager talk. These statements often include untruths, such as "you can do it" when the employee actually can't or "great job" when it really wasn't, and may be more damaging than helpful when employees see through the hype. The generalized statements of encouragement shown below may, in a limited way, help build employees' confidence if the statements are thoughtful and accurate.

Generalized PMT that may be helpful when performance is lagging includes the following "talk."

—"Stick with it. You're getting there."

—"Don't give up. You can do it."

—"I'm impressed. I can see progress every day."

—"Keep at it. You'll get there."

—"Great job. Hang in there."

Generalized PMT that may be helpful when there has been a failure includes "talk" such as the following.

—"Don't worry about it. It's history now."

—"It wasn't your fault. Don't sweat it."

—"Hey, no need to cry over spilled milk."

—"Learn from what happened, and try harder next time."

—"You'll get another chance. You'll show 'em then."

A more effective means of positive manager talk is the use of specific statements that focus on what is causing a slump in the employees' B1. Specific PMT should include (1) statements related to the specific B1 cause that is to be overcome, or has been overcome, or should have been overcome and (2) statements specifically expressing your confidence that the employees "can" perform. In both kinds of statements, be truthful. This cannot be stressed enough. Say only what you believe.

To illustrate this, two specific sets of PMT will be presented. The first set of "talk" focuses on responses to employees whose performance has been lagging. The second set represents responses when employees have failed in their attempts to perform. Within each set, each response focuses on one B1 cause, with the responses covering all the B1 causes cited in chapter 2. Employees react well to this kind of positive manager talk.

When employee performance is lagging, specific PMT that will boost employee B1s includes the following "talk."

—"I know you've been concerned about not having all the skills needed for this job, but I've been watching your work closely the last few weeks and it looks good. I'm very pleased."

—"Now that we've agreed on some more realistic performance requirements for you, I know you will meet all of them."

—"You seem more confident about your work already, now that we've clarified the details of your job structure. You seem to know exactly what to do, when to do it, how to do it, and what the expected results are. You'll do fine."

—"I know it's tough to do a good job with limited resources, but you're doing very well, considering the budget constraints."

—"I know our growth and constant backlog of orders is a problem for you with our always switching you from one machine to another and often to machines you've never operated. Every time you step up to a different piece of equipment you're probably saying, 'I'll never learn to operate this one.' But you always seem to do a good job. I've never seen anyone with the knack to pick things up so fast on any and all of our equipment. I'm always confident you'll do a good job no matter what you are asked to do."

—"I can see how you could interpret my management style on this project as meaning I don't have much confidence in you. But that's not how I feel. The reason I have to know everything that's going on is that my boss and the client call me several times each day for updates and to ask all kinds of questions about the project. They expect me to know what's going on. That's the only reason I ask you a million questions. You really are doing a good job. And I let my boss and the client both know you are."

—"You told me yesterday you were having doubts about being able to do your job because of some problems you had in your last job. It may be hard to forget those things completely, but I want you to know your work here has been very good. You have proved to me that you can do it. I have total confidence in you. I know you can handle this job."

When employees have failed at some part of their job, specific PMT such as the following will help employees with low B1s:

—"It was our fault. We threw you into the fire without preparing you for it. We know that now. You have a lot of potential. You'll do fine."

—"We were foolishly expecting the impossible. That was our fault. No one could have done a better job. That's something to be proud of."

—"I agree with you. It would have helped to focus earlier on developing some structure for your job. Most of your problems stemmed from the lack of structure. If you had gotten started off on the right foot, I know you would have done well. Next time you'll know, and you'll do fine."

—"Actually, your job has a lot of structure as you can see now that we've gone through everything. If you had known this, I know your performance would have been much better. As for the future, I know you'll be doing a good job."

—"I know this thing didn't turn out the way you expected, but I hope you aren't questioning your ability. I'm surely not. It's obvious we didn't give you the resources you needed to get the job done the way you wanted."

—"I know you're disappointed, but don't interpret this to mean you're not a capable person. You're very capable. No one can succeed every time. This project was destined to fail because of organization politics. There was nothing anybody could have done."

—"The client is a perfectionist. That's why I asked you to do the work over. That doesn't mean you can't handle this job. Nobody can do perfect work all the time."

Whatever you do, don't underestimate the importance of positive manager talk. Employees want it, and they actually need it—far more than most managers realize. Knowing that you believe in them is important to employees. Their beliefs about effort leading to performance depend in part on you, on your beliefs about their effort leading to performance. When you think they can do it, tell them so. It influences their B1. Positive manager talk is not hard to do.

SUMMARY

There you have it. Thirteen distinctly different solutions for B1 problems. Two of the thirteen, namely PST and PMT, are universal in that they can be and should be used whatever the cause of the employee's B1 problem. The other eleven are situational, meaning they are appropriate depending on which of the B1 causes are affecting the employee. Each of the eleven is useful, but each has its time and place. Use them when they fit. You'll be pleased with the results.

What do you think? Can you choose the appropriate B1 solution, depending on the cause of the B1 problem? Can you implement each solution, following the guidelines presented in this chapter? What is your B1 for each of these skills? Rate yourself using the 10-point B1 rating scale. Take a minute to do this. OK, what do you think? Most managers at this stage in learning about B1 solutions have a pretty high B1, usually with a rating of 7 or higher.

The B1 solutions presented in this chapter are simple and straightforward. This typifies one of the attractive features of applying the expectancy theory of motivation. It is easy to use. Another appealing feature is that it gives results. If you apply the solutions as prescribed here, you will get results, too.

4

Diagnosing Performance-Outcome Problems

Everyone has experienced the frustration of not getting what they deserve. This happens when good performance goes unnoticed. It happens when promises are made but not kept. It happens when managers do not have the authority to give employees what they deserve. It happens when organizations do not believe in taking care of their people. Whatever the reason, employees often question whether or not they will get what they deserve. Employees often conclude, "I will not get it." This is the belief that performance will not lead to outcomes (B2). In expectancy theory terminology, this is a performance-outcome problem. When this problem occurs, employee motivation suffers, and so do effort and performance.

The prevalence of performance-outcome problems, where employees believe "I will not get it," is widely recognized in all organizations. Employees and managers at all levels are very much aware of these problems. People discuss them openly. Some are vocal about them with their managers. Others say little, believing it would not help and might even hurt.

From the manager's perspective, what does this mean? First, every manager has some employees, perhaps a large percentage, whose motivation, effort, and performance suffer because they don't believe performance leads to outcomes (B2). Second, these problems may go unnoticed for a long time, in part because many employees do not bring them to the attention of their superiors. Third, performance-outcome problems have a long-lasting negative impact on motivation, effort, and performance. Once the problems are discovered, it takes weeks, even months, to convince employees that outcomes really are tied to performance.

The expectancy theory of motivation offers a powerful way to deal with performance-outcome problems. Numerous strategies for identifying and solving, even preventing, these problems are presented in chapters 4 and 5. This chapter focuses on diagnosing problems, and the next offers numerous practical solutions.

Diagnosing performance-outcome problems (B2), like diagnosing effort-performance problems (B1), requires the two skills of (1) obtaining and (2) interpreting the needed information. Attention will be given to the second skill first, to make the learning process easier. This chapter will focus first on interpreting B2 information, with the remainder of the chapter devoted to obtaining B2 information.

INTERPRETING B2 INFORMATION

As you interpret B2 information, two things must be done. First, you must diagnose the level of the employee's B2. The employee will believe, "I will get the outcome if I perform," or "I will not get it," or "I'm not sure." If the employee's B2 level is other than the "I will" belief, the second thing you want to do is to diagnose what is causing doubts about performance leading to outcomes. Let's focus first on diagnosing B2 levels, then look at diagnosing causes.

Diagnosing B2 Levels

Your diagnosis of B2 levels is aided by applying a 10-point rating scale similar to the one used in chapter 2 for rating B1. You should use a rating of 10 when you think employees are "certain" performance will lead to the outcome. Statements like the following suggest a 10 rating: "I'm sure I will get it," "I am positive I'll get it," "I'm certain I will get it," "I know I will get it," "There is no question I will get it," etc.

Ratings of 7, 8, or 9 are used when you think employees believe it is "likely" that performance will lead to outcomes. When employees say things like the following, ratings in the 7-8-9 range are appropriate: "I'm fairly certain I will get it," "I feel really good about the chance of getting it," "The odds of getting it are really in my favor," "The chances of getting it are much better than even," "It isn't guaranteed, but I am almost certain I'll get it," etc.

B2 ratings of 4, 5, or 6 are appropriate when you sense that employees are thinking "maybe I will get it." These "maybe" ratings fit when employees say the following: "I have a 50-50 chance of getting it," "I believe the odds are about even for getting it," "I have a fair chance of getting it," "The odds of getting it are slightly in my favor," "Getting it is a toss-up," etc.

Ratings of 1, 2, or 3 should be used when employees believe it is "unlikely" they will get the outcome. Here are some examples where these "unlikely" ratings apply: "It is possible, but not likely, I will get it," "There is only a slim chance I'll get it," "Getting it is not impossible, but next to it," "The odds of getting it really are stacked against me," "I have about one chance in ten of getting it," "Getting it is unlikely," etc.

A B2 rating of 0 should be used when you feel employees believe it is "impossible" for performance to lead to the outcome. This rating is used when employees say the following: "I am certain I will not get it," "There is no way I will get it," "I'm positive I will not get it," "It's impossible to get it," "There is no way in the world I will get it," etc.

Things employees say represent one of the most important kinds of B2 information you will be interpreting. There are a lot of ways employees express performance-outcome beliefs (B2). Several common ones are shown following this paragraph. Read each one and interpret the employee's B2 level using the B2 rating scale. What is each employee's belief about the likelihood that performance will lead to outcomes? When you have done this, continue reading to see how your ratings measure up.

1. "I feel absolutely certain I will get the promotion if my department maintains current production and profit levels for six more months."
2. "This project is great. Everything I do on it is fulfilling."
3. "It doesn't matter whether I do a good job on this or not. I'm convinced I will not get anything out of this."
4. "I hate this job. I don't get anything from it at all."
5. "I think I have a 50-50 chance of getting a bonus if I keep up the good work."
6. "I believe the odds are about 9 to 1 that I will get special recognition if we have the best safety record."
7. "Why should I break my neck around here. The chances of getting rewarded for it are slim to none."

It is fairly easy to diagnose B2 levels for the seven employees represented here because each comment is specific and directly related to their beliefs about the likelihood that performance will lead to outcomes. The "absolutely certain" in response 1 means that a B2 rating of 10 is appropriate. A B2 rating of 10 also is appropriate for the employee in response 2, who says "everything is fulfilling." (Fulfillment is an intrinsic outcome, an outcome received from doing the work itself, rather than an extrinsic outcome that someone else gives the employee.) Response 3 is at the other end of the rating scale with a B2 rating of 0, based on "convinced I will not get anything." At the same end of the rating scale is response 4, where the employee says "I don't get anything," indicating a B2 rating of 0. A "50-50" chance, as in response 5, is in the middle of the scale and has a B2 rating of 5. Response 6, like response 3, is very specific and indicates a B2 rating of 9. In the final response, a B2 rating of 1 ("slim") or 0 ("none") appropriately describes the employee's belief about performance leading to outcomes. How did your ratings compare with these? Most of them probably were pretty much on target. If not, rethink them and review the B2 discussion above and in chapter 1.

Employees often are not specific and direct when making statements that reflect performance-outcome beliefs (B2). Even so, you will find it relatively easy to interpret their comments and diagnose B2 levels. Some examples are presented following this paragraph. Read each comment and diagnose the B2 level by assigning a value using the B2 rating scale. Then continue reading to see how good your "guesses" are.

1. "Promises, promises. That's all we ever get."
2. "That's what I like here. You always get what you deserve."
3. "Sometimes you get rewarded, sometimes not. You never know."
4. "Some parts of my job are challenging, some are not. But overall it's not bad."
5. "Why produce more? Everybody gets treated the same."
6. "I get very little sense of accomplishment from my work."
7. "Pay, promotions, just about everything is tied to performance here."
8. "The union contract determines what you get, not how you perform."

Employees often exaggerate when they have a low B2. This likely is the case in response 1, where the employee is saying, "All we ever get is promises, never outcomes." If taken literally, this would be interpreted as earning a B2 rating of 0. Taking the possibility of exaggeration into account, a B2 rating somewhere in the "unlikely" range on the scale (1, 2, or 3) may be more accurate. However, diagnosing an employee's B2 level is a guessing game. Yet, exactness is not necessary. Close is close enough. It makes little difference whether you diagnose this employee's B2 as 0 or as 1, 2, or 3 because all represent beliefs so low that the employee would not be very motivated.

When employees have high B2s, they may tend to exaggerate somewhat, but not as much. Consequently, it generally is appropriate to interpret high B2 comments literally. With this in mind, the "always" in response 2 suggests a B2 rating of 10. However, a 9 rating, or even and 8, doesn't really change your diagnosis. This employee believes outcomes will be forthcoming if performance is what it should be.

What about the "sometimes you do, sometimes you don't" comment in response 3? This would be interpreted as "maybe I will, maybe not." This clearly is a "maybe" belief with a B2 rating in the 4, 5, or 6 range being appropriate. Response 4, with "some parts of my job are challenging, some are not," suggests a B2 rating in the "maybe" range like that for response 3. (Challenging work is an intrinsic outcome.) However, the "but overall it's not bad" comment may push the rating into the lower part of the 7, 8, or 9 "likely" range. A 6 or 7 rating would be a good guess.

Response 5, if taken literally, would deserve a B2 rating of 0. If everybody is treated the same, this means employees get identical outcomes no matter how they perform. For example, everyone gets a 4 percent pay raise. Taking the possibility of exaggeration into account, a B2 rating in the "unlikely" range (1, 2, or 3) may be more appropriate. As with response 1, it makes little difference whether you rate this employee's B2 a 0, 1, 2, or 3. The bottom line is that the B2 is low and the employee is not very motivated.

Response 6 would have a low B2 rating. "Very little" indicates that the employee believes that feeling a sense of accomplishment from the work is "unlikely." (Sense of accomplishment is an intrinsic outcome.) This suggests a B2 rating of 1, 2, or 3, or maybe as high as 4 if the employee seems to be exaggerating how bad the situation is. Again, it makes little difference whether you pinpoint the rating. This employee doesn't believe that getting a sense of accomplishment from the work is very likely.

Response 7, like the first six responses, allows for closeness but not precision in your B2 diagnosis. But remember, close is close enough. The "just about everything is tied to performance" suggests the employee is not absolutely certain about performance leading to outcomes in every case, but clearly indicates that the employee believes it is likely. A rating somewhere in the "likely" range of the scale (7, 8, or 9) is called for, probably toward the upper end of the range. Again, exactness is not necessary. Whether you rate the B2 as 7, 8, or 9 is unimportant. This employee believes outcomes will follow performance.

Response 8 is a strong statement indicating a weak B2. If the "union contract, not performance," does determine outcomes, then that's that. This employee's B2 is low, very low. A B2 rating of 0 could be an accurate diagnosis here.

Diagnosing B2 is a guessing game, and precision is neither possible nor necessary. Take the information you have and make your best guess about the employee's B2 level. Get more information and guess again. After looking at several pieces of information, your guesses will narrow in on a B2 diagnosis that will be close enough to let you know if there is a problem.

Let's take your learning process another step forward by introducing two other dimensions. One is to look at B2 information related to specific performance-outcome relationships. The other is to predict employee motivation levels, based on the diagnosis of B2 levels. Look carefully at the following information and diagnose the B2 level for each employee and decide if each is motivated.

1. Sales commission—"Sure. They always pay."
2. Performance bonus—"The chances are real good. Nothing's guaranteed, but I would be very surprised if I didn't get it."
3. Company car—"I've been promised a car for two years. I'm hopeful I'll get one, but the chances are a little less than 50-50."
4. Promotion now—"No. I'm not eligible for another year."
5. Overworked—"That's for sure, unfortunately."
6. More responsibility—"Probably. They usually pile more on when you do a good job."

In response 1, the salesperson is saying, "When you make a sale (perform), you always get a sales commission." That is, "I believe with certainty that a sales commission follows a sale." This employee's B2 for a sales commission is at the highest possible level. The B2 rating is 10. Is this salesperson motivated? You don't know. Remember, motivation comes only when three conditions are met, as discussed in chapter 1, when the person (1) believes effort leads to performance (B1), (2) believes performance leads to outcomes (B2), and (3) believes outcomes lead to satisfaction (B3). Because all this information is not known, you can conclude only that the salesperson's B2 for a sales commission works in favor of motivation. That is, the sales commission does not prevent motivation.

You may feel somewhat discouraged at this point, realizing how many pieces of information are needed to diagnose an employee's motivation level, not to mention diagnosing causes and then selecting and implementing solutions. Actually, the whole process is easy. You already are developing many individual skills that collectively will enable you to diagnose and solve motivation problems better than you ever dreamed. Just stay with it!

The employee in response 2 is saying, "The chances are real good I'll get a performance bonus—nothing is guaranteed, but I'd be surprised if I didn't get it." This person is not certain of getting a bonus (B2 is not 10), but almost certain. A B2 rating of 7, 8, or 9 would be appropriate here. Is this employee motivated? We don't know. Because you do not have B1 and B3 information and have only limited B2 information, you can conclude only that the B2 for a performance bonus works in favor of motivation.

Response 3, with "the chances are a little less than 50-50," indicates a B2 rating of about 4 for getting a company car. Is this employee motivated? Even though the B2 is not high, it may not be holding back this employee's motivation, as the employee still is "hopeful" of getting the car. In this case, with no B1 and B3 information and a B2 level that is difficult to interpret, the most that can be said is that this employee's B2 may not be a problem. Notice what has happened here. You see that sometimes it is possible to know a B2 level and still not know its effect on employee motivation. That is, when the B2 is at the 4-5-6 midrange, borderline level, it is difficult to know whether the "scales" are tipped against or in favor of motivation. (The same is true for B1.) But it means you may not have to do much to tip the situation in favor of motivation.

A new dimension is introduced with response 4, the time element. Thus far in discussing B2 the focus has been on the short run: "If you perform, do you believe the outcome(s) will follow, soon?" In response 4 the employee is saying, "No, I don't believe I will get a promotion now." In fact, the employee is saying, "It's impossible to get it now because according to the way things are done here, I am not eligible until next year." A B2 rating of 0 is appropriate. Does this keep the employee from being motivated? It may not. That depends on the answer to another question. Does the employee believe a promotion will be forthcoming next year? If the answer is no, this employee's low B2 for a promotion will work against motivation, assuming the employee wants a promotion. If the answer is yes, the high B2 for a promotion will work in favor of motivation, if a promotion is desired by the employee. This is an interesting point. It is possible for employees to be motivated even when they have a low B2. If employees do not expect to receive an outcome until later and find the future time frame acceptable, a low B2 for receiving the outcome immediately is irrelevant to their motivation.

Three new dimensions are introduced with response 5. One is "when" the outcome is received. Another is who gives the outcome. The third is the way the employee values the outcome. The employee is saying, "It's certain that if I do a good job on this, I'll be overworked." When is the outcome of being overworked received? It doesn't come after the work is completed. Instead, being overworked comes at the same time the work is being performed. Who gives the outcome? It is not the boss, but the employee who "gives" it by choosing to do the work. (This state of being overworked is an intrinsic outcome, that is, an outcome that accompanies doing the work itself.) How is the outcome valued? Being overworked is dissatisfying to most employees. What does all this mean?

Because the outcome of being overworked comes with doing the work, performance guarantees receipt of the outcome. That is, the B2 rating is 10, as indicated by the employee who is saying, "It's for sure I'll be overworked, unfortunately." The "for sure" indicates the B2 level and the "unfortunately" indicates the dissatisfaction with being over-worked. This is a situation where an employee is certain of getting something that is not wanted. How does this affect the employee's motivation? Obviously it is a push in the direction of not being moti-vated. To overcome this, outcomes that are satisfying to the employee must be offered that outweigh the dissatisfaction of being overworked, and the employee must believe those outcomes will be received.

In chapter 1, it was emphasized that a high B2 is necessary for an employee to be motivated. But as you can see from response 5, a high B2 does not necessarily contribute to employee motivation. Specifically, a high B2 for an outcome that yields dissatisfaction works against mo-tivation. This is suggested in response 6 as well. The "probably" com-ment in response 6 is the same as saying, "It is likely I will get more responsibility if I perform well on this." A B2 rating on the "likely" part of the rating scale indicates a B2 of 7, 8, or 9. How does this high B2 affect employee motivation? It depends on how the employee views the outcome. If more responsibility is dissatisfying, as it is for some employees, the situation is the same as in response 5; the employee expects to get something not wanted by performing. This works against motivation. If more responsibility is satisfying, the high B2 works in favor of motivation.

What do you think? Can you diagnose B2 levels by interpreting things employees say? That is, what is your B1 for diagnosing B2? It probably is high (a 7 or 8 rating), and it should be. If not, reread chapter 1 and this chapter, being sure you (1) understand each point, (2) think about situations when you are asked to do so, and (3) practice B2 diagnosis where indicated. If you do this, you will be able to say, "I can do it."

Diagnosing B2 Causes

Let's turn our attention now to the other half of B2 diagnosis. The focus thus far has been on the skill of diagnosing B2 levels. Now the emphasis will turn to the skill of diagnosing B2 causes. Remember, you first diagnose the employee's B2 level. If you find a problem, the cause(s) must be diagnosed as the basis for moving ahead to select and imple-ment a solution. This dual emphasis will be accomplished through the use of several short cases.

Read the following cases and do two things with each. First, diagnose the employee's B2 level. Use the B2 rating scale when doing this. Second, diagnose the B2 cause(s) for any B2s that are low enough to hinder employee motivation.

Case 4-1—Interpreting B2 Information Obtained by Communication. Ray worked for a firm in the service industry and was responsible for delivering services directly to clients. Here is what he said to his manager one day. "Look, you say my work isn't up to what it should be and that's why I never get a raise like everybody else and why I'm never considered for a promotion. Well, I think my work is as good as the next guy's. Oh, sure, sometimes the guys complain that I'm too slow or not careful enough, but that's just because I'm not the most popular guy around. They have to gripe at somebody." How low is Ray's B2? What is causing it to be low?

In Case 4-1, Ray, who never gets a raise like everybody else and never is considered for a promotion, understandably has a low B2. He believes it is very unlikely that outcomes ever are tied to what he considers good performance. A B2 rating of 2, or maybe 1 or even 0, would be appropriate here. What is causing this low B2? Ray says, "My work is as good as the next guy's," but others do not agree. The manager has said that Ray's "work isn't up to what it should be." And coworkers openly say Ray is "too slow" and "not careful enough." It seems Ray thinks his performance is better than it actually is. The cause of Ray's low B2 is the misperception that outcomes are not tied to performance. In reality, his performance "isn't up to what it should be," and he is getting outcomes accordingly.

Case 4-2—Interpreting B2 Information Obtained by Communication. As a faculty member at a major state university, Dr. Bell's performance was widely recognized as being head and shoulders above everyone in his department in terms of the three primary measures of performance: teaching, research, and service. Though his department head always made sure Dr. Bell got the largest pay raise, Dr. Bell went to his boss with these comments after the most recent pay increase: "When you told me about my pay raise, I was really excited, and I mentioned how pleased I was to be working here because it's the kind of place where performance pays off. I'm not sure I feel that way now, not after hearing that a couple of people got more than I did. Everybody knows they didn't deserve anything. I guess I was wrong. Performance doesn't seem to count." What was Dr. Bell's B2 initially? What is it now? What caused the change?

Dr. Bell in Case 4-2 actually got the largest pay raise in his department, but he thinks he didn't. His B2 up to now has been high, as indicated by his "performance pay off" comment, with a B2 rating in the 8-9 range. But now he is confused and is doubting his previously held belief about the performance-outcome relationship. A B2 rating in the 4-5-6 range probably fits him now. The doubting comes after hearing about a couple of people who "got more" when they "didn't deserve anything." In reality, they did not get bigger raises. Dr. Bell's emerging B2 problem is caused by his misperception of inequity.

The B2 diagnosis in Cases 4-1 and 4-2, like all others so far in this chapter, has been based on information received through communication with the employee, that is, on things employees say. There are other ways of obtaining B2 information, including (1) observation, (2) performance analysis, (3) organization analysis, (4) manager analysis, and (5) B2 history analysis. In the cases that follow, each of these ways will be illustrated. The remainder of the chapter will then provide an in-depth discussion of each way to obtain B2 information. Even though B2 information can and does come from different sources, you will find that interpreting it is no different from what you have done earlier in this chapter. You will see this as you work with the remaining cases and continue diagnosing B2 levels and causes.

Case 4-3—Interpreting B2 Information Obtained by Observation. Robert, an experienced production supervisor with a major manufacturing company, was already having second thoughts about moving to a lesser-known firm. He made the change because management had assured him things would be great with their "new system." The employees Robert was supervising had long referred to their place of employment as the "hellhole." They had been treated poorly for a long time with low pay, poor benefits, and nothing but push, push, push. They felt management didn't care, and it showed. The employees were capable of producing and wanted to, but they didn't because they were not rewarded when they did. Shortly after Robert was hired, management announced a new system where "everything will be based on performance." Robert watched his employees as the new program was announced and saw nothing but doubt and skepticism on their faces. After two months Robert noticed that nothing much had changed with the employees even though there were some signs that management was keeping its word. Poor performance was still the word of the day. There was no progress toward improvement, and no change in effort. Everyone still had the same bad attitude and negative feelings. They still complained a lot and continued to be dissatisfied with their jobs. Robert sensed a definite "wait and see" attitude. What were employee B2s before the new system was announced? What are they now? What is causing them to be where they are now?

Robert's observations in Case 4-3 are cause for concern. His job is to get workers to produce, yet he finds himself in a situation where his employees are not responding to the new incentive system he thought would make his job easier. Employee B2s have been low for a long time, probably in the 0-1-2-3 range. Robert's observations tell him that the B2s are not changing even though the new "everything based on performance" program has been in effect for two months. What is causing B2s to stay at the same low level? It takes time, usually a long time, to erase a low B2. It isn't done in weeks, and usually not in months. A lengthy and repeated tying of outcomes to performance is required. B2s are still low for Robert's employees because of the recency of tying outcomes to performance. It takes time to change B2s.

Case 4-4—Interpreting B2 Information Obtained by Performance Analysis. John was exceptionally bright and always performed well. He worked with ease, seldom having to work late, and always seemed free of the pressure felt by other employees. John was not reaching his full potential, but because he was a top performer his manager did not push him. Suddenly, John's performance declined substantially. He began doing only what was required—no more, no less. Shortly before the decline began, John was passed over for a promotion in favor of a couple of hard-working but average performers. What was John's B2 before his decline in performance? What happened to it when he was passed over for the promotion? What did being passed over mean that caused the change in his B2?

John's initial performance in Case 4-4 was fine and gave no hint of a B2 problem. Pinpointing his B2 prior to the decline in performance is difficult, but it must have been at the 6 or 7 level, at the least, or it would have been low enough to show up in his performance. The sudden and substantial decline in performance obviously signals a problem. The key to the performance analysis here is tying the decline in performance to a recent event that immediately preceded the decline, namely, being passed over for a promotion. This single event resulted in a substantial lowering of John's B2 level, which in turn reduced his motivation, effort, and performance. To John, being passed over meant "outcomes are not tied to performance."

Case 4-5—Interpreting B2 Information Obtained by Organization Analysis. Eliot was a young management consultant with a Ph.D. in business. He had started his own company and was working with a new client, a government agency, to improve productivity. After analyzing the organization, he came to the conclusion he had expected. "This is a well-established bureaucratic system where everything is based purely and simply on politics. Nothing depends on how well employees do their jobs. A few managers measure employee performance and try to reward those who perform well, but these managers receive no support or encouragement from above. They have little control over raises, promotions, and many other outcomes valued by high performers. Employees have no reason to perform better. That's the way it is, the way it always has been, and the way employees see it." What is the B2 for these employees? What is causing their B2s to be as they are?

The results of the organization analysis presented in Case 4-5 are not uncommon for government units at the federal, state, and local level. Eliot's analysis reveals an organization where outcomes are a function of things unrelated to performance. Outcomes simply are not tied to performance. This causes B2s to be low, very low. A B2 rating of 0 would not be inappropriate for most of these employees. Selected employees who work for competent managers may have somewhat higher B2s, but this would be the exception.

Case 4-6—Interpreting B2 Information Obtained by Organization Analysis. Eliot met the chairman of the board of one of the largest corporations in the United States while on a U.S. Department of Commerce trade mission to Saudi Arabia. The chairman asked Eliot to take a look at the corporation's manufacturing operations to see what could be done to motivate employees to do a better job. A summary of Eliot's analysis of the organization went something like this: "All of the manufacturing operations are unionized, and the unions are strong. Everything is based on seniority. Employees have no incentive to work harder. Managers at all levels have their hands tied with union contracts and consequently can do little, if anything, to motivate workers to perform better." How low are employees B2s? What is causing them to be low?

The organization analysis in Case 4-6 describes a company that not only does not tie outcomes to performance, it cannot. Union contracts prevent it. Employee B2s obviously are low, approaching a B2 rating of 0 for most employees, all because outcomes cannot be tied to performance. Even if the organization and its managers wanted to, it cannot be done.

Case 4-7—Interpreting B2 Information Obtained by Manager Analysis. Betsy was finishing her first year of managing a group of eight women in the financial services industry when she analyzed her management behaviors. "I have to admit that Susan does more work and better work than anybody else in my department. She gets rewarded well for her work. She was happy about it, too, until she found out some of the other women have higher salaries. There are good reasons for that. The other women don't give me a hard time. Susan is hard to get along with. She is arrogant, outspoken, and tactless. She had good ideas, but that embarrasses me sometimes. She intimidates people sometimes, including me. As long as she treats me as she has been doing, I don't see why I should treat her any better. After all, she gets rewarded well for what she does." What was Susan's B2 before discovering the salaries of the others? What is it now? Why the change?

The manager analysis in Case 4-7 describes the familiar situation of a manager being unfair to an employee. Betsy is giving outcomes based on factors other than performance. As a result, Susan's B2 has dropped. A prior rating in the 7-8-9 range and a current rating in the neighborhood of 3-4-5 probably would be good guesses of Susan's B2. The sudden drop was caused by inequity. Susan was getting basically what she deserved, based on her performance. However, what she was getting was not equitable relative to others.

Case 4-8—Interpreting B2 Information from B2 History. Andrea's brother Mark was the family favorite. Mark always got the most attention and praise, even if Andrea got better grades or did more work around the house or played a better ball game. This continued through elementary school, high school, and college. Mark took a job with a young, growing company. He performed well and advanced rapidly. Andrea went to work with an old, established major corporation. She performed well too, but her work went unrecognized in the size and bureaucracy of the organization. After a while she took another job, hoping her work would be recognized in a different environment. It wasn't. She didn't stay long. She's in a new job now. What was Andrea's B2 as a youth? What was her B2 in her previous job? What is it now? Why?

Andrea has a long history of outcomes not being tied to performance, as indicated in Case 4-8. In both her personal and work life, Andrea never seemed to get what she felt she deserved. It is difficult to pinpoint a B2 rating, but somewhere in the 2-3-4 range probably is fairly close. In any event, her B2 has always been on the low side. She has just started a new job. What is her B2 now? With the long history of a low B2, the best guess is that it is low now. It may be a little higher because a new job often represents new hope, but it is unlikely to be substantially different. She'll "wait and see" before changing her beliefs much about the performance-output relationship.

The eight cases discussed here have pointed out the six major causes of B2 problems: Case 4-1—Ray has a "misperception," in this case wrongly perceiving that outcomes are not tied to performance. Case 4-2—Dr. Bell also has a "misperception," this time the incorrect perception that an inequity has occurred. Case 4-3—Robert's employees have low B2s because of the "recency of tying outcomes to performance." Case 4-4—John's B2 dropped when he concluded that "Outcomes are not tied to performance." Case 4-5—The government employees are aware of the fact that "outcomes are not tied to performance." Case 4-6—The union employees, as well as their managers, know that "outcomes cannot be tied to performance." Case 4-7—There is "inequity," and Susan knows it. Case 4-8—Andrea has a long "history of outcomes not being tied to performance." When you diagnose an employee's B2 as low, look for one or more of these six factors to be causing the problem.

OBTAINING B2 INFORMATION

Obtaining B2 information usually is easier than getting B1 information. Employees with B1 problems often try to cover up feelings of inadequacy, even to the point of lying. Who wants to confess "I can't do it" to the boss? Employees have a different feeling about B2 problems because they are caused by someone else, someone who isn't giving them what they deserve. When employees believe outcomes are not tied to performance, they want to remedy the situation. Consequently, they are more likely to speak up, particularly when encouraged to do so.

The same "guess and guess again" approach suggested for diagnosing B1 also is recommended for B2. This means continuing to obtain B2 information until initial and revised guesses about B2 levels and B2 causes are confirmed. There are six ways to obtain this information: communication, observation, performance analysis, organization analysis, manager analysis, and B2 history analysis. It normally is not necessary to use all these methods to diagnose the B2 for a single employee, but it is better and safer to use more than one. All of them, however, will be needed at one time or another.

Communication

Communication with the employee is the best way to obtain information about B2 levels and all six of the B2 causes. This is accomplished with the same communication philosophy used with B1, that is, to "ask, shut up, and listen." Employees want to tell you when they have a problem, and they will if you use this simple approach. The same three ways to ask (open questions, direct questions, and clarifying questions) and the same four ways to actively listen (restating, summarizing, responding to nonverbal messages, and responding to feelings) that are discussed for B1 in chapter 2 can be used to obtain B2 information from your employees. Some of your questions and active-listening techniques will focus on B2 levels, while others will focus on B2 causes. Some will focus on employee B2s relative to extrinsic outcomes, while others will focus on intrinsic outcomes. With all this in mind, let's see how to do it.

When asking questions, it is best to start with one or more open questions. This "opens the door" for employees to talk. Open questions do not direct or limit the way employees respond. Instead, they allow and encourage employees to say whatever is on their minds. As a result, you obtain more and better information. Some standard open questions that have proven to work well are shown following this paragraph. Notice that different questions are required for obtaining information about B2 levels and B2 causes. The B2 level questions are asked first; if a B2 level problem is diagnosed, B2 cause questions should follow.

To Diagnose B2 Level

1. "What do you think about the way employees (you) are treated here?"
2. "What is your opinion about the way we reward employees (you)?"
3. "What are your thoughts about the way rewards are tied to performance?"
4. "How do you feel about the way we reward performance?"
5. "What is your reaction to the way we treat employees (you)?"
6. "How do you think we measure up in giving employees (you) what they (you) deserve?"
7. "You've seen how employees (you) are rewarded (treated) here. What do you think?"

To Diagnose B2 Causes

8. "What's causing you to believe employees (you) are not getting the things they (you) deserve?"
9. "What's happened to make you think employees (you) are not being rewarded the way they (you) should be?"
10. "What's making you question the way employees (you) are being treated?"
11. "Why are you having doubts that we are fair with our employees (you)?"
12. "What's causing you to believe that employees (you) are not getting what they (you) deserve?"
13. "What's happened to make you think employees (you) are not being rewarded as they (you) should be?"
14. "What's making you question the way we treat employees (you)?"
15. "Why are you having doubts about our treating our employees (you) fairly?"
16. "What's causing you to believe outcomes (rewards) are not tied to performance?"

You can see from these questions that an employee's B2 is formed not only by whether he or she is receiving outcomes tied to performance but also by whether outcomes are tied to performance for other employees. If an employee sees others getting outcomes based on performance, the employee will expect the same treatment, that is, will have a high B2, unless there is evidence to the contrary. Likewise, if others are not getting outcomes based on performance, the employee will expect the same and therefore have a low B2. Because of this, you can get an idea of an employee's B2 level by asking questions about the performance-outcome relationship of others.

Open questions, like those in the previous list, should be followed by direct questions. Using these, you can direct employee comments to specific information that is important to your diagnosis. In contrast to open questions, direct questions enable you to zero in on specific things employees may have said or implied or may not have mentioned yet. Some direct questions will yield information about B2 levels, others about B2 causes. Standard direct questions of both types that have been proven to be effective are as follows.

To Diagnose B2 Level

1. "Do you believe we reward employees (you) based on their (your) performance?"
2. "Do you think employees (you) are getting what they (you) deserve?"
3. "Are employees (you) being treated fairly?"
4. "Have we been meeting employee (your) expectations?"
5. "Are things working out the way employees (you) want them to?"
6. "Have we been following through on our commitments to employees (you)?"
7. "Does it seem that when employees (you) perform well, they (you) get what they (you) are looking for?"
8. "Do you believe that when employees (you) produce more, they (you) get rewarded for it?"
9. "Does it look as if everybody is treated the same regardless of performance?"
10. "Do you believe outcomes (rewards) generally are tied to performance here?"

To Diagnose B2 Causes

11. "Do you think this is a clear-cut case where employees (you) could be getting outcomes (rewards) based on performance, but are not?"
12. "Do you feel as if we are in a situation here (unions or bureaucracy or whatever) where it is impossible for managers to give rewards based on performance?"
13. "Are you having trouble believing we are serious about the new push to give people what they deserve, after so many years of not doing so here?"
14. "Have you been in a lot of situations in the past where you didn't get what you deserved?"
15. "Do you think some people are treated differently than others, and therefore unfairly, when it comes to giving out rewards like pay raises, promotions, and whatever?"

Two things about these questions. First, for cause questions 11 through 15, each asks employees to give information about a different B2 cause. That is, each question directs the employee to respond to a specific thing that may be causing a B2 problem. These direct questions allow you to obtain information to pinpoint B2 causes. Second, can you recognize and name the five B2 causes indicated in questions 11 through 15? You may want to refer back to the list of B2 causes presented earlier in this chapter. Identify the causes in the five questions, then check yourself in the next paragraph.

The B2 causes that are the foci of questions 11 through 15, respectively, are (1) outcomes are not tied to performance, or misperception that outcomes are not tied to performance; (2) outcomes cannot be tied to performance; (3) recency of tying outcomes to performance; (4) employee history of outcomes not being tied to performance; and (5) inequity in tying outcomes to performance, or misperception of inequity in tying outcomes to performance. How did you do in identifying the B2 causes? Maybe not perfectly, as this was your first attempt. No need to worry. You'll get two other chances to practice shortly.

The third kind of question you will find indispensable is the clarifying question. The purpose obviously is to get clarification, and the value is immeasurable. Here's why. In the first place, most people are not great communicators. They often (1) don't say what they mean, (2) don't mean what they say, (3) say things ambiguously, and (4) leave out critical information. Second, employees often are hesitant, for whatever reasons, to tell you readily all you want to know or even everything they want to tell you. Clarifying questions provide a very effective way to deal with employee difficulty and hesitancy in communicating the information you need. The questions are simple to formulate and use. Here is a list of standard clarifying questions that are guaranteed to work.

1. "Can you be more specific?"
2. "Could you give me a couple of examples?"
3. "Would you give me more details?"
4. "Can you tell me more?"
5. "Can you tell me exactly what you're thinking?"
6. "Can you help me understand that better?"
7. "What else can you tell me?"
8. "I'm not sure I understand." (Same effect as a question.)

Now come active-listening techniques to facilitate communication with employees as a way of obtaining B2 information. The same four techniques discussed in chapter 2 for B1 diagnosis can be used for diagnosing B2. They are restating, summarizing, responding to nonverbal messages, and responding to feelings. The same advantages to each one discussed in chapter 2 apply here. You may want to review them quickly before moving ahead.

Restating is repeating, in your own words, a key point the employee has made. The restating accomplishes several things. It shows employees you are listening and understand what was said. It allows them to correct or complete your restatement. It encourages them to talk more and give you additional information. It makes employees feel good to know you are listening, understanding, and making it easy for them to talk. All of this makes your job of diagnosing the employee's B2 easier and more effective. Examples of restating are shown below. As you read them, identify the B2 causes in restatements 7 through 12.

To Diagnose B2 Level

1. "So, the way you see it, outcomes (rewards) for the most part are tied to performance here."

2. "What you are saying is that we could do a little better job of giving employees (you) what they (you) deserve."

3. "Sounds like you think things are way out of line, with some employees getting a lot more than they deserve while the others are getting far less."

4. "It is your opinion, then, that everybody is being treated pretty much the same no matter how they perform."

5. "So you feel that we promise a lot, but often don't come through with it."

6. "As far as you are concerned, then, you're confident about being treated right as long as you do a good job."

To Diagnose B2 Causes

7. "You've heard that a couple of people you think produce the same as you got bigger pay raises, and you feel that's unfair."

8. "So it's hard for you to trust what anybody promises because you seldom got what was promised in the past, even when you really deserved it."

9. "You seem to be saying that our emphasis on rewarding people for performance is so new that it is too soon to believe it is for real."

10. "Sounds like you are convinced that outcomes seldom, if ever, are based on performance."

11. "The way you see it, the system here makes it impossible for people to get rewarded based on how good a job they do."

12. "Basically you're saying that giving everybody a 5 percent pay raise is just another example of management not caring whether you produce or not."

The B2 causes in restatements 7 through 12, respectively, are (1) inequity, or misperception of inequity, in tying outcomes to performance; (2) employee history of outcomes not being tied to performance; (3) recency of outcomes being tied to performance; (4) outcomes are not tied to performance, or misperception that they are not; (5)

outcomes cannot be tied to performance; and (6) outcomes are not tied to performance, or misperception they are not.

Summarizing is the active-listening technique of restating two or more things. In the case of B2 diagnosis, summarizing what the employee has said is what is relevant to the diagnosis, not summarizing things you may have said. You may summarize at any point in the discussion, and more than once if necessary, but definitely at the end of the discussion to bring closure to the B2 discussion. The advantages of restating apply to summarizing. Examples of summarizing information about B2 levels and B2 causes are shown following this paragraph. As you read items 4 through 8, identify the specific B2 causes in each one.

To Diagnose B2 Level

1. "Let me summarize. You feel that you have done a good job for us, but you keep getting passed over for a promotion and are beginning to lose confidence in our commitment to reward people who deserve it."

2. "So you're saying that most of the employees in our unit are beginning to see clearly that if you do a good job, you get rewarded, and if you don't perform, you don't share in the rewards."

3. "Let me recap what you've said. You worked harder than ever for four months on the conversion project, did more work and better work than anybody else, and never got anything for it, not even thanks. Now you're wondering if doing a good job even matters."

To Diagnose B2 Causes

4. "I'm hearing three things. You believe your work is much better than Bill's. You know he's making more money than you. And you think that's unfair."

5. "So that's the story of your life. Work hard, do a good job, and never get rewarded for it. And you think you see the same thing happening here."

6. "You seem to be making three main points. Nobody really has ever been held accountable around here. People are seeing a few attempts toward more accountability, but not enough has happened yet to convince anybody that things are going to be different."

7. "Everybody knows who does a good job and who doesn't, yet the same people get the rewards no matter what. Nobody has a reason to be more productive."

8. "So you're saying you want to get ahead, but there is no way except through seniority in the union. You want to move further and faster than the union allows, so you're thinking about looking for another job with more opportunity."

The B2 causes in summaries 4 through 8, respectively, are (1) inequity, or misperception of inequity, in tying outcomes to performance; (2) employee history of outcomes not being tied to performance; (3)

recency of outcomes being tied to performance; (4) outcomes are not tied to performance, or the misperception they are not; and (5) outcomes cannot be tied to performance.

Responding to nonverbal messages is another active-listening technique for obtaining B2 information. It encourages employees to talk about things they may not mention otherwise, things that often are critical to diagnosing their B2 accurately. The idea is to watch for and pick up nonverbal messages and to respond to them rather than passing up the opportunity to obtain B2 information. Your response to nonverbal messages should include two components. First, specifically state the nonverbal message you have picked up ("the look on your face," "nod of agreement,"etc.). Second, state the performance-outcome relationship you want the employees to talk about ("across-the-board pay raises," "special recognition for performance," etc.). Some typical examples of responses to nonverbal messages are as follows.

1. "Judging from the look on your face, you're not surprised that we're giving across-the-board pay raises again."
2. "I noticed nods of agreement when staff members were given special recognition for performance yesterday."
3. "You looked shocked when it was announced that one of your coworkers had gotten the only promotion."
4. "You haven't stopped smiling since the corporate office gave you special recognition for the project work you just completed."
5. "You looked skeptical in the morning meeting when the plan was announced to develop better performance measures to tie pay more closely to each employee's contribution."
6. "You look as if you feel cheated not being selected to be in the new 'fast track' program."

The final active-listening technique for obtaining B2 information is responding to feelings. This is an excellent technique, because showing feelings about a B2 issue suggests a willingness, maybe even an eagerness, by employees to share what they are thinking. This is a great opportunity to obtain B2 information. By responding to employee feelings, you not only take advantage of this opportunity but also make the employee feel good by encouraging the open sharing of feelings. As you respond to employee feelings, do two things. One, name the feeling the employee is showing (anger, frustration, happiness, hurt, satisfaction, depression, joy, excitement, relief, eagerness, discouragement, disgust, rejection, sadness, apathy, etc.). Two, state the performance-outcome relationship you want the employee to talk about. Some common examples of responding to feelings are as follows.

1. "You sound angry about being passed over for a promotion after working so hard for it."
2. "It's frustrating to be the one who always has to stay late when something important needs to be finished."
3. "You really seem happy about your promotion."
4. "It hurts when you don't get something you really deserve."
5. "You seem satisfied with the way things turned out after we finally realized you were the one who kept us from losing our biggest client."
6. "Seems like you've been a little depressed since you heard we were bringing in an outsider rather than giving you the unit manager position."

As you can see, one of the essential ways to obtain B2 information is communication with employees. The key is to ask questions (open, direct, and clarifying questions), "shut up," and listen (restate, summarize, respond to nonverbal messages, and respond to feelings). It is not difficult to ask questions and listen in the way suggested here. Simply use the standard questions provided and follow the active-listening examples. You will do fine.

Observation

Observing employees can be a good way to obtain B2 information. Although you cannot depend on observation alone to diagnose B2 levels and causes, it can be a good starting point. In fact, observation may give the first clue that a motivation problem exists. Once you are aware of a problem, any piece of information obtained through observation can be valuable, maybe even the key, to the "guess and guess again" approach for diagnosing B2. Although observation can be particularly helpful for identifying one of the main causes of B2 problems, that outcomes are not tied to performance, it may also give clues to the presence of any of the other B2 causes.

What do you observe? In one sense, you should watch for anything and everything that could suggest employees are either concerned that outcomes are not tied to performance or pleased that they are. Fortunately there are a few specific things to keep your eyes on. Let's take a look at them, keeping in mind that although a conclusive B2 diagnosis will not come from observation alone, a valuable piece may be added to the diagnosis puzzle.

Observation of performance can tell you something about the B2 of your employees. If observed performance is where you want it to be, there is little reason to expect a B2 problem. But what if performance isn't where you want it? Poor performance may be indicating that the employee has a low B2. Let observations of poor performance be your signal to obtain additional information to assess B2 levels more accurately.

In addition to performance, three other related factors can be observed—progress, amount of effort, and kind of effort. Each is a substitute for observing performance, especially when performance is difficult to measure or observe. If observed progress and effort seem satisfactory, there is no reason to suspect a B2 problem. When progress and effort are unsatisfactory, a B2 problem is just one of several possiblities, but one to be checked out. Look to surrounding circumstances for evidence of factors known to cause B2 problems. Doing so may well lead you to a key piece of information in determining B2 levels and causes.

Let's go back to Case 4-3 to see how observation can be used to help diagnose employee B2s. In this case Robert, the supervisor, is comparing observations of employees before and after the company announcement of a new system where "everything will be based on performance." Robert's observations after two months led him to conclude that "nothing much had changed."

Specifically, Robert observed that performance was still poor and that there had been no progress toward improvement and no change in effort. Furthermore, employees still had a bad attitude and the same negative feelings; they continued to complain a lot and remained dissatisfied with their jobs. As the case points out, these were employees who could perform well and wanted outcomes to be tied to performance. Given this knowledge and Robert's observations, you can make a reasonably conclusive diagnosis that B2 levels are low and that they are low because the recency of the new system has not provided sufficient time to overcome the long history of outcomes not being tied to performance.

What do you think about Robert's observations? Were they difficult to make? Not really. It is easy to observe poor performance, lack of progress, no change in effort, bad attitudes, negative feelings, lots of complaints, and dissatisfaction. What's so special about what Robert did? There are three things. He knew he should observe, he knew what to observe, and he knew how to translate the observations into a B2 diagnosis. Doing it is the easy part. Recognizing the need to do it is the first step. Do it and you'll do it well.

Performance Analysis

Analyzing employee performance is another good way to obtain B2 information about your employees. This analysis is particularly useful in identifying B2 problems caused from outcomes not being tied to performance. If employee performance is meeting performance requirements, there is little reason to expect a B2 problem. But what if actual performance is less than required? This tells you there is a problem of some kind, and it may be a B2 problem. It is necessary to look to the circumstances surrounding the situation to determine if a B2 problem exists. What are the situations? There are two. What are the circumstances? There are many.

One situation is where employee performance takes a downturn from what previously has been satisfactory. What are the circumstances surrounding the downturn? If the downturn came soon after performance standards were raised or new work methods were instituted, the circumstances give reason to suspect a B1 problem, not B2.

But what if the circumstances that preceded the downturn in performance included one or more events known to cause B2 problems? This category includes events that indicate outcomes are not tied to performance (the employee is unfairly passed over for a promotion, for example) or events that suggest inequity (such as one employee seeing another who had a reputation for poor performance getting a bigger pay raise). Such B2-related circumstances suggest that the downturn in performance could be the employee's reaction to recent evidence that "outcomes are not tied to performance," that "I'm not getting what I deserve." These circumstances are only a basis from which to guess, but they provide a starting point. The performance analysis suggests a B2 level that may be low and perhaps suggests possible B2 causes. Take a first guess, and then guess and guess again as you obtain more B2 information.

The other situation is where employee performance has not yet reached the required level. Again, looking at the circumstances may tell you something useful. If the employee was untrained when hired and has not received adequate training since, your best guess is that the employee doesn't have the skills (no training) and therefore does not have the motivation ("I can't do it") to perform. This circumstance suggests a B1 rather than a B2 problem.

Different circumstances, however, might lead you to make an initial guess that the employee's B2 is the problem. Suppose the employee has all the needed skills but does not put out the effort necessary to meet performance standards. Further, suppose you know the employee has a history of "bad" experiences, like quitting the last two jobs "because I did everything and did it well, and all I ever got was promises." This circumstance suggests that the employee's B2 level may be low and further suggests that the employee's B2 history may be causing the problem.

As performance analysis is used, keep in mind that employee performance also may turn down or never reach required levels because of misperceptions that keep employees from being motivated. There are two kinds of misperceptions. One, employees often perceive their performance to be higher than it is and therefore view outcomes as being less than they ought to be. The result is a low B2. Second, employees often perceive outcomes to be less than they are and therefore view their performance as deserving more. Again, the result is a low B2. In both cases, outcomes are not perceived to be closely tied to performance, although they are.

How do you find out if employees have either of these misperception? You can ask. Regarding perception of performance, here are some examples of useful questions:

—"How do you feel about your performance?"
—"How do you think your performance is coming along now?"
—"How do you see your work compared to everybody else's?"
—"Would you give me a rundown of exactly what you have accomplished?"
—"How do you see your actual performance compared to performance standards?"

With respect to perception of outcomes, here are some examples:

—"What are the main things you feel you're getting out of your work?"
—"What do you value most in your job?"
—"What are some of the things you'd like to be getting from your work but aren't?"
—"What do you most want that you're not getting?"

These and related questions give employees a chance to say things that enable you to recognize misperceptions regarding performance and outcomes.

In addition to employee perception, employee potential also is a consideration in performance analysis. Earlier it was stated that if employees were meeting performance requirements, there was little reason to suspect a B2 problem. However, a B2 problem is possible in this instance. Some employees can meet performance requirements with little effort, that is, without being very highly motivated. For these employees, you should compare their actual performance not only with required performance but also with their performance potential. If you find that actual performance is less than their potential, you have identified an employee whose motivation could be higher. That is, you have an employee whose B2 may not be low but may be as high as it could be. If an employee's actual performance equals performance potential, there is no reason to suspect a motivation problem of any type.

You can see that performance analysis can be a useful way to obtain

B2 information. Analyzing employee performance levels relative to performance requirements and performance potential, keeping employee misperceptions in mind, can yield valuable B2 information.

Want to try your hand at performance analysis? Take another look at Case 4-4. What was John's actual performance compared to performance requirements before and after his performance decline? What does this suggest about his B2 level before and after? What was his actual performance compared to his potential before and after the decline? How does this affect your diagnosis of his B2 level?

An analysis of John's performance indicates quite a bit about his B2. John's good performance initially, where actual performance exceeded performance requirements, suggests that his B2 was on the high side. How high? This is hard to pinpoint, but his B2 had to be at least at the 6 or 7 level, or else he would not have been motivated to perform so well. His performance decline to a level equal to performance requirements indicates a lowering of his B2. But how low? The fact that he was meeting performance requirements, though not exceeding them as before, suggests that his B2 probably did not go below the 4 or 5 level. That is, he believed that outcomes were tied to performance enough that he did not want to take the risk of letting performance drop below the minimum required level.

Let's take a look now at John's actual performance compared to his potential and how that affects the B2 diagnosis. Initially, when he was performing well, his performance fell short of his full potential. This indicates he wasn't fully confident about outcomes being tied to performance. This suggests that his initial B2 was on the high side, but on the lower end of the high side (at 6 or 7). That is, his B2 was not low but it was not as high as it could be.

Noticing a decline in employee performance is not difficult, if you are watching. You know this signals some kind of problem, possibly a B2 problem. Linking performance declines to events known to affect B2 levels, like being passed over for a promotion or failing to get a well-deserved pay raise, helps identify B2 problems and their causes.

Organization Analysis

Organization analysis is another way of obtaining information to diagnose B2s. It helps identify several causes of B2 problems, including (1) outcomes are not tied to performance, (2) inequity of outcomes among employees, (3) recency of tying outcomes to performance, and (4) outcomes cannot be tied to performance. What factors do you examine when analyzing the organization? How do they affect employee B2s?

Perhaps the most important factor is the organization's belief about tying outcomes to performance. Do the leaders in your organization believe that employees perform better when they get what they deserve? If leaders truly believe this, key decisions will reflect it; and much will be done to insure that employees are rewarded on the basis of performance. Employee B2s will be on the high side, though B2 ratings as high as 9 and 10 generally are not to be expected. If the leadership in the organization does not believe in tying outcomes to performance, little will be done to give employees what they deserve. Consequently, employee B2s generally will be low, with B2 ratings as low as 2, 1, or even 0.

The second factor to consider when doing this kind of analysis is the degree of the organization's freedom from barriers that make it difficult, even impossible, to tie outcomes to performance. Entrenched bureaucracy, in federal, state, and local governments as well as in some older and larger corporations, and labor unions erect major barriers to tying outcomes to performance. Employees in these organizations typically have extremely low B2s, bordering on the lowest possible B2 rating of 0. Organizations that are free of such barriers at least have the opportunity to do something to tie outcomes to performance. Whether employee B2s are on the high side or not depends on what the organization does.

The third factor to evaluate when doing an organization analysis is the encouragement the organization gives managers to tie outcomes to performance. Does the organization insist that managers measure employee performance, and does it use those measures when conducting performance evaluations and making decisions about pay raises, promotions, and other rewards? Are managers evaluated and rewarded according to the way they tie outcomes to performance for their employees? Managers do what they are encouraged to do, especially what they are rewarded to do. When managers receive encouragement and rewards for tying outcomes to performance, employee B2s will tend to be high. If there are little or no encouragement and few if any rewards, employee B2s will be low.

The fourth factor to be considered in organization analysis is the extent to which employee performance can be measured. This can pose a real challenge. How do you measure performance when research requires years for discovery or inventions take years to develop? How do you measure a manager's performance in nonprofit organizations or public relations efforts in any organization? When measuring performance is difficult or next to impossible, or extraordinarily costly and time consuming, performance tends to go unmeasured. When this is the case, there is no basis for tying outcomes to performance. B2s likely will be on the low side. However, the fact that measurement is possible does not insure that B2s will be high, but at least there is a chance they can be.

The fifth factor to look at in organization analysis is the availability of outcomes, especially resources, to tie to performance. Resources simply may not be available for pay increases, bonuses, company cars, extensive benefits, retirement plans, paid vacations, complimentary tickets to concerts or athletic events, etc. Other outcomes may not be available, such as promotion opportunities, as is the case in some organizations with slow growth, low turnover, and few employees nearing retirement age. When outcomes are not available, there is little to tie to performance, and employee B2s will be low. When outcomes are available, the door is opened for giving employees what they deserve and establishing high B2s.

Organization analysis is a simple and straightfoward way to obtain information for diagnosing employee B2s. The information usually is readily available and obtaining it normally is not difficult. Looking at the five organizational factors can do a lot to help you understand the B2 of your employees.

A word of warning is necessary here. Doing an organization analysis often is discouraging. You likely will find that many of the factors analyzed are not favorable in your organization. This means that the B2s of your employees are not high, certainly not as high as you would like, and may well be considerably lower than you had originally been thinking. Even more discouraging is the realization that your ability to improve employee B2s is constrained by your organization, maybe severely constrained. But don't give up and say "I can't." Not yet, anyway. There may be some solutions that will work for you.

The use of organization analysis to obtain B2 information can be seen in Case 4-5, which deals with a government agency that hired a consultant to help improve productivity. Read the case again and pick out the key information that relates to organization analysis, then compare your list with the consultant's.

The main points in the consultant's organization analysis are that (1) the agency believes in a reward system based on politics, not performance; (2) it is bound by an entrenched bureaucracy that poses many barriers to the concept of tying outcomes to performance; (3) while some managers do measure employee performance, they are not encouraged to tie outcomes to performance; and (4) mangers who take the initiative to do so on their own do not have control over the resources necessary to reward high-performing employees. What about the diagnosis? Obviously B2 levels are low. The cause? Outcomes are not being tied to performance.

Case 4-6 also deals with organization analysis. Read this case again and identify which of the five factors in the organization analysis is dominant. When you have decided, continue with this paragraph. The manufacturing company represents a situation where (1) organization beliefs about tying outcomes to performance do not matter, (2) encouraging managers to tie outcomes to performance does not matter, (3) the extent to which employee performance can be measured does not matter, and (4) the availability of outcomes does not matter. None of these four factors matter, because a strong contract by a strong union is such a dominant factor that the company is prevented from tying outcomes to performance.

What are your conclusions about organization analysis after seeing it done in Case 4-5 and Case 4-6? Is it difficult? No, not really. It is easy to obtain information about any of the five factors. The information is readily available. Getting it is easy, if you know what to get. And now you know. It's simple. Just do it.

Manager Analysis

Now comes manager analysis as a way of obtaining information to diagnose the B2s of your employees. Manager analysis is a self-analysis of the things you do that influence employee beliefs about performance leading to outcomes (B2). As a manager, you have a greater influence over the B2s of your employees than anything or anyone else. Are you having the kind of influence you want? An objective analysis of what you are doing can answer this question. This can help identify several causes of B2 problems: (1) outcomes not tied to performance, (2) inequity of outcomes among employees, (3) recency of tying outcomes to performance, and (4) outcomes that cannot be tied to performance.

Analyzing the way you manage can be painful. The truth can hurt, especially if it points a finger at you. But the truth can help, if it's used to identify and solve problems. The truth in this case comes from analyzing six factors about yourself.

The first is whether or not you believe in tying outcomes to performance. This is the starting point. If you don't believe outcomes should be directly related to performance, you will do little to tie them together, and your employees will have low B2s. Do you really believe that both you and your employees will benefit considerably by giving employees what they deserve? Believing this, even strongly, doesn't guarantee high B2s for your employees, but it's a step in the right direction.

The second factor to analyze is the extent to which you control the outcomes your employees want. Although you may not have control over all of the resources you need, like money for pay raises, and may not have the authority to decide who gets promoted, you always have control over certain outcomes like praise, recognition, job assignments, employee involvement in decision making, and the full range of outcomes associated with the management style you choose to use with employees. This can go a long way toward keeping B2s at a reasonably high level. However, B2s will not be as high as they could be if you had more control over resources.

Your ability to measure employee performance is the third factor to look at in manager analysis. Outcomes simply cannot be tied to performance when you cannot measure performance. Can you measure the performance of all of your employees? If not, the B2s of some will be low. Figuring out how to measure performance can be easy. Your employees may even be willing to help, especially those who want to see outcomes tied more closely to the results of their efforts. Yet, being able to measure employee performance doesn't insure high B2s. What else must be done?

You also must have the ability to establish a satisfactory performance/outcomes schedule. This is the fourth factor to evaluate when doing a manager analysis. You must identify appropriate outcomes for various levels of performance, that is, you must create a performance/outcomes schedule. The schedule must be satisfactory not only from your own perspective but also from the perspectives of both the organization and the employee. This is no simple matter and requires significant capability. Unless you can do this, employee B2s cannot be expected to be high.

The fifth factor to consider in the manager analysis is another ability, that of tying outcomes to performance as planned, in accordance with the performance/outcomes schedule. Following a schedule seems simple, but two major problems often arise. They were mentioned earlier in the discussion of the causes of B2 problems. One is that employees may be left with the misperception that outcomes are not tied to performance. The other is the misperception of inequity, as employees compare outcomes they receive relative to others. These problems stem from the way managers communicate with employees when giving outcomes. It takes a focused effort to leave employees with a complete and accurate perception.

The sixth and final factor to evaluate when doing the manager analysis is the extent to which you actually tie outcomes to performance. Are you really tying outcomes to performance? Even if you measure up favorably on each of the other five manager factors, doing this job still may be difficult. One reason is time. You may not have enough time, or take enough, to do everything and do it right. Having a high need for acceptance and approval from your employees is another reason. Because of this need, you may find it difficult to give what is deserved, instead feeling pressure to give what your employees want. Are you actually tying outcomes to performance? This is the bottom line to the self-analysis of the way you manage.

So there you have it: manager analysis, another way to obtain information for diagnosing the B2s of your employees. Analyzing the six factors about yourself is relatively simple, if you can be objective. The results will give you greater insight into the performance-outcomes beliefs (B2s) of your employees.

A very strong warning accompanies this manager analysis. The results can cause considerable self-doubt. You probably will not evaluate yourself favorably on all of the factors. You may conclude that you are causing some, perhaps many, of the B2 problems your employees are experiencing. This is no cause for real concern. You can learn how to turn this situation around. It is easy, as you will see in the next chapter when B2 solutions are discussed.

Case 4-7 deals with manager analysis. As you reread this case, how would you evaluate Betsy in terms of the six factors used for a manager analysis? Based on your evaluation, how would you expect Betsy's way of managing to affect the B2s of her employees? How does your evaluation compare with the following? Betsy does not really believe in tying outcomes to performance (factor 1). She believes in partially tying outcomes to performance. This is evidenced by her giving Susan a smaller raise than those given some of the less-productive employees on the basis of measures not directly related to performance, such as "Susan gives me a hard time—is hard to get along with—is arrogant, outspoken, and tactless–embarrasses me—and intimidates me." Not believing in tying outcomes to performance means Betsy is not establishing a satisfactory performance/outcomes schedule (factor 4). Although she seems to have adequate control over outcomes (factor 2), apparently knows how to measure employee performance (factor 3), and probably can tie outcomes to performance as planned (factor 5), her failure to believe in tying outcomes to performance (factor 1) results in her not doing so (factor 6). How does this affect the B2s of Betsy's employees? You know the answer. It makes them realize that outcomes are tied to performance in only a limited way. Most of Betsy's employees probably would have B2 ratings in the midrange (B2 = 4, 5, 6) at best.

B2 History Analysis

Although all the ways to get B2 information—communication, observation, performance analysis, organization analysis, and manager analysis—are important, an employee's B2 history deserves special treatment. There are five reasons. First, each employee's current B2 is determined largely by past beliefs about performance leading to outcomes. Second, it is difficult, if not impossible, continually to make an accurate diagnosis of current B2s without knowledge of the employee's past. Three, although it is not particularly difficult to learn to recognize the diversity of influences that go into the ultimate formation of an employee's B2, it takes time. Four, obtaining information about an employee's B2 history and interpreting it are more difficult than the other ways of getting B2 information. Five, an employee's B2 history is the only way to identify one of the primary causes of B2 problems, an employee history of outcomes not being tied to performance. With this in mind, let's move ahead to see how B2 histories can make your job go more easily and better.

B2 history refers to the employee's past beliefs about the likelihood that performance will lead to outcomes. These beliefs develop in several ways and have a significant influence on the employee's current B2. Let's take a look at this developing and influencing process.

Over time, all employees develop both a general B2 and a B2 for each specific outcome. Examples of how employees express their general B2 (gB2) are "I usually get what I deserve" (gB2 = 7, 8, 9) or "I hardly ever get what I deserve" (gB2 = 0, 1, or 2) or "Sometimes I get what I deserve, sometimes I don't (gB2 = 4, 5, or 6). A B2 for a specific outcome might be expressed as "I've really done a good job and I'm almost certain I'll get a good pay raise this year" (B2 = 8 or 9 for a good pay raise) or "There's so much favoritism here that I don't have much of a chance for a promotion anytime soon" (B2 = 0, 1, 2, or 3 for a promotion soon) or "From what I hear, I think I have a pretty fair chance of getting some kind of special recognition for my work on the project" (B2 = 5, 6, or 7 for special recognition).

Several things are suggested by a close analysis of a large number of B2 histories. First, gB2s seem to be developed initially during youth. Early experiences tend to lead young people to conclude, "Yeah, I usually get what I deserve" (gB2 = 7, 8, or 9) or "Life's not fair" (gB2 = 0, 1, or 2). Second, once a low gB2 is formed, it tends not to improve much over time; when it does, it rises only after a lengthy period of repeatedly receiving outcomes based on performance. Three, when a gB2 is high, it may take only a few situations of not receiving what is deserved to cause the gB2 to drop. How much it drops and how quickly is a function of the number of times deserved outcomes are not received, how important the outcomes were, and how deserved they were, that is, how cheated the person feels.

How does an employee's gB2 develop? The developmental process takes hold first during youth and continues as personal and work-related events in the employee's adult life exert a major influence. Many events in an employee's youth contribute to the formation of the gB2, that is, contribute to the employee's general belief about whether or not outcomes are tied to performance. Two categories of events are commonly mentioned by employees: (1) the extent to which teachers, parents, other significant adults (grandparents, neighbors, coaches), and peers gave them outcomes based on their performance and (2) the extent to which significant others (family members, friends, heroes) received outcomes based on performance. If a youth starts seeing that people do not get what their performance deserves, the tendency is to see only that; and the belief that performance does not lead to outcomes hardens. It takes a long history of seeing outcomes tied to performance to erase a history that has firmed up the belief that "people don't get what they deserve."

Two striking conclusions can be drawn from the events that play a primary role in developing a young person's gB2. One, it is not surprising that B2 problems develop early in life for many people. The events that cause gB2s to be low are typical in the lives of many youth, but those that cause gB2s to be high are not. Two, the gB2 is developed not only from events that affect individuals directly but also from events they see affecting others. This carries over later in life. Adults look at the experiences of others as well as their own in the evolution of their gB2s.

Let's see how this developmental process continues into adult life. Adults experience many events in their personal lives that contribute to the formation of gB2s. This can be summarized as (1) the extent to which their spouses, children, friends, and significant others give them outcomes based on performance and (2) the extent to which significant others get outcomes based on performance. Unfortunately, it is commonplace in the personal lives of many adults not to receive outcomes based on performance and to see the same happen to others. Such events have a strong influence on the general beliefs employees hold about outcomes being tied to performance. This is coupled with the rather uncommon occurrence of events that contribute to the formation of high gB2s.

In addition to the events in an adult's personal life, there are many work-related events that go into the formation of the employee's gB2. Events that occurred in previous jobs, as well as in the employee's current job, are part of the formation process. Discussions with employees indicate that two factors in previous and current jobs contribute significantly to the formation of gB2s. The first is the extent to which outcomes have been tied to their performance. Organization(s) that give across-the-board raises and promotions based on seniority are prime examples of organizations not tying outcomes to performance. Managers who give rewards based on favoritism, politics, and loyalty rather than performance teach employees that they can generally expect outcomes not to be based on performance. The second is the extent to which outcomes have been tied to performance for others they know. The gB2 of employees is determined not only by what happens directly to the employee but also by what is happening to others. The pervasiveness of negative events in most organizations leaves little doubt about why many employees believe outcomes generally are not tied to performance. Although they acknowledge some exceptions, in which specific outcomes are tied to performance, many employees believe it is uncommon to see outcomes closely related to performance.

How, then, is an individual's gB2 formed, given all of these possible events in a person's youth and adult life? It is not the nature of these events alone that is responsible. The relative frequency of the events is a primary determinant of the level of an individual's gB2. If the vast majority of the events an individual experiences shows outcomes being tied to performance, the individual forms the general belief that outcomes usually are tied to performance (gB2 = 7, or 8, or 9). However, if only a small percentage of the events experienced indicates that outcomes are being tied to performance, the individual forms the general belief that outcomes seldom are tied to performance (gB2 = 1, or 2, or 3).

If the nature and relative frequency of events combine to determine the level of an individual's gB2, what determines the strength of the belief? That is, what determines how firmly the belief is held? The strength is primarily a function of the amount of accumulated evidence. An older employee who has observed for twenty years that outcomes seldom are tied to performance will have a more strongly held belief (gB2) than a young employee who has observed the same thing over only a two-month period. The gB2 for both may be at the 3 or 4 level, but the belief formed by hundreds of events over twenty years is stronger than the younger employee's newly formed belief.

Four facts that emerge from B2 histories are surprising. The first is the overwhelming number of employees who have gB2s that are low. The experiences of many employees have left them believing it is more the exception than the rule that outcomes are tied to performance, believing that "I generally do not get what I deserve," believing that being cheated and treated unfairly simply is the way it is.

The second surprising fact is how firmly entrenched most low gB2s are. When a lengthly history of outcomes not being tied to performance is followed by recent events in which deserved outcomes are being given, long-held beliefs are not abandoned quickly. Instead, employees tend to hold onto beliefs formed by a long history of events stretching back to their youth. It takes a new and lengthy history of outcomes being tied to performance to erase a strongly held general belief that outcomes are not tied to performance.

The third surprising fact is how quickly and how far high gB2s will drop. When recent events indicate outcomes are no longer being tied to performance, after years of getting what was deserved, employees tend to change their beliefs considerably and quickly. It does not take many recent events for employees to start believing that outcomes are no longer tied to performance, that the good days are over, and that things will never be the same. This happens especially if recent events immediately follow new ownership, new management, or getting a new boss. It takes only a few recent events where outcomes are not tied to performance to erase a strongly and generally held belief that outcomes are based on performance.

The fourth surprising fact is how readily most employees will reveal their gB2s when given the chance. Remember from our earlier discussion on gB1 in chapter 2 that employees tend to be embarrassed to admit, "I don't have much confidence generally in my ability to perform well even when I try." With gB2 it is very different, for at least two reasons. First, saying "I don't think I generally get what I deserve" does not reflect anything negative about the individual, as is the case of B1 with the person admitting "I can't." Second, when employees believe, "I don't get what I deserve," they tend to say it, even complain about it, because they want the wrong to be made right. There is little reluctance among most employees to reveal their beliefs on this matter.

All of this discussion about an employee's gB2 is important, but knowing an employee's gB2 is a step away from where you need to be to motivate your employees. The real issue is the employee's B2 for specific outcomes, like the belief about whether performance will lead to a pay raise, a promotion, or praise from the boss, for example. Why is B2 rather than gB2 the real issue? In short, because employees typically base their actions on B2s for specific outcomes, not directly on their gB2s. That is, B2s rather than gB2s are the basis for deciding whether to put out the effort to perform.

The gB2 is important, however, because it influences B2s for specific outcomes. For example, a new employee who brings a low gB2 to the job, believing "I never get what my performance deserves," is promised a pay increase in six months if performance is good. What is the employee's B2 for a pay raise in six months? Does the employee believe the promise of a new boss in a new organization or continue with the well-founded belief that "I never get what I deserve?" While the employee may want to believe the promise, the gB2 tends to prevent the B2 from being high. Because of the fact that employees' gB2s do influence B2s for specific outcomes, it is essential for you to know the gB2 for each of your employees.

While an employee's gB2 is important, looking at it alone can be misleading. The B2 for a few specific outcomes may be different from the gB2. Two examples. One of your employees may have a low gB2, believing "I seldom get anything I deserve," yet have a high B2 for a specific outcome such as "my boss always tells me when I've really done a good job and I like that." As a manager you need to know this.

Or an employee may have a high gB2, believing "when I do a good job, I usually get the things I want and deserve," but at the same time have a low B2 for a specific outcome such as "I feel my performance justifies a promotion right away, but everybody says I haven't been here long enough." Again, as a manager you need to know this.

Why is B2 history important? The answer is in the pattern. First, the employee's B2 history forms the employee's gB2, the belief about whether outcomes generally are tied to performance or not. Second, the employee's gB2 is a major influence on the employee's B2 for specific outcomes. Third, the employee's B2 for specific outcomes is one of the three determinants of the employee's motivation. Remember, from chapter 1, that motivation is determined by three things—the belief about effort leading to performance (B1), the belief about performance leading to outcomes (B2), and the belief about outcomes leading to satisfaction (B3).

Where do you get an employee's B2 history? Although it is possible to get bits and pieces from people who know the employee, this is not a feasible way to get what you need when you need it. The best way is to get it directly from the employee. You will get a more complete, more accurate B2 history this way. The information must be gathered over a period of time.

How do you get an employee's B2 history? The best way is to focus on four areas of B2 history, looking at the extent to which employees believe outcomes have been tied to performance in their (1) youth, (2) personal lives, (3) previous jobs, and (4) current position. This is accomplished by getting employees to talk, especially during informal conversations, when they are more likely to feel free to discuss matters of this nature. The best way to do this is to use the "ask, shut up, and listen" approach discussed earlier.

What questions do you ask to get the employee's B2 history? Some standard questions known to be helpful are listed following this paragraph. Don't forget to use all the active-listening techniques of restating, summarizing, responding to feelings, and responding to nonverbal messages, when appropriate. Just ask and listen, and ask and listen, until you eventually have the B2 history for the employee. Don't expect to get a complete history in one conversation. It may take weeks or even months. Be patient, but use everything employees tell you to construct a B2 history that will help you better understand and manage them.

1. "When you were growing up, did kids pretty much think that the world was fair, that they would get what they deserved?"

2. "When you were growing up, did you generally get what you deserved when you did things well?"

3. "Who were the first people to try to teach you that performance pays off? Were they right?"

4. "What was it like at other places you've worked in terms of people getting what they deserved if they did a good job?"

5. "Have most (any) of the organizations you've worked in rewarded you primarily on the basis of performance?"

6. "Who were the best managers you ever had in terms of tying outcomes to performance? How did they go about doing it for you?"

SUMMARY

So there you have it. In this chapter you have seen six practical ways to obtain B2 information, through communication, observation, performance analysis, organization analysis, manager analysis, and B2 history analysis. There are two purposes for the B2 information obtained in these ways. One is to diagnose the B2 level of your employees, thus enabling you to identify which employees have motivation problems stemming from low B2s. The other purpose is to identify B2 causes, thus making it possible for you to select appropriate solutions and implement them effectively. Each of the six methods will provide information needed to diagnose B2 levels and causes. As mentioned previously, it isn't necessary to use all of them in any one situation, but each one will prove valuable at one time or another. They are easy to use. Simply follow the process suggested for each, and you will be able to gather the B2 information you need.

5

Solving Performance-Outcome Problems

When dealing with performance-outcome problems, where employees do not believe outcomes are tied to performance ("I'm not getting what I deserve"), managers often are faced with a frustrating dilemma. They may find themselves in a position where they can honestly say, "My hands are tied." This happens, for example, when managers do not have the authority to make pay and promotion decisions. Unfortunately, managers cannot tie outcomes to performance when the outcomes are out of their control. This causes considerable reluctance to deal with B2 problems. Even when managers do have control over outcomes, they still may be reluctant because of an uncertainty about how to move ahead.

Manager reluctance to tackle performance-outcome problems (B2) can be overcome easily by keeping three things in mind. One, you can go a long way in dealing with B2 problems simply by concentrating on the outcomes you do control. Every manager has control over some of the outcomes employees want, like being kept informed, having the opportunity to give input, being treated with respect, being appreciated, being given a word of praise, etc. Rather then focusing on what you can't do, concentrate on what you can do. Two, most B2 problems can be solved with a few simple, practical solutions. Three, there are some effective ways to deal with B2 problems that seem impossible to solve.

How do you go about solving performance-outcome problems (B2)? Once you have obtained B2 information, interpreted it, and identified B2 problems and their causes, as discussed in chapter 4, the next step is to choose appropriate B2 solutions and implement them. Different solutions are called for depending upon the causes of the B2 problem. Seven solutions are presented in this chapter: tying outcomes to performance, creating and maintaining equity, leveling, preference shifting, transfers, terminations, and changing employee perceptions. Selecting the appropriate solution will be easy because you know how to identify B2 causes. Likewise, you will be able to readily implement the solutions by following the straightforward and practical guidelines presented in this chapter. All of the solutions take into account the fact that managers seldom have control over all the outcomes employees want. Some of the solutions are designed for employees who have B2 problems that cannot be solved.

TYING OUTCOMES TO PERFORMANCE

Tying outcomes to performance is the only solution for three of the six causes of B2 problems discussed in chapter 4 and is a partial solution to one other. It is the only way to raise low B2s that are caused when (1) outcomes are not being tied to performance, (2) outcomes have only recently been tied to performance, and (3) employees have a history of outcomes not being tied to performance. It is a partial solution when inequity is the cause and serves to maintain equity once it is restored.

When implementing this solution, keep one thing in mind. It takes time to erase low B2s. This is different from many B1 problems where B1s can go from low to high practically overnight, for example, with a few days of skill building. Not so with low B2s. Tie outcomes to performance once, and employees say, "That's only once." Do it a second time and they say, "Two times doesn't mean things have changed." With the third time they may say, "Maybe things are going to be different, but let's wait and see." It may take four, five or even more times before employees start believing that "outcomes really are tied to performance." In some cases, the duration is very long. For example, improving the B2 for pay raises or promotions may take some time if the span between giving these outcomes is fixed at six or twelve months, as often is the case. But this is the exception. The B2 for most outcomes can be increased dramatically over a much shorter period of time. But it does take time, and patience.

What is involved in implementing this solution? Two things are required to tie outcomes to performance effectively. First, choose the appropriate method. Second, apply it, using a prescribed process.

First, method. There are four. Two are good, two not so good. The first is positive reinforcement. The idea is to reinforce, in a positive way, good performance. This is done by giving employees outcomes they want when they perform well. When performance is good, give pay raises, promotions, company cars, bonuses, a better office, praise, recognition, a word of thanks, or work that is more challenging, more creative, or more fulfilling. Give something. Give anything, as long as it has value to the employee, that is as long as the employee gets satisfaction from it. If you want your employees to do a good job, they must believe they will be rewarded for it. That is, they must have a high B2. They must believe that outcomes are tied to performance. Giving positive reinforcement is one method to develop this belief.

The second method is avoidance. The idea behind avoidance is that employees will perform well to avoid something undesirable, like being fired, being yelled at, having the boss gripe and complain, being given the dirty work, having to travel a lot, working the night shift, etc. Avoidance is the method of withholding outcomes that yield dissatisfaction when employees perform well. Consistent use of avoidance will cause employees to conclude that outcomes are tied to performance. That is, B2s will increase. But avoidance causes problems. Although the fear of getting something bad seems to motivate employees, at least in the short run, continually using this method has adverse side effects. Employees tend toward minimally acceptable performance, rather than excellence, and bad relationships develop between employees and managers when avoidance is used. When this happens, managers are faced with a losing battle in motivating employees to perform well.

Punishment is the third method. The idea is to punish employees when performance is poor. That is, outcomes that employees do not want are given when performance is poor. Consistent use of punishment shows employees that outcomes are tied to performance and therefore increases B2s. Although some employees seem to be motivated by the fear of punishment, the side effects are damaging. Not only do punished employees perform at minimally acceptable levels and have poor relationships with their managers, but they also tend to get back at their managers by deliberately creating problems.

The fourth method of tying outcomes to performance is extinction. The purpose of extinction is to extinguish poor performance. This is done by withholding desirable outcomes previously given when performance was poor. Employees who in the past received raises, promotions, praise, or recognition when they performed poorly would no longer receive such outcomes for poor performance. A familiar example of this is when adults laugh and give attention to a child for "cute" misbehavior. This encourages the child to continue the inappropriate behavior. One way to extinguish the child's bad behavior is to start withholding the desirable outcomes previously given (laughter and attention) each time the child subsequently displays the bad behavior. Repeated nonreinforcement will cause the behavior to decrease and eventually disappear. This is extinction.

The ideal way to effectively tie outcomes to performance is to use a combination of positive reinforcement to encourage good performance and extinction to discourage poor performance. Avoidance and punishment also will strengthen B2s, but with the cost of creating adverse side effects, as mentioned earlier.

Positive Reinforcement

So much for the methods of tying outcomes to performance. What about the process? What process should be followed to apply the two recommended methods effectively? A set of specific, concrete steps have emerged over years of research and practice. They work, and you can make them work for you. Let's look at positive reinforcement first, then extinction.

Positive reinforcement is the five-step process of (1) measuring employee performance, (2) identifying performance that merits reinforcement, (3) deciding which outcomes to give as reinforcers, (4) determining how much of each outcome to give, and (5) giving the outcomes. Step 5 is a particularly important, but often overlooked, step in the process. The actual giving of outcomes must be handled with care, or the impact of the positive reinforcement will be greatly diminished. You'll see this shortly.

The process is easiest when these three circumstances fall into place at the same time: (1) when performance is measurable, like units produced or sold; (2) when outcomes are measurable, like dollars for a production bonus or a sales commission; and (3) when a performance/outcomes schedule already is established, such as a specified dollar amount per unit produced or a percentage of sales for a sales commission. When these circumstances come together, the positive reinforcement process is straightforward. First, measure the employee's easy-to-measure performance. Second, third, and fourth, check the performance/outcomes schedule to determine if the performance merits reinforcement and, if so, which outcome(s) to give and how much. Fifth, give the outcome(s) to the employee.

Giving positive reinforcement requires more attention (1) when performance is not readily measurable; (2) when determining the amount of an outcome to give is somewhat troublesome, as in the case of praise, recognition, and autonomy, for example; and (3) when there is no predetermined performance/outcomes schedule. The same five-step process for providing positive reinforcement is used in these circumstances, but the steps are more involved. Let's see how.

First, determine how well employees have performed. But how, when performance is not easy to measure? The guideline is to go for specifics, not for generalities, which can be misleading. This can be done in several ways. One, continually observe what your employees are doing. Two, regularly have employees brief you on what they are doing, how they are doing it, and how well it is being done. Three, gather and analyze performance data, including looking at (1) end results, especially in relation to results expected, cost, and any problems that may have been created; (2) the way end results were achieved; and (3) any factors that made the performance either difficult or easy, such as budgets, human resources, time, or standards. Four, get the reaction of people close to the performance, including coworkers, other managers, and customers or clients, and anyone else in a position to help you better understand the employee's performance. Following these steps will give a good indication of how well the employee is performing.

Second, identify performance that should be reinforced. This can be deceptive. In a sense, it is a simple step. Exceptional performance stands out. It is usually visible even if you're not looking for it. You'll recognize exceptional performance when you see it. But this is part of the deception. Performance that is good but not exceptional sometimes goes unnoticed, particularly if daily activities run at a hectic pace. Identifying performance that should be reinforced requires a constant, conscious effort. For many managers, this is difficult.

Third, decide which outcome(s) to give. How is this done when there is no performance/outcomes schedule? There are several things to do here. One obviously is to determine which outcomes are valued by the employee, that is, which ones are satisfying. This is the subject of chapter 6 and will be discussed at length there. However, determining which outcomes employees prefer is not enough. You must also consider other factors that influence the decision, like company policy and precedent that must be followed, availability of outcomes (like promotion opportunities, dollars in the budget for raises, etc.), and equity relative to other employees.

Fourth, decide how much of each outcome to give. How big should the raise be? How much praise should you give? How much recognition? How many privileges? How much authority, responsibility, autonomy, and power? Deciding how much is tough. The answer is to give as much as the performance deserves. This is what tying outcomes to performance is all about. Unfortunately, the "how much" can't be precisely computed. "As much as performance deserves" must be weighed against, and perhaps adjusted in view of, other factors such as how much the employee wants, how much the employee expects, how much you can give within the constraints of policy and precedent, availability of the outcome, and equity relative to other employees.

Fifth, give the outcome(s). This is a step that does not always get enough attention. The way outcomes are given is more important and more involved than first meets the eye. The importance lies in the necessity that employees see outcomes received as being tied to performance. If this is not clearly seen, B2s will not improve as much as they could. Saying "nice job" or "your raise was approved" isn't enough. It doesn't insure that employees will see the performance-outcome connection.

Giving outcomes involves three parts. Getting necessary approvals may be required, depending upon your authority and the nature of the outcome. Giving a pat on the back is one thing, but getting the OK for promotions and raises can be a major undertaking. This can be a problem. Outcomes may be delayed so long that their effect is diminished. Employees may hear about outcomes first through the grapevine, thereby diminishing the impact.

The second part is to talk with the employees and clearly point out the performance that has led to the outcomes about to be given. Saying "you've been working hard" or "your work has been good" isn't enough. Indicate the time period of the performance. Then be specific about the work done, the results achieved, the extent to which expectations have been met, the contribution to department and organization goals, etc. Be specific and clear so that employees will understand what they have done that has led to the outcomes being received.

Part three is giving the outcome(s), doing so in such a way that the employees clearly know what is being given. Saying "we're giving you a promotion," or "you're getting a raise," or "the vice president singled you out for outstanding performance" is not enough. Give details about a promotion, like the position title, when it takes effect, what the duties are, etc. Be specific about the amount of a raise and when it becomes effective. Indicate how an employee was singled out, exactly what was said, who was in the meeting, what the reaction was, etc. Give details to help employees know exactly what they are getting.

Let's take a look at a situation where this five-step process for giving positive reinforcement can be applied. Read Case 5-1. Go through each of the five steps, focusing on how you would handle steps 3 through 5. What would you do if you were Turner? How would you go about tying outcomes to performance?

Case 5-1—Tying Outcomes to Performance Using Positive Reinforcement. Turner had been trying for weeks to finalize a half-million dollar contract to do some training for a state agency. The decision makers for the agency wanted the support of key managers from around the state before entering into the contract. These were the managers who would be sending people to the training. Agency officials were having trouble getting the endorsements they wanted, even though they had met with the managers several times to explain the program. Turner suggested having the managers go through a one-hour segment of the training to experience it firsthand, then decide whether to support it or not. Everyone agreed this would be a good way to reach an informed decision. Turner's staff was nervous as twenty or so managers and agency officials began filing into the meeting room. The staff included (1) Higgins, Turner's best project manager, who was to give an overview of the program and answer questions; (2) Elmer, the best trainer, who was to conduct a segment of the training; and (3) three others to help with setting up the room and to talk with the guests before and after the session. All the staff did a good job, but Elmer stole the show by conducting a flawless one-hour training session that resulted in the group's overwhelming endorsement of the program. Elmer, who had always been an above-average performer, was truly exceptional on this day. The contract was signed the next week.

What did Turner do in the situation described in Case 5-1? Turner knew from observing Elmer's work, from performance reviews, from Elmer's self-reporting, and from the reports of employees and clients that Elmer did very good work (step 1). He also recognized Elmer's exceptional performance in demonstrating a segment of the training program (step 2). Turner was aware of Elmer's willingness to take on the high-pressure task, to spend a lot of time preparing and rehearsing for it, and yet to keep up with his regular duties (part of step 2). Turner decided to give three outcomes he knew to be important to Elmer, namely, praise, recognition, and money (step 3). But how much of each outcome (step 4)? Turner decided that (1) the highest possible praise was appropriate, (2) Elmer's contribution should be recognized among all key persons in the company, and (3) a $2,000 cash bonus was appropriate.

How did Turner give the outcomes (step 5)? Immediately after the meeting ended, Turner called the five staff members together and thanked each of them for their contribution to the success of the meeting, naming specific things each had done to contribute. He saved Elmer for last, and said, "The training you did today was the best I have ever seen. It couldn't have been better. The group could not have been more impressed. We'll get the contract. Thanks for making it possible." When the contract was signed, Turner sent an announcement to everyone in the training unit and all managers in the chain of command, including the president. The contribution of all staff members was noted, with a full paragraph about how Elmer's performance was the deciding factor. Elmer became a celebrity for a few days as he received a lot of attention, including a word of praise from several higher-ups. Turner had to get approval for the cash bonus, but he found no opposition in view of the widespread acknowledgment of Elmer's contribution. When Turner gave Elmer the check, he made it a point to recap the highlights of Elmer's recent performance to be sure Elmer knew exactly what the check was for. As the result of this positive reinforcement and the way it was handled, Elmer and all the employees in his unit concluded, "Do a good job here, and it pays off." Everyone's B2 was strengthened.

Extinction

Let's look at the other side of the story now. Remember, positive reinforcement is giving desired outcomes for good performance. What should you do when performance is not good? This is where extinction comes in. It is used to extinguish poor performance. Extinction is withholding desired outcomes that were previously given for poor performance when you want to extinguish the poor performance. What is the process for using extinction? Let's look at the steps.

Extinction is the process of (1) measuring employee performance; (2) identifying performance that should be improved; (3) deciding which outcomes to withhold, in total or in part; (4) determining how much of each outcome to withhold; and (5) withholding the outcomes. Let's take a look at these steps, but first a word about the reality of using extinction.

Withholding desired outcomes takes courage. It requires taking a definite stand in opposition to poor performance. It means working with employees who are disappointed by not getting what they want and risking their rejection because of it. As a result, managers often choose to do nothing about poor performance. This is especially true for managers whose need for acceptance is greater than their need to perform. But doing nothing is doing something. Here's what happens.

Doing nothing about poor performance means treating employees as if their poor performance is OK. Desired outcomes are not withheld. Instead they are given. In doing so, the manager avoids employee disappointment and rejection. This is a tempting choice. But giving desired outcomes for poor performance reinforces poor performance. It causes employees to conclude, "Hey, I can do a poor job and still get what I want." That is, employees believe that outcomes are not tied to performance (low B2). This results in problems with motivation, effort, and performance. Giving employees what they want when they perform poorly not only tells them poor performance is OK, it may actually motivate them to perform poorly.

The five-step extinction process recommended for withholding desired outcomes is simple and straightforward. It parallels the steps for giving positive reinforcement, and the same approach can be used for steps 1 through 4 of extinction. Step 5, withholding outcomes, deserves comment, however, because it involves more than meets the eye. As a result, it often gets shortchanged. When this happens, the benefits of using extinction and the impact of steps 1 through 4 are diminished considerably. So, what's involved in the final step? What should you do? It depends. There are two kinds of situations. One is where outcomes, such as raises and promotions, are withheld for performance over a period of time. The other involves outcomes withheld immediately upon performance completion, such as praise, recognition, and other forms of approval. Let's take a look at step 5 in each of these situations.

When outcomes are withheld for performance over a period of time, as with raises or promotions, step 5 has four parts. The first is to indicate that the outcome normally given for poor performance is being withheld. Be clear. "You are not getting a raise this time" or "You were not recommended for a promotion" or, "Your promotion was not approved" is better than beating around the bush. The second part is to explain why. The explanation should include two things: (1) a statement of the performance that is required to receive the outcome and (2) a summary of the employee's performance. Be specific on both. Saying, "Your work hasn't been up to par" or, "We're disappointed in your results" isn't enough. What time period is involved? What work hasn't measured up? What were the results? How does actual performance compare with what is required to receive the outcome? Be prepared. Have evidence to back up what you say. Don't come across as arbitrary, subjective, or biased. The idea is to help employees see that their performance has not been good enough to get the outcome they want. The third part of step 5 is to indicate that when performance reaches the required level, they will get the outcome. Encourage them. Leave them with hope. Leave them believing that outcomes are tied to performance and that if they perform they will get what they want. Part four is to address the B1 issue. The employee has failed to meet performance requirements, as you have pointed out, and a B1 problem may exist. Check it out by diagnosing the employee's B1, and move ahead as appropriate depending upon the result of the diagnosis.

When outcomes are withheld immediately upon performance completion, as with praise and recognition, step 5 has three parts. The first is to point out how the work needs to be improved. Be specific and complete. Point out exactly what must be done to make the work acceptable. The second part of step 5 is to do nothing and say nothing. This means withholding the desired outcome. Do not give praise, recognition, approval or anything for the poor performance. If you must give a desired outcome, don't give it for poor performance. Give it for "wanting to do this right" or "putting a lot of time into it" or other positive behaviors you want to encourage. Although you don't want to reward poor performance, neither do you want to make it seem OK. Resist the urge to say "it's OK" or "don't worry about it," particularly when employees show disappointment and hurt. Saying and doing nothing also means not making critical comments about the work. This would be a form of punishment, as discussed earlier. The third part of step 5 is to determine if there is a B1 problem and, if so, to deal with it as appropriate.

Let's take a look at a situation that involves a decision that will affect an employee's B2. Read Case 5-2. If you were the manager, how would you handle it? What would you do and what would you say to the employee whose performance is less than desired?

Case 5-2—Tying Outcomes to Performance Using Extinction. Daisy was a joy to work with. You would have to look long and hard to find anyone else so kind and gentle and sweet. She was loyal to her boss, Will, and worked harder than anybody else in the office. However, the quality of her work wasn't always the best, for two reasons. One, she tried to do too much too fast. Two, sometimes she did not fully understand Will's expectations, mainly because he often wasn't clear when giving instructions. One day she went into Will's office to give him a short summary of four categories of data he had requested her to work up. She stood there while he looked over it, desperately wanting his approval for a job well done. If he realized what she had done, as she had discovered only moments ago, it would take another hour to recompute the fourth section, and she wasn't up to it today. As soon as Will glanced at the fourth category of summarized data, he knew something was wrong. The numbers didn't look right. Then he realized that all the first-quarter data had been left out of the summary. Daisy was sensitive. Will seldom pointed out mistakes like this, because he was afraid she would be hurt. He did have time to correct it himself before his meeting, if he put some less-pressing work on hold. What should Will do?

Case 5-2 presents a situation in which the manager feels it would be almost cruel not to give Daisy the approval she is seeking. Why hurt her by pointing out the mistake? What harm would follow from his saying "nice job" or "thanks" or "just what I needed"? Maybe none, if Daisy didn't know her work was done incorrectly. But she did. Managers seldom really know how employees view the quality of their work. Is giving employees undeserved outcomes to make them feel good worth the risk of having them conclude that "outcomes are not tied to performance?" Approval is a desired outcome for Daisy, as it is for most employees, and giving it for a piece of work that is less than satisfactory only serves to reinforce poor performance.

Case 5-2 clearly is a situation that calls for extinguishing poor performance by withholding approval. What should Will do? Following the five-step process for extinction, Will already has evaluated the employee's performance (step 1) and identified what should be improved, that is, including first-quarter data in the summary (step 2). Now what?

What else should be done? Step 3 calls for Will to decide what outcome(s) to withhold. This is easy. Withhold approval, the outcome he has been giving her in the past for poor performance. Step 4 is to determine how much of the outcome to withhold. Since three-fourths of the work is correct, it is fine to give some, but not total, approval. Step 5 is to withhold the outcome. How should Will do this? He could say something like "Daisy, you've done a nice job on the first three parts of this, but it looks like the first-quarter data are missing from the fourth category" (part one of step 5). Stop. Let her respond. She probably will volunteer to correct it; but if she doesn't, ask her to do so. There is no need to say or do anything else, certainly no need to scream and shout or to say, "It's OK," or "Don't worry about it," or "I'll fix it" (part two of step 5). With this, Will has tied outcomes to performance by withholding the desired outcome, namely, the total approval Daisy wanted, in view of the less-than-satisfactory performance.

The information given in Case 5-2 is inadequate to determine the level of Daisy's B2. But it doesn't matter. Whether her B2 is high or low, the manager should do the same thing. Outcomes should be tied to performance, in this situation by withholding the desired outcome. This will reinforce a high B2 or improve a low B2, whichever the case may be.

Tying outcomes to performance is essential. It is the sole solution to three of the six causes of B2 problems and is a required part of the solution to a fourth. Outcomes are best tied to performance by using positive reinforcement and extinction. Both are necessary. You must use them. Employee motivation will be less than desired if you don't, and so will effort and performance.

CREATING AND MAINTAINING EQUITY

Inequity exists when employees do not get what they deserve relative to others. There are two kinds of inequity. An employee may be either underrewarded or overrewarded, relative to others. That is, an employee may be getting less than deserved, or more, compared to other employees. Inequity is the result of not tying outcomes to performance among all employees. When inequity exists, what should you do? Can you afford to create equity? Can you afford not to? Take a look at Case 5-3 and decide what should be done.

Case 5-3—Creating Equity. Scott was hired to manage the department that had been headed for years by Mr. Johnson, who had recently retired. Soon after taking over, Scott started hearing a lot of stories about how unfair Mr. Johnson originally had been to the first women employees he was forced by top management to hire. He'd rather have men any day than women, he often had said. Scott noticed that the salaries of the several women hired initially by Johnson still were considerably less than those of any of the men, but also less than those of the more recently hired women, whose pay was comparable to that of the men. The women hired originally had the same qualifications as the men or better, but they were given much lower starting salaries. Also, they had not received any pay raises for their first three years, although they seemed to be paid on the basis of their performance thereafter. It appears that Johnson came to believe that women could perform as well as men, but he never corrected the inequity that he created with the three initially hired women, who were still in the department. Should Scott do anything about this situation or not?

Before discussing Case 5-3, let's take a look at how inequity affects the B2s of employees. The impact differs depending on the employees' current B2. For employees who already have low B2s, inequity confirms, even strengthens, the belief that outcomes are not tied to performance. With inequity, low B2s do stay low.

For employees with high B2s, inequity weakens their belief about the performance-outcome relationship. When high B2 employees see others being underrewarded, they become aware that "if it can happen to others, it can happen to me." With this realization, B2s decline. When employees with high B2s see others being overrewarded, a more damaging thing happens. High B2 employees may be getting what they deserve relative to their own performance; but, relative to the overrewarded employees, they feel cheated. This causes them to conclude, "If they're getting that much, I should be getting more." With this comes the belief, "I'm not getting what I deserve," and B2s are lowered.

How do you solve inequity problems and thereby improve employee B2s? A two-part solution is required. The first part is a new, or renewed, focus on tying outcomes to performance for all employees. This addresses both underrewarding and overrewarding by minimizing the creation of additional inequity and begins the process of narrowing the inequity gap. Existing inequity is not erased with this approach, but with time a narrowing of the gap can occur.

Some inequity, however, is so profound that the narrowing process would be quite lengthy. This gives rise to the need for a second solution that works swiftly to achieve equity. Appropriately, it is called instant equity. How is the solution used with underrewarding? What about using it with overrewarding?

Underrewarding first. Let's say the pay for some employees is far less than it should be, both in terms of performance and relative to other employees. Tying the next annual pay increase to performance over the past year is a start in dealing with the inequity. But some "catching up" needs to be done. The pay for these employees should be instantly raised to an equitable position. Although this is not a popular notion because of the money involved, it is something that should be done if motivation, effort, and performance are important. Once equity is established, it is maintained by continually tying outcomes to performance.

When overrewarding is the problem, instant equity is achieved with the reverse of catching up. There should be a "cutting back" of outcomes. If an employee's salary (or position, type and/or location of office, fringe benefits, etc.) is in excess of what it should be, both in terms of performance and relative to other employees, the inequity can be swiftly resolved through a cutback. This is not a popular solution for most managers because cutting back takes guts. But so does living with all the problems caused by the overrewarding, both the problems of motivation, effort, and performance caused by the inequity and the related problems of absenteeism, turnover, jealousy, lack of cooperation, infighting, etc. The alternative is to not have cutbacks, but to make it clear that the new focus on tying outcomes to performance applies to everyone regardless of inequities in the past.

What does all this mean in terms of Case 5-3? What should Scott do? What would you do? It really is a simple decision. Employees should be treated fairly. So, create equity. Give the three women a one-time pay increase to bring their compensation to an equitable level. Thereafter, continue, as Johnson had done, to tie outcomes to performance. Although the decision may be simple, implementing it may not be. You likely will have to explain and justify such a decision many times and many ways before getting final approval. But it is a decision that will pay off. It will have a positive impact on the motivation of all employees over a long period of time and consequently on their performance as well. It is a decision that may be hard to measure in terms of dollars and cents, but you will not go wrong by treating employees fairly.

LEVELING

There are occasions when certain outcomes cannot be tied to performance. Organizations have ways of doing things that are not going to change. Whether it is entrenched bureaucracy, union contracts, corporate policy, or other factors, certain outcomes simply cannot be tied to performance. Promotions often are based on seniority or on organizational politics rather than on performance. Pay raises sometimes are determined by union contracts or by a policy of giving across-the-board raises. Other factors, like the reduction of middle managers, economic instability, cash flow problems, shrinking markets, or downsizing, also may mean that outcomes cannot be tied to performance for long periods of time.

How do employees respond when outcomes cannot be tied to performance? Some accept it and perform only at the level necessary to keep their jobs. Others blame the organization, perhaps even their manager, and become filled with resentment and bitterness. They tend to perform poorly and often to cause problems as a way of getting back at those who are depriving them of what they deserve. Other employees hang on to a false hope that things will get better. However, their performance will drop below their level of capability. In every case, B2 levels are far below what they could be; and employee motivation, effort, and performance suffer.

When outcomes cannot be tied to performance, what should you do? That is, when outcomes are not tied to performance and there is nothing you can do about it, what should you do? It is time to level with employees. Leveling is the solution of last resort before turning to transferring or terminating the employee. It is used when everything else has failed, when you have given up ("I can't do it"), and when you are unwilling for things to continue as they have been. Leveling is used because there is a chance that the employee will come up with a solution when confronted with your decision not to tolerate problems with motivation, effort, and performance any longer and with your willingness to take whatever action is necessary to deal with the situation.

The results of leveling are varied. One, some employees will have options and will pursue them, either quitting to take a new job or transferring within the organization. Two, others who do have options will conclude that things would not be any better elsewhere. Three, some employees will realize they do not have other job options. In the latter two cases, employees come to the realization that improving performance is in their best interest. Whatever the result of leveling may be, it is better for the manager and the organization than a current situation filled with problems in motivation, effort, and performance.

How do you go about leveling with employees? Are there any steps to follow? Yes. There is a pattern that works. Let's look at the steps by applying them to a situation that calls for leveling. Read Case 5-4 and diagnose the motivation problem. How low is the employee's B2 level? What is causing it to be low? Then consider the possible solutions to this B2 problem. Why is leveling the best solution?

Case 5-4—Leveling. When Richard was hired, he had been out of work over a year. During his first four months as head of shipping and receiving for a small manufacturing company, he had performed well.

Then things started changing. Customers started complaining about shipments being wrong and late. Paperwork errors caused problems with inventory counts and customer billing. The warehouse was in a mess, and procedures that had been well established were no longer being followed. Richard admitted things were not going well. He was vocal about (1) how much he wanted to be promoted, (2) how promotions should be based on performance, not seniority, and (3) how he could hardly make himself come to work in view of this injustice. Richard liked the company, but he knew that its stability, low turnover, and a promotion policy based on seniority gave him little opportunity for a promotion. How would you handle this situation with Richard?

What is the problem described in Case 5-4? Richard's declining performance is the result of a motivation problem. Promotions are based on seniority, not performance. This has caused a B2 problem, with a B2 level at or near 0. He has concluded he will not advance in the company, at least not for a very long time. What are the possible solutions? Given the cause, the possible solutions are (1) leveling or (2) termination. Leveling is the solution of last resort before terminating Richard.

How should leveling be used with Richard? There is an eight-step process you can use. The discussion of each step will be followed by its application to Case 5-4. The first step in leveling is to indicate that poor performance is not acceptable and why. Let employees know exactly where they stand. This is not a time to scream and shout and be critical, but don't tiptoe through the tulips, either. Be objective and call it the way it is. Be specific and clear. Do not leave any room for doubt.

Manager: "Richard, I wanted to talk with you about the quality of your work over the last couple of months. The number of shipments that have been wrong and late has more than doubled, and customers are complaining. The increase in paperwork errors is a big problem. And the warehouse is very disorganized. You started out doing a great job, but your performance the last two months has not been acceptable."

Next, indicate that you are unwilling to tolerate unacceptable performance any longer. Mean it when you say it, and say it as if you mean it. There is no need to be harsh or threatening, but don't beat around the bush. Be firm. Be cool and objective, rather than getting hot and emotional. The idea is to make it clear where you stand. Unacceptable performance cannot continue. That's the message.

Manager: "Things simply cannot continue this way any longer."

Third, point out that the situation is not going to change. Be clear about this. Do not leave any room for hope. False hope is a problem, and any belief that things will change should be dispelled. This means making it clear that the outcome cannot be tied to performance, and will not be. Explain why, so that the employee understands the circumstances and the fact that the situation is beyond your control.

Manager: "I can see you don't agree with our promotion policy. The company has been very successful. Employees like it here, and they are rewarded for their loyalty, dedication, and long-term commitment. This is not going to change. I couldn't change it if I wanted to."

Fourth, present the options. The possibilities are that the employee quits, gets fired, or improves performance. This is not a time for ambiguity. Employees need to know where they stand. Let them know what happens if performance improves and what happens if it doesn't. Be sure they see that continuing to perform poorly is not an option.

Manager: "I want to be open with you about where you stand now. I hope you will get things running smoothly, as they were a couple of months back, but you would need to show progress immediately. If not, you will have to leave."

Then, point out that this is the employee's decision. Make it clear that the employee can choose to quit or to improve performance and that not choosing to improve means choosing to be terminated. This employee choice is important. It gives employees control over their destiny, and it gives you a better chance of getting to a good decision.

Manager: "This is your decision. You can stay, provided you start turning things around right away. If you decide not to do this, you will in effect be choosing to leave. It's up to you."

Sixth, establish a deadline for the employee to make a decision. Set a day and time. Make it the employee's responsibility to come to you. Also, indicate the consequences of not making the decision on time. The main consequence should be the loss of the opportunity to decide. Do not have a misunderstanding here. Make it clear that if the employee doesn't decide, you will.

Manager: "I'd like you to give me your decision by the end of the day Thursday. If I don't hear from you by then, I'll decide how to handle it."

Next, be sure the employee understands you have the authority to decide, with the necessary backing to make your decision stick. Don't bluff on this. Be certain you have the authority and support needed. This is no time for a mistake. The employee may challenge you. Don't just say you have the authority and backing. Give some evidence, if nothing more than a few details of the results of a meeting you had with your boss to discuss the situation.

Manager: "I told the people above me how I wanted to handle this with you. They agree this is the best way, and they expect me to let them know the outcome first thing Friday."

The eighth and final step is to offer your help in making the decision and in implementing it. Indicate your willingness to further explore the options, answer questions, react to ideas, etc., as the employee works through making a decision. In addition, point out your willingness to help in finding another job or improving current performance. The idea is to be caring, helpful, and supportive. There is no need to be otherwise. This is a difficult and stressful situation for the employee, and part of your job as a manager is to help in working through it. Remember, all of your employees will be watching and judging how you do this.

Manager: "This is a hard decision for you to make. If I can help you think through it or do anything else, be sure to let me know. If you decide to leave, I'll do whatever I can to help you get another job. If you choose to stay, I'll help in any way I can to get things back on track. I want this to be a good decision for you as well as for everybody else here. Let me know if I can help, and I'll see you on Thursday."

This eight-step process for leveling places the responsibility for solving the performance problem squarely on the shoulders of the employee. Doing so is appropriate when you have exhausted all possible options available to you other than getting rid of the employee through termination. This gives employees an opportunity to pull themselves out of their own problems. Leveling gives employees one final chance to turn things around using their own initiative. This is a better option than moving directly to termination, which is the next step if employees cannot engineer a turnaround on their own.

PREFERENCE SHIFTING

All employees experience changes in preference for outcomes. The change usually comes about in two ways. One type occurs gradually over a long period of time, like preferences for raises and promotions giving way to an increasing desire for job security and retirement benefits as employees get older. In other cases preference shifting comes abruptly because of a traumatic experience, like the death of a family member that produces a dramatic and long-lasting preference for more time with the family rather than getting ahead at work. In both cases, circumstances are the moving force behind the changes.

As changes in preference take place, changes in motivation occur. Let's say an employee has a strong desire for a promotion but, believing promotions are based on politics, has a low B2. This may reduce the employee's motivation quite a bit. As the employee learns more about the job, the desirability of it may diminish considerably. When this happens, the employee's B2 would be unchanged, but the low B2 would no longer hold back the employee's motivation level, as the outcome is no longer desired. The same could be true with an undesirable outcome an employee was receiving. If the employee's preference for it changes from negative to positive, motivation would improve. That is, preference changes can improve employee B2s and thereby improve motivation, effort, and performance.

Preference shifting refers to changes in employee preferences for outcomes. The shifting can be initiated by the manager as a solution to B2 problems that are caused when outcomes cannot be tied to performance. The idea is to show employees how they will be better off by wanting one outcome less and another more. Let's see how preference shifting works.

Some employees have jobs where the work itself is not rewarding. Suppose there is no practical way to redesign these jobs to make them more rewarding. Furthermore, suppose some of the employees have no opportunity for another job because of lack of skills or unwillingness to relocate or a tight labor market or whatever. Basically the employee is stuck in a job where the work itself is not rewarding. There are two options. One is for the employee to live with things the way they are, going to work day after day with dread and frustration, constantly wishing and hoping things would get better and experiencing mounting discontent, even misery, and stress as a result. The other option is to undergo a change in preferences whereby more emphasis is placed on the positive aspects of the job and less on the negative.

The manager is stuck, too. Stuck with employees who have low B2s and motivation, effort, and performance that are not where they could be. The manager has three options, two of which are unattractive. One is to live with the situation, probably only to see it worsen. Another is to terminate the employee and hire a replacement with a better job match. The third option is preference shifting. In this option the manager helps employees undergo a change in preferences. How can this be done?

How can you initiate preference shifting? Some specific steps can be taken. Step one is level with employees so that they will realize the situation is not going to change. They have to come to grips with the fact that no matter how much they want the work itself to be more rewarding, or how much they want certain extrinsic outcomes, nothing can be done about it. The second step is to help employees understand that, by not quitting their job, they are choosing to stay in a situation where outcomes cannot be tied to performance. Many employees blame others for things they choose for themselves, and helping them take the responsibility for this decision is a necessary step. Step three is to convince employees they can be happier with their choice if they will shift preferences. Show them how easy it is to get hung up on things they don't have or things they don't like, how hard it is to see anything else, and how only they can change the way they feel about those things.

The fourth step in preference shifting is helping employees accept the fact that they are like most other employees in the sense that they can't have everything they want, that this is normal, and that to think otherwise is unrealistic. Step five is to show employees how they can get out of the dissatisfaction rut by focusing on the positives they have rather than the negatives. Have them identify the parts of the work itself that are rewarding, even though it may be only one or two things, or help them identify other things about their jobs that they like, such as the pay, growth and development opportunities, promotion opportunities, the freedom and independence they have, or not having somebody on their back all the time. The idea is for employees to accentuate the positive.

Sometimes preference shifting comes quickly and easily, sometimes not. Don't expect results overnight, but don't be surprised if it happens quickly. However, being patient is important because it takes time for some employees to lay down their hostility toward the situation and accept things the way they are. Helping employees change preferences often is a test of persistence. Sticking with it improves your chances for success.

TRANSFERS

Transferring employees can solve B2 problems caused when outcomes cannot be tied to performance. This means getting employees into jobs where the outcomes they want (B3) are tied to performance (B2). Of course, they must be able to handle the job (B1), too. With this in mind, let's take a look at some specific steps that make transfers work.

The first step is to get the employee's agreement that a transfer is the best option for solving the problem at hand, namely, a B2 problem. This can be done by helping the employee understand and evaluate the available options. This begins with presenting the options to the employee. Let's say the employee's current performance is acceptable, though not at the level it could be because certain outcomes cannot be tied to performance. The option here is for the employee to stay in the job and not have any hope of things improving. If performance is unacceptable, the options are to improve performance or get fired. Regardless of performance, the employee can choose to quit. The final option is to be transferred to another position in the organization. Once the options are presented, you can lead the employee through an evaluation of them. If the employee prefers an option other than being transferred, fine. Go with it. But if the choice is a transfer, you can move ahead with the support and involvement of the employee.

The next step is to determine what a good job match would be for the employee. To do this you have to identify all of the employee's skills. That is, where would the employee have a high B1? Then, identify what the employee wants. In other words, what outcomes would be satisfying (B3)?

The third step is to identify jobs the employee can handle (B1) where desired outcomes (B3) are tied to performance (B2). Talk to the personnel department. Get the word out to other managers. Let people know what you are looking for. Be specific about the skills the employee has. Also be specific about what the employee wants, that is, the outcomes it would take for the employee to be motivated to perform well. This helps others identify transfer opportunities that potentially will be good job matches.

The fourth step is to facilitate the transfer process, working with both the employee and those who might want the employee to transfer to their unit. This facilitation consists of giving information to both sides, asking questions, and encouraging each side to focus on making a good job-matching decision, so that the transferred employee will have a high B1, B2, and B3 in the new position.

The idea here is not simply to dispose of your problem by transferring it somewhere else. Helping the employee get a good match not only helps the employee, it helps the organization and it helps you. It helps you especially with other employees. A caring, concerned manager who treats employees right (B3) is important to most people. Demonstrating this with regard to the transferred employee has a positive impact on the motivation of all of your employees. Handling a transfer in the right way pays off for you.

TERMINATIONS

When all else fails to solve B2 problems caused when outcomes cannot be tied to performance, terminating the employee is the only solution that remains. While this is an option feared by employees and managers alike, terminations actually are much easier than managers believe and less painful than employees expect. Doing it the right way makes it better for everyone.

The approach recommended for terminating employees is a continuation of the leveling process. That is, the first step in the termination process is to level with the employee, using the same eight steps in the leveling process outlined earlier. The basic message communicated when leveling is that the "shape up or ship out" decision is completely in the hands of the employee. The employee chooses whether or not to improve performance. Choosing not to improve is choosing to leave.

The second step is to acknowledge and follow-up on the employee's decision of intent. The employee may say, "I am not willing to improve my performance, and I intend to quit." In this case, simply accept the decision and work out the necessary arrangements. On the other hand, the employee may say, "I am unwilling to improve, and I intend to make you fire me." This decision also should be accepted and carried out in accordance with the guidelines of your organization.

Other employees may say, "I intend to improve my performance because I don't want to be fired." When this is the employee's decision, it is critical to carefully spell out the conditions of continued employment. How much does performance have to improve? How long does the employee have to show these improvements? How will the improvement be measured? It also is critical that the consequences of their actions are spelled out. What happens if performance is improved as required? What if it isn't improved? What happens if improvement is followed by a decline in performance? Employees who choose to perform better have a right to know all the conditions and consequences. Don't be ambiguous. Spell it out. Give employees every chance to turn the situation around.

When employees decide to improve rather than be fired, the third step is to wait and watch. Because the termination decision now rests with the employee's performance, the idea is to watch for performance improvement and wait for the end of the period given for improvement to take place to see what the termination decision will be. It is important to keep in mind that the decision is in the employee's hands, not the manager's.

Step four is to confirm and carry out the employee's decision. The decision is confirmed by reviewing the performance results and is carried out by (1) meeting with the employee to present performance results and state the resulting decision and (2) taking other necessary steps. If the decision is not to terminate, the employee should be given positive reinforcement for performing well and encouragement to continue doing so, as well as stressing the conditions for continued long-term employment and the consequences if performance should decline again. If the decision is to terminate, the employee should be given official notification and other necessary steps should be taken in accordance with your organization's termination procedures. That's it. The employee made the decision. It is your job to carry it out.

This method of terminating employees removes much of the emotion and stress normally associated with it. Using this clear-cut, step-by-step approach that is based on employee choice it makes it easier and less painful for both you and the employee.

Another step sometimes is a helpful addition to the process, especially for managers who have a great deal of concern for the personal well-being of their employees. This step is for managers who tend to worry about terminated employees, about the impact termination has on their lives, its effect on their families, and what will happen to the employees. It is a step for managers who tend to feel responsible for the employee's termination decision. It is a step that precedes the first step of leveling.

What is this other step? It is the step of preparing mentally to terminate employees. It has four parts. First, realize that you and your work unit will be better off without employees who do not carry their share of the performance load. You can see this by comparing the consequences of employees leaving with those of their staying on as poor performers. Second, realize that employees will be better off in the long run by leaving. This can be seen by thinking about the impact on employees who come to a job every day where desired outcomes cannot be tied to performance. Third, realize that the time to deal with poorly performing employees is now. Waiting only allows a bad situation to get worse. Fourth, realize that with this approach you are giving employees a chance to avoid termination; if they are terminated, it is by their own choosing.

CHANGING PERCEPTIONS

Employees do not always perceive things accurately. These misperceptions often result in B2 problems. They can lead employees to the conclusion that outcomes are not being tied to performance when they really are. When motivation, effort, and performance decline because of misperceptions, what can you do?

Employee perceptions can be changed by using an established pattern of communication. It is a pattern that works. It has two steps. First, identify the specific misperception that is causing the employee to believe incorrectly that outcomes are not tied to performance. Second, give evidence to clarify the misperception. That's it. Two things.

The starting point is to identify the misperception. There are at least nine possibilities. Some are much more common than others, but you are likely to see all of them at one time or another. This list will help you recognize them more readily. Which ones have you seen recently? Think of your employees as you read about the nine misperceptions discussed here. Do you see any that fit? Here are the nine.

One, employees may not fully understand the performance/outcomes schedule. That is, they may not understand what they are supposed to get for performing in certain ways. This misunderstanding is understandable because (1) the schedule may not be completely formulated, (2) the manager may not have a full awareness or understanding of it, and (3) the manager may fail to communicate it to employees.

Two, employees may overestimate their performance and therefore believe outcomes are less than what is deserved. This is very common. Even when employees get what their performance deserves, they feel cheated because they see their performance as being more and/or better than it really is. Case 5-5 describes this kind of situation. How would you handle Charlie when he questions his pay raise?

Case 5-5—Changing Perceptions. Charlie is a machine operator in a metal fabrication plant. His production rate is fine, but he does sloppy work. This shows up in two ways. One, he has a lot of waste. This is expensive, because the cost of metal is a significant part of the total cost of each unit produced. Second, the rejection rate of his finished units is high. Units that do not pass inspection sometimes can be reworked, but normally they are scrapped. This is very costly because of the cost of both the material and the labor involved. Charlie, like other machine operators, is paid by the hour. He is not pleased with his most recent pay raise, his second one in fourteen months of employment. How would you handle Charlie if he complained about his pay raise?

The following dialogue, based on Case 5-5, illustrates how to change an employee's perception when outcomes are viewed as being less than deserved because performance is overestimated.

Employee: "I don't think it's fair that I got the smallest pay raise again."

Manager: "Why is that, Charlie?" (step 1—question to identify the misperception)

Employee: "Because I produce as much as everybody else, that's why." (step 1—misperception identified)

Manager: "The pay increases were based strictly on performance data. Frankly, Charlie, your numbers just weren't as high as the other guys'."

Employee: "I don't believe that. I work as hard as they do."

Manager: "Let me pull the file and you can take a look. OK, here it is. Let's look at it together. The record shows that during the past six months you produced fewer units and had more rejects and scrap than anyone else.

That's why your raise wasn't quite as high as the other guys'."(step 2—give evidence to clarify the misperception)

Employee: "Yeah, but what you're saying isn't right. I produced practically as many units as everybody else. Look at the numbers. They don't lie."

Manager: "You're right, Charlie. You did produce nearly as many as everybody else, but when the number of rejects and amount of scrap are considered, you're not as productive. We look at all of that when we decide what kind of pay raise to give." (step 2—more evidence to clarify the misperception)

Three, employees may undervalue the outcomes received and therefore believe outcomes are less than deserved. This happens sometimes, for example, when employees do not see the full growth and development value of being given more responsibility or do not fully appreciate either the recognition or promotion potential in being selected for a special assignment or do not see the real dollar value of a retirement plan. It also happens when employees do not realize they have received, or will receive, a certain outcome. Such misperceptions can occur for an employee whose letter of recognition gets lost, or an employee who never knows that the manager praised work of the employee to a vice president, or the employee whose notification of promotion is delayed for weeks by in-house politics.

Four, employees may underestimate performance and therefore believe their outcomes are more than deserved. Employees sometimes do not recognize the value and contribution of their performance; and when they get what they deserve, they feel that it's too much. "I don't deserve this" is the response. Admittedly, this is not common; but it does happen. The conclusion is, "Outcomes are not tied to performance."

Five, employees may overvalue outcomes and therefore believe their outcomes are more than deserved. This cause is on the rare side, too, but does happen occasionally. It occurs when employees believe something means more and/or is worth more than it is, like a corner office or a company car. Or when employees mistakenly think an outcome has been received when it hasn't been, like employees believing their boss has been giving them a lot of credit with other executives.

Six, employees may mistakenly believe that effort equals performance and therefore believe their outcomes are less than deserved. If the last two causes are rare, this one makes up for it. Many employees think they should be rewarded for effort rather than results. They firmly believe outcomes are deserved if they come to work and put out a reasonable amount of effort. In their minds, how much they produce and its quality should have no bearing on the outcomes received.

Seven, even in situations where equity has been established, employees may incorrectly perceive things as unfair. That is, employees sometimes see inequity even when there is none. When this happens, employees conclude that "outcomes are not tied to performance," even though they are. Case 5-6 describes this kind of misperception. How would you handle it?

Case 5-6—Changing Perceptions. Robyn has been a salesperson for a printing company for four years. All salespersons are paid a salary and commission. After the most recent pay raise, word got out that Brennerman had received a bigger salary increase than any of the other salespeople. This caused quite a stir. In the first place, everyone believed his sales lagged behind those of everybody else, especially during the last year or so. Second, he was widely viewed as an obnoxious, loud-mouthed braggart who lied about his sales exploits. Robyn was so upset about the situation that she decided to express her feelings to the boss. She had just finished her best year ever and felt the whole pay raise situation was very unfair. How would you handle Robyn if she came to you?

The best way to deal with employees like Robyn in Case 5-6 is to use the two-step process for clarifying misperceptions described earlier: (1) identify the cause of the misperception and (2) give evidence to clarify it. Here is one way to apply these two steps to the situation described in Case 5-6.

Employee: "I'm not as happy with my raise as I thought I was."

Manager: "Why is that?" (step 1)

Employee: "I found out what 'Bigshot' Brennerman got. Everybody knows he's not selling much, and he gets a bigger raise than several of us who had our best year." (step 1)

Manager: "I don't know what you heard, but I'll be happy to show you, and anybody else who's interested, what the salary increases were. It's no secret. Here, take a look for yourself." (step 2)

Employee: "According to this, Brennerman didn't even get a raise."

Manager: "That's right."

Employee: "He lied to us!"

Manager: "I can assure you that the numbers on this sheet are correct."

Eight, employees also may incorrectly perceive the recent tying of outcomes to performance as only a temporary situation in spite of a solid, long-term management commitment. This can stem from several things, including a general distrust of management or a lack of awareness of the commitment that has been made. Whatever the reason, this perception leads to the conclusion that "outcomes really are not tied to performance, except for occasional brief periods."

Nine, employees with a history of outcomes not being tied to performance may incorrectly perceive the current situation as being the same as the past, even though it may be quite different and much better. Their history can be blinding, keeping them from seeing what is happening and causing them to interpret it inaccurately. Consequently, they do not see outcomes as being tied to performance.

The common element in these nine situations is that employees are not accurately seeing things the way they are. Each of these misperceptions can lead employees to wrongly believe that outcomes are not tied to performance. When misperceptions are causing B2 problems, the solution is simply to correct the misperceptions. Employee perceptions can be corrected easily when the cause of the misperception is identified and when evidence to the contrary is presented.

SUMMARY

Seven solutions have been presented in this chapter for solving B2 problems, namely, tying outcomes to performance, creating and maintaining equity, leveling, preference shifting, transfers, terminations, and changing employee perceptions. The appropriate solution depends on the cause of the problem. You will find that solving B2 problems comes easily when you first determine the cause(s), then select the appropriate solution(s), and implement each one according to the guidelines presented in this chapter.

The greatest barrier to solving performance-outcome problems (B2) is manager reluctance, and for good reason. Remember, B2 problems are not solved overnight. When employees believe outcomes are not tied to performance, giving deserved outcomes once or twice is not enough. You must link outcomes to performance frequently and over a long period of time to erase B2 problems. Managers are at a disadvantage in doing this when they do not have control over the necessary outcomes, as often is the case. Managers simply must do the best they can with what they have. This will be enough, however. You know how to solve B2 problems, as outlined in this chapter, and you can do wonders with your employees. Although B2 problems cannot always be solved as quickly and completely as desired, you can see substantial improvements in employee motivation, effort, and performance. It is unrealistic to expect overnight success. Progress comes from taking one step at a time. You are prepared to do this. Just follow the guidelines recommended in this chapter. Give it a try. You can do it. You'll see.

6

Diagnosing Outcome-Satisfaction Problems

Everyone experiences dissatisfaction at one time or another with the rewards of the job. Employees may not be getting the rewards they want most, like a good pay increase, the right promotion, and genuine appreciation. Or maybe they are given something that has little, if any, value, like an insincere word of praise or a certificate for years of service. Sometimes employees are rewarded with things they don't want, like more responsibility or assignment to a special project. And frequently they are put into jobs where the work itself is not rewarding. When any of this happens, employees often conclude, "I am not getting what I want," or "I don't like what I am getting." Both of these are the belief that outcomes do not, or will not, lead to satisfaction (B3). In expectancy theory terminology, this is an outcome-satisfaction problem. The result is a decline in motivation, effort, and performance.

Outcome-satisfaction problems, where employees believe "I don't get what I want" or "I get what I don't want," permeate every organization. Employees discuss these problems openly with each other. They blame the organization, and often their own manager, when they are not satisfied with the rewards of their job. While some employees are quite vocal about this with their manager, others are reluctant to mention it.

From the manager's perspective, what does this mean? First, every manager has employees whose motivation, effort, and performance suffer because they are not satisfied with the rewards of the job. Second, the presence and depth of these problems may go unnoticed for a long time. Third, the impact can be very damaging. Employees who are not satisfied with rewards have problems with motivation, effort, and performance. The problems are intensified as employees feel cheated, become resentful, and place blame.

The outcome-satisfaction belief (B3) represents the third and final condition that must be met for employees to be motivated to perform well. As stated in chapter 1, employees are motivated only when they (1) believe effort will lead to performance (B1), (2) believe performance will lead to outcomes (B2), and (3) believe outcomes will lead to satisfaction (B3). The stronger these beliefs, the greater the employees' motivation to perform.

The expectancy theory of motivation offers a simple, yet powerful, way to prevent as well as to identify and solve outcome-satisfaction problems. A variety of strategies for doing this are presented in chapters 6 and 7. The emphasis in this chapter is on diagnosing problems, while the focus of chapter 7 is on practical solutions.

Diagnosing outcome-satisfaction beliefs (B3) follows the pattern used for diagnosing effort-performance beliefs (B1) and performance-outcomes beliefs (B2). The same two skills are required: (1) how to obtain the needed information and (2) how to interpret it. As in the previous discussions on diagnosing B1 and B2, attention is given to the second skill first. This chapter, then, focuses first on interpreting B3 information and then on obtaining it.

INTERPRETING B3 INFORMATION

As with B1 and B2, two things must be done when interpreting B3 information. The first is to diagnose the level of the employee's B3, the extent to which employees believe that "outcomes are not, or will not be, satisfying." If the employee's B3 level is a problem, the second step is to diagnose the cause. That is, what is causing the employee to believe the outcomes being given or offered do not or will not lead to satisfaction? Our attention will turn first to B3 levels, then to the causes.

Diagnosing B3 Levels

The diagnosis can be done in the context of two different time frames, the present and the future. If you are looking at employee motivation in a current job, the question is, "How satisfying does the employee believe the current outcomes are?" This is the employee's current B3. If you are planning (1) to make changes in an employee's job, either in the work itself or in its extrinsic outcomes; (2) to promote or transfer the employee; or (3) to hire a new employee, you naturally need to consider the employee's motivation in the future circumstances. You want to know the employee's future B3. The question, is "How satisfying does the employee believe the future outcomes will be?"

Is there a difference between the ways you diagnose a current or a future B3? No, the approach is the same. The same diagnostic techniques can be used, too. There are two important points to note, however. The first is that employees often find that the amount of satisfaction derived from outcomes once they get them is different from how satisfying they believed the outcomes would be. How often have you heard comments like the following from employees after they finally get something they have wanted for a long time?

—"This isn't the way I expected it to be."

—"I thought this would mean more than it does."

—"I'm not enjoying this as much as I expected."

—"This is worse than I ever imagined."

—"This is a pleasant surprise."

In view of this, you need to be cautious when making decisions based on an employee's future B3. The satisfaction may not be what the employee expected, and employee motivation may not be what you anticipated.

The second point is that a current B3 is, by definition, valid. A current B3 has a strong information base, having been derived by the employee from current empirical evidence. That is, the employee is getting certain outcomes and knows how satisfying they are. However, the amount of satisfaction an employee derives from outcomes may change. When this happens, the current B3 changes. This means that you can have confidence in a current B3 that is properly diagnosed, as long as it is indeed current.

With this in mind, how do you go about the diagnosis? Diagnosing B3 levels is best done by using a rating scale that is similar to, but not identical with, the ones used for rating B1 and B2 levels. The B3 scale ranges from -10 to $+10$ and reflects the fact that employees view some outcomes as satisfying and others are dissatisfying (-10, -9, . . . -2, -1, 0, $+1$, $+2$, . . . $+9$, $+10$). That is, employees see some outcomes positively and others negatively. A B3 rating of -10 represents maximum dissatisfaction and $+10$ maximum satisfaction.

One of the most important kinds of B3 information you will be interpreting is what employees tell you. Employees express outcome-satisfaction beliefs (B3) in numerous ways. Several common ones are shown following this paragraph. Read each one and interpret the employee's B3 level using the B3 rating scale. What is each employee's belief about how satisfying the outcome is or will be? When you have done this, continue reading to see how your ratings measure up.

1. "I want that promotion more than anything else I've ever wanted in my life!"

2. "I'm over my head in debt. If I don't get a good raise, I'm dead. Nothing else matters."

3. "If there is one thing I can't stand, it's being criticized all the time, especially when you're doing your best. I hate that more than anything."

4. "The last thing I need is more responsibility. I have too much now, and it's killing me. I can't take any more."

5. "I don't like business travel, but it's not enough to get too upset about."

6. "Job security? It would be nice, but it's not a big deal to me."

How did you do? When employees want something "more than anything" (as in response 1) or want something so much that "nothing else matters" (as in response 2), B3 ratings of +10 are appropriate. At the other extreme, ratings of −10 fit when employees refer to something with statements like "hate it more than anything" (as in response 3) or "can't take it any more" (as in response 4). Extremely strong statements are easy to interpret. Others are not a problem, however, for two reasons. First, the recommended "guess and guess again approach" means you make your best guess and continue gathering information until you feel confident about your interpretation. Second, remember that precision is not necessary and "close is close enough." That's why sometimes your first guesses may lie within a range. Take response 5, for example. How is a statement like "I don't like it, but it's not enough to get too upset about" to be interpreted? First, as we know it represents dissatisfaction, a negative rating is called for. But how much dissatisfaction? As a first guess, let's say the B3 probably is in the −1, −2, −3 range and leave it at that. The same is true for statements like "it's nice, but no big deal"(as in response 6). This suggests satisfaction, but not a lot, so that guessing a B3 in the +1, +2, +3 range is a good first guess. How did your ratings compare with these? They probably were pretty close.

How about a little more practice? Let's take a look at a few more ways employees express B3 information. Read the following statements and rate each one using the B3 rating scale. Then continue reading to see how your interpretations stack up.

1. "The thing that matters most to me is doing work I enjoy."

2. "Getting promoted would be the worst thing that could happen to me. I would hate the work, the hours, the travel, and the pressure."

3. "I'd love to get one of the new reserved parking spaces. People notice that kind of thing. On a scale of one to ten, I'd give it a six."

4. "I don't like making so many presentations, but I guess things could be worse."

5. "Getting one of the new corner offices would be OK, I guess. But that sort of thing isn't all that important to me."

6. "The thing I love more than anything else is being around people. Nothing would be as bad as having to work alone. I wouldn't last long in that kind of job."

The B3 ratings for these are as follows. "The thing that matters most" (response 1) and "The thing I love more than anything else" (response 6) are the kind of statements that deserve a +10 ratings. Equally clear are statements like "The worst thing that could happen" (response 2) and "Nothing would be as bad" (response 6) call for −10 ratings. Sometimes employees are equally clear in another way as they make very specific statements about outcomes like "on a scale of one to ten, I'd give it a six" (response 3), clearly suggesting a B3 of +6. "I don't like it, but things could be worse" (response 4) indicates dissatisfaction, but how much? A first guess somewhere around −2, −3, or −4 is close enough. "It's OK, but not all that important" (response 5) indicates a B3 in or near the +2, +3, +4 range. How did you do this time? These were pretty easy, weren't they?

Let's look at a few that are more difficult. They are listed following this paragraph. Assign a B3 rating to each one, then compare your ratings with those shown after each employee's response. It is particularly difficult to pinpoint B3 levels in responses 5 through 10. If you disagree with the ratings shown here, don't worry. Your guesses may be better. However, your rating should match those given in terms of positive (+) and negative (−) value.

1. More travel—"Flying terrifies me." (rating = −10)
2. Relocating—"That would be traumatic for me and my family." (rating = −10)
3. More challenging work—"You couldn't do anything that would mean more to me." (rating = +10)
4. A cash bonus—"If I ever needed some extra cash, now is the time!" (rating = +10)
5. Promotion—"I want it more than anything!" (rating = +10)
6. More responsibility—"Sure. A little more would be fine, I guess." (rating = +2, +3, +4)
7. Attend management training program—"It probably would have some value." (rating = +3, +4, +5)
8. Improved retirement benefits—"I'm only 23. Retirement plans don't mean that much." (rating = +1, +2, +3)

9. Give up one of your job functions—"I don't want to give it up, but it's not a life-or-death matter." (rating = -3, -4, -5)

10. More employees to supervise—"The employees I have give me enough headaches, but I guess a few more won't kill me." (rating = -3, -4, -5)

It is time now to change the focus away from individual outcomes. Not only do employees have B3s for individual outcomes, as discussed so far, but they also have B3s for sets of outcomes. The sets can be made up of (1) intrinsic and/or extrinsic outcomes; (2) outcomes derived from the individual, the work environment, the manager, and/or the organization; and (3) outcomes currently received or outcomes potentially available in the future. Sets that commonly are important to employees include (1) intrinsic outcomes the employee is currently receiving in the job, (2) extrinsic outcomes the employee would expect to get in a different job, (3) all outcomes the employee is getting in the present job, or (4) all outcomes the employee would like to be getting in the current job. Employees can have B3s for each of these sets of outcomes, and for many others.

Let's turn our attention now to the interpretation of B3s for sets of outcomes. Employees express beliefs about sets in a variety of ways. Several are shown following this paragraph. Read each response and guess the employee's B3 rating for the set of outcomes referenced. Notice that some responses refer to more than one set of outcomes. When you finish, continue reading to see how your ratings compare.

1. "All things considered, I don't think I could be much happier in my job. Everything is great. I don't have any complaints." (Current job—all outcomes being received.)

2. "This is the worst job you could imagine. Nothing good and everything bad. I've been trying to get out from day one." (Current job—all outcomes being received.)

3. "Now that would be the ideal job. I've had my eye on it for a while. Even talked to a couple of guys that work there. They say it's about as close to perfect as a job can get." (Another job—all outcomes expected in that job in the future.)

4. "There's good and bad in every job. In mine, the good outweighs the bad, but just barely." (Current job—all outcomes being received.)

5. "I keep thinking I'm going to leave. If things were just a little better, the good would outweigh the bad and I think I could live with it." (Current job—all outcomes currently being received.)

6. "This is a great company. I love the people I work with, and I couldn't have a better boss. I get just about everything I want. The only problem is that I don't enjoy my work anymore. I just don't like what I'm doing. Sometimes

I can't stand the thought of doing it another day." (Current job—extrinsic versus intrinsic outcomes being received.)

7. "I'm not getting everything I want now, but I'm pretty well satisfied. The things that excite me the most are all of the opportunities if I can get that next promotion. I'll be in heaven." (Current job—all outcomes being received; future position—all outcomes expected.)

The B3 levels for each of these are approximated as follows for responses 1 through 7, respectively:

1. The set of outcomes in this employee's job are about as satisfying as they can be. A B3 rating in the $+8$, $+9$, $+10$ range is appropriate.

2. The set of outcomes could not be much worse in this employee's job. The B3 rating would be in the -8, -9, -10 range.

3. This employee is thinking about another job, one believed to offer a set of outcomes as satisfying as any could be. A B3 rating in the $+8$, $+9$, $+10$ range fits here.

4. All things considered, this set of outcomes offers minimal satisfaction. A positive but low rating is appropriate here, something in the $+1$, $+2$, $+3$ range.

5. The bad outweighs the good now, but just barely, for this set of outcomes. This suggests a rating in the -1, -2, -3 range.

6. This employee's B3 for the set of extrinsic outcomes being received is in the $+8$, $+9$, $+10$ range, but the B3 for the work itself (intrinsic outcomes) is in the -8, -9, -10 range. The overall B3 for all outcomes combined seems to be negative ("can't stand the thought of doing it another day"). How negative? This is a hard one to call. Probably in the -7, -8, -9 range.

7. Here is an employee with a B3 rating in or near the $+6$, $+7$, $+8$ range for the set of outcomes currently being received. This employee believes that nothing could be more satisfying than the set of outcomes expected if the promotion comes through. This suggests a B3 rating of $+9$ or $+10$ for the set of outcomes envisioned in the future.

What do you think? Do you feel confident about diagnosing B3 levels based on things employees say? If you have followed this discussion, and especially if you have thoughtfully diagnosed the B3 levels in all of the examples so far, you should be able to say, "I can do it."

Diagnosing B3 Causes

So much for the first part of B3 diagnosis, namely, diagnosing B3 levels. Our attention turns now to diagnosing B3 causes. Short cases will be used for this focus, with each illustrating one or more causes of B3 problems. The cases will give you an opportunity to identify the causes as well as an opportunity to continue practicing how to diagnose B3 levels for sets of outcomes. Simply read each case carefully, determine B3 levels and causes, and compare your diagnosis with the analysis that follows each case.

Case 6-1—Interpreting B3 Information Obtained by Communication. Scottie had worked hard to keep Nance out of promotion consideration for a position not in her best interest and instead got her appointed to head up an important project that had top management visibility. Now she was looking across her desk at Nance. She hoped Nance wouldn't bring up the parking issue again. Too many people resented young employees who got reserved spaces, and Scottie intended to protect Nance by not assigning her one. Scottie started the meeting by asking, "How are things going?" Nance was hoping for this discussion. "There is only one opening now for a promotion, and I'm not being considered for it. I'll die if I don't get it. That's more important to me than anything in the world. I have to get promoted before anyone else in the group I was hired with. That's been my goal from the beginning. It's my obsession. Well, that's the first thing. Then there is the deal about reserved parking. I've asked about it several times. I know for a fact there is at least one space that is unassigned. Why can't I have it? That's important to me. I've worked hard enough to deserve it. Then there is the new project I was just assigned to head up. Why me? I mean, is it really that important?" What is Nance's B3 for the promotion? For reserved parking? For heading up the project. What is her B3 for the full set of outcomes she is currently receiving? What is causing this to be lower than it could be?

How do you interpret the B3 information Scottie has obtained by communicating with Nance, as presented in Case 6-1? Since the promotion is "more important than anything in the world," a B3 guess with a $+10$ rating would be on the mark. Her B3 for a reserved parking space probably is in the $+6$, $+7$, $+8$ range—important, though less so than the promotion. The "why me—is it really that important" comment suggests a B3 for heading up the project that is slightly positive $(+1, +2, +3)$ at best, and may be even slightly negative $(-1, -2, -3)$. Even though Nance may be receiving a lot of very positive outcomes in her job, their value probably has been overshadowed by her concern about not getting promoted, not getting a reserved parking space, and heading up a project whose importance she questions. This would suggest a B3 for the total set of outcomes that is positive, but not very positive, in the $+4$, $+5$, $+6$ range or perhaps on the lower side of it. What is causing Nance's B3 to be lower than it could be? Two things. One, she is overvaluing outcomes not received, the promotion and the reserved parking space. She has greatly overvalued the promotion, to the extent that it has become what is called an outcome obsession. Two, she is undervaluing an outcome received, heading up the project.

Case 6-2—Interpreting B3 Information Obtained by Communication. In April, eight months after being promoted, Frank told his boss, "I want to thank you again for the promotion. I'm worker longer and harder, and accomplishing more than ever before. It's exciting. I never thought I could enjoy a job so much. I like everything about it, especially the money, having more responsibility, and the travel." In May, Frank's oldest son was killed in an automobile accident. In June, Frank told his boss, "I've lost a lot of enthusiasm for my job. It seems that all I do is work and travel. I never have any time for my family. If anything else comes open, I'd sure like to know about it." In August, Frank's boss called him in to discuss an opening that might better suit Frank's needs. Two days later, Frank talked it over with his boss, saying, "The new position seems to have everything I'm looking for, especially more time for my family. You know how important that is to me now. But I do have one concern. I'm not sure I would enjoy the work. I've done that kind of thing before, and it's just not something I enjoy. I don't know what to do." What was Frank's B3 in April for the total set of outcomes in his new job? What was it in June? What caused the change? What is his B3 in August for the total set of outcomes in the new position he is considering? What is causing it to be on the low side?

Case 6-2 illustrates the impact of changing and conflicting values on an employee's B3. For April, a B3 rating in the $+8$, $+9$, $+10$ range is a good guess because Frank likes everything about his job. Following the death of his son, Frank wanted to change jobs to have more time with his family. All things considered, Frank no longer wanted the set of outcomes his job offered. This means his B3 in June would be described best by a negative rating, in the -1, -2, -3 range, if not lower. Why this change? It was caused by a change in values, a change initiated by the death of his son. Frank started placing more value on his family and less on his job and career. Changed values are a common cause of B3 problems. What about the new job available to him? Frank seems to like all of the extrinsic outcomes associated with the job (a B3 rating in the $+5$, $+6$, $+7$ range, maybe higher), but feels that the intrinsic outcomes would not be rewarding at all (a B3 rating in the -4, -5, -6 range, perhaps worse, would be appropriate), with an overall B3 that is slightly positive ($+1$, $+2$, $+3$) at best and may be slightly negative (perhaps in the -1, -2, -3 range). Why so low? This low B1 is caused by conflicting values, a conflict between the value Frank places on doing work that is enjoyable and the value of having time with his family.

Case 6-3—Interpreting B3 Information Obtained by Communication. On March 4: "Thanks for asking, but that's just not a position I'm really interested in pursuing," George tells Dennis, his boss. "The extra money doesn't make up for the added pressure and having to relocate." March 8: Dennis meets individually with each department member to notify them of pay raises. For the third consecutive time, George received the largest raise, in terms of both dollars and percentage increase, because of his consistently high performance. March 10: George storms into Dennis's office and says, "I'm upset. First I hear that Tom got a bigger raise than I did. Then I hear Walt is probably going to get the position you asked me about last week. That's not fair. I'm more qualified than he is. I've been here longer, and I deserve the promotion. I can handle it. Relocating is no big thing. And the extra money would be nice." March 17: Dennis offers the position to George. March 19: George meets with Dennis and says, "I just don't know if this promotion is what I want or not. One minute it sounds great. The next minute it doesn't. I can't make up my mind." What is George's B3 on March 4 for the set of outcomes associated with the new position? What is it on March 10? And March 19? Why the change? What is George's B3 on March 10 for the set of outcomes he is receiving in his current job? What was behind the change?

Two separate B3 issues are involved in Case 6-3. One deals with George's current job. On March 10 George is upset because he believes someone else got a bigger pay raise. It isn't possible to pinpoint George's B3 level based on this information alone, but one thing we know for sure. His B3 for the pay raise and his B3 for the total set of outcomes in his current job are lower than they were before he came to believe someone got a bigger raise. Why? The lowering of his B3 is the result of George's believing that Dennis has not been fair in the way pay raises were given. George placed less value on his pay raise after he heard Tom got a bigger raise. This is called undervaluing an outcome and is one of the causes of George's low B3.

The other B3 issue in Case 6-3 focuses on George's B3 for the set of outcomes associated with the new position. Let's look at how this B3 changes over a two-week period. On March 4, George is not very interested in the outcomes of the position. His B3 for the new position definitely is lower than his B3 for his current job; otherwise, the new position would have been more appealing. It is difficult to guess exactly what the B3 level for the new position is. If it is positive, it is low (in the +1, +2, +3 range) and may be negative, though it is hard to say how negative. On March 10, however, George's B3 for the same position is very positive, obviously more positive than for his current job. A B3 rating in the +6, +7, +8 range or higher probably would be a good guess. Then on March 19, what is it? This is tough to guess, tough because George doesn't even know. He can't make up his mind. He has confused values, which are causing him to have a B3 problem.

He is confused about what he wants, about what he values. Confused values can cause frequent, even dramatic, shifts in an employee's B3.

Case 6-4—Interpreting B3 Information Obtained by Observation. Bert was an assistant to the president of a small company. He was good with numbers, could write well, and liked to work alone. His job mainly involved gathering and analyzing data and preparing and writing reports. Bert was a hard worker, performed extremely well, and enjoyed his job—until it changed. Over a period of several weeks, it changed quickly. He no longer gathered and analyzed data, but he continued to write reports and had started writing letters, speeches, and proposals for the president. His job had become a writing job. Everything else remained basically the same. Except Bert. He didn't put as much effort into his work, and his performance dropped off. There was a change in attitude, including resentment for having to work late occasionally. He began to complain about little things, and appeared overall to be dissatisfied with his job. All these changes in Bert were very noticeable because he had always been such a model employee. Compare Bert's B3 for the set of outcomes associated with his job before and after the change. What caused the change?

Case 6-4 presents an interesting and very common situation that is simple to diagnose. Bert's B3 for the set of outcomes before the change in duties was very high, probably a rating in the +7, +8, +9 range; otherwise, his performance and behavior would not have led to the "model employee" designation. After the change in his job, negative changes were observed in his performance, effort, attitude, complaints, and satisfaction. How should these observations be interpreted, in the context of Bert's B3? These changes, individually and collectively, indicate a decline in Bert's B3, to the point of being just barely positive, like a +1, +2, +3 rating, and perhaps worse, with a rating in the −1, −2, −3 range or lower. The key in this situation is that everything in his job remained basically the same except for the change in duties. There is no reason to believe Bert's B3 for extrinsic outcomes changed, as the same outcomes continued to be available. Instead, it appears that the lowered B3 centers on the intrinsic outcomes associated with the new duties. That is, the cause of this B3 problem is that the work itself is no longer rewarding.

Case 6-5—Interpreting B3 Information Obtained by Skills Analysis. David had been in the maintenance department for about six years and could repair any piece of equipment the company used or made. Although his technical skills were the best, his people skills were not that strong. He was basically a quiet person who preferred working alone. When he talked, he went straight to the point. There was no pretense about him. Some employees thought he was a little rude, but nobody had any real complaints about him. David didn't have any complaints either.

He liked his job. Because David did such good work, someone suggested having him do sales and service work with clients who had service contracts on equipment purchased from the company. What is David's B3 for his current job? What would you expect it to be for the new one? What is the cause for the difference?

Case 6-5 indicates that David "likes his job," suggesting a very positive B3 (in the +6, +7, +8 range or higher), but the skills analysis (David's technical skills are strong but his people skills are not) suggest a B3 problem for the new job. A B3 rating in the neighborhood of −4, −5, −6, or worse would be a good guess. Why? For one thing, David would expect to get some outcomes he does not value. The skills analysis shows that David doesn't have the people skills for the job. He might put it this way, "I like to work alone, but in the new job I'd have to be nice to everybody, have to put up with stupid questions, unrealistic demands, and complaints, and in general be hassled by somebody all the time. I'd open my big mouth and then I'd be in trouble. My boss would be complaining and hassling me, too. I don't need any of that." David also would not be getting some things he likes. He wouldn't be working alone, wouldn't have the satisfaction of doing a good job, wouldn't be recognized as the best, wouldn't get much praise for his work, wouldn't get nice pay raises, and wouldn't enjoy his work very much. He definitely would have a B3 problem, which would be caused by a combination of three things: (1) not receiving valued outcomes, (2) receiving outcomes not valued, and (3) work that itself is not rewarding.

Case 6-6—Interpreting B3 Information Obtained by Job Analysis. James is a graduate of one of the top business schools in the country, with a degree in management. He is proficient with computers, but his strength and love lie in dealing with people. He interviewed with a national consulting firm and was offered a position as a junior consultant. He gladly accepted, thinking it was the perfect job for him in the first stage of his career. When he reported to work, he was asked to shift into a position working on computer applications for clients. He agreed to do so. James, like his coworkers, spends most of his time working alone, doing the following tasks: (1) He specializes in a limited number of computer applications within two application areas. (2) He is given job assignments that are small parts of large computer applications for major clients. (3) He produces work to meet the job specifications provided. (4) He turns over completed work to someone else, who integrates the various parts and follows through with implementation to meet client needs. The notes taken in the initial job interview with James show that he said, "There are two things I hate. One is doing things that required precision and attention to detail. I have little tolerance for it. The other is doing the same thing over and over. I get bored quickly." What is James's B3 for each of the following individual outcomes: (1) dealing with people, (2) work that involves precision and attention to detail, and (3) work that is repetitious? What is James's B3 for (4) the total set of outcomes expected in the junior consultant job and (5) the total set of intrinsic outcomes currently being received in the computer job? What is causing James's B3 problem in the computer job?

In Case 6-6, let's look at individual outcomes first, then the sets. As James "loves" dealing with people, his B3 for doing so probably would have a rating in the +8, +9, +10 range. Because he "hates" work that requires precision and attention to detail and work that is repetitious, his B3 rating for both likely is somewhere around −8, −9, −10. James's B3 for the total set of outcomes expected in the junior consultant position probably was a rating in the +8, +9, +10 range, because he viewed it as the "perfect" job. If he had gone into that position as planned, what would you guess his B3 to be for the set of outcomes actually received (as opposed to expected)? It would be lower. Things never are as perfect as expected.

What about James's B3 for the intrinsic outcomes of the computer job? A quick job analysis reveals that (1) James works alone, (2) the work requires precision and attention to detail, and (3) there is considerable repetition in job assignments. When this is compared to what James likes and dislikes, you see that the work itself denies him one thing he "loves" and gives him two things he "hates." Based on this, the best guess is that James places a negative value on the intrinsic outcomes of his job, maybe as negative as a −8, −9, or −10 rating. What causes this B3 problem? Two things cause it: (1) not receiving valued outcomes (dealing with people) and (2) receiving outcomes not valued (precision/detailed work and repetition).

Case 6-7—Interpreting B3 Information Obtained by Work Environment Analysis. James likes being around people, enjoys the interaction, likes the fellowship, wants to fit in, has a need to be accepted, likes to influence others, and needs recognition and positive reinforcement from his peers. He has a computer job (see Case 6-6) in which there is no direct contact with clients and little involvement with his manager. Unlike James, his coworkers went to technical universities, majored in technical areas, and have technical skills and interests. They talk about different things, dress differently, look and act differently. They have little in common with James. Consequently, they have rejected him as a member of the work group. Interaction with them is minimal and is confined to a few short weekly meetings. James finds the meetings unpleasant and goes only when forced to do so. What is your best guess about James's B3 for the set of outcomes he is receiving from coworkers? What is causing his B3 not to be higher?

An analysis of the work environment in Case 6-7 suggests that valued outcomes (interaction, acceptance, influence, etc.) are not made available to James in his work environment. There is no opportunity to receive them from clients and little opportunity of getting them from his manager. Instead, he is receiving outcomes not valued, namely, rejection by coworkers, limited interaction, unpleasant interactions, low-quality fellowship, forced attendance at unpleasant meetings, and probably being ignored rather than receiving recognition and being criticized rather than receiving positive reinforcement. James's B3 for the rejection probably is at or near the maximum (B3 = −9 or −10), with his B3 for the each of the other outcomes following not too far behind (probably in the neighborhood of B3 = −5, −6, −7, or −8). It seems safe to guess that James's B3 for the full set of outcomes being received is very negative, like a B3 rating of −8, −9, or −10. Two things are causing this B3 to be so low: (1) not receiving valued outcomes and (2) receiving outcomes not valued.

Case 6-8—Interpreting B3 Information Obtained by Organization Analysis. For five years, the company hired large numbers of young, aggressive, ambitious, well-educated managers who advanced rapidly over the next twelve to fifteen years because of the company's rapid growth and expansion. Salaries doubled and tripled, opportunities for growth and development were unlimited, and jobs were very secure. As these managers reached the age range of thirty-five to forty, the company's growth diminished considerably. For five years now, it has been a stable company, with sales that normally increase annually at about the same rate as inflation. Profitablity has declined, there have been some cutbacks among hourly workers and managers, and compensation and benefits have not kept pace with the industry average. Except for the cutbacks, few middle-level and higher-level managers have left the company. What has happened to B3 levels for individual outcomes like money, advancement, growth and development, and job security among managers aged thirty-five to forty? What changes have occurred to B3 levels for the total set of outcomes these managers receive now compared to those of the past? What impact does this have on their motivation to work?

The organization in Case 6-8 has undergone some changes that have had an impact on worker motivation. For most managers aged thirty-five to forty, the value they placed in the past on individual outcomes such as money, advancement, growth and development, and job security probably was relatively high (B3 = at least +5). The value likely has remained high, perhaps even increasing in the case of money (to support bigger houses, finer cars, children approaching college age) and job security (with age and a threat of job loss with cutbacks). How satisfying are the outcomes these managers are receiving now, in total, compared to the past? Until the last five years, things couldn't have been much better for these managers. The B3 for outcomes received probably was in the +7, +8, +9 range. But recently, compensation and benefits haven't kept up with growing needs, managers have not advanced into positions they had hoped for, personal growth and development have slowed, and job security is uncertain. Overall, most of these managers probably are less satisfied now, with B3s likely in or near the +2, +3, +4 range. What does this mean? These managers are less motivated than they once were. Their B3 for outcomes available in jobs held by their friends and neighbors likely is more attractive, causing them to spend considerable time thinking about, and perhaps exploring, other job opportunities. What caused these diminished B3s? Valued outcomes were not being received.

Case 6-9—Interpreting B3 Information Obtained by Organization Analysis. Funding for faculty raises at a large state university was equal to 3 percent of last year's salary levels. Three percent was considerably less than the inflation rate at the time. Each school within the university received its proportional share of funds, along with authorization to allocate it for faculty raises in the way deemed most appropriate. Most schools elected to give 3 percent raises to each faculty member. In one school, for example, salaries for the previous year varied from approximately $30,000 to $40,000 annually. The already high cost of living in the area was increasing because of rapidly rising inflation. Most faculty members were barely getting by financially. What was the B3 for a substantial raise? What was it for the 3 percent raises? What caused B3 levels to be what they were?

The employees earning $30,000 to $40,000 in Case 6-9 were struggling to make ends meet, given the cost of living and the inflation rate. Consequently, their B3 for getting a substantial pay raise was very high (in the +8, +9, +10 range). What was the B3 for the 3 percent raises they actually received? That is, how satisfying were the raises? Not very, in view of what they needed and hoped to get. B3 ratings in the +2, +3, +4 range probably would be appropriate. What about the B3 for the few high performers who deserved much more? The small amount of satisfaction they received (+2, +3, +4) was further diminished, maybe to the 0, +1, +2 range, because of the inequity of giving everyone the same 3 percent raise regardless of performance. This was particularly true of a young faculty member making $30,000 who performed well and received a 3 percent ($900) raise while seeing a low-performing older person making $40,000 also getting a 3 percent ($1,200) raise. This is not much incentive for a high performer and yields little satisfaction. The low B3 levels for everyone are caused by (1) not receiving valued outcomes and (2) undervaluing outcomes received. Inequity further compounds dissatisfaction for anyone who performs better than the lowest performers.

Case 6-10—Interpreting B3 Information Obtained by Manager Analysis. Kevin had just finished college and was in his first job. He was only twenty years old, but his performance was exceptional. Jay, an extremely competent middle manager who everyone agreed was on the way up, took notice of Kevin's work and wanted Kevin in his department. When Jay talked with him about it, Kevin was very open in pointing out that he performed best with (1) opportunities for growth and development, (2) frequent interaction with his manager, (3) detailed feedback on his performance, and (4) recognition when he performed well. With Jay's assurance, Kevin agreed to come into the department. Kevin's performance was outstanding. He was the kind of person you could give an assignment to and know it would be done right without ever having to check on him. This worked out well for Jay because he was responsible for a major profit center and had enormous demands on his time. He met with Kevin only occasionally, and those meetings were confined to giving Kevin his next assignment. Jay viewed these meetings as important to Kevin because Jay always selected assignments that were challenging and allowed, actually forced, Kevin to acquire the skills and experience he needed to advance rapidly in the company. What was Kevin's B3 for the set of four outcomes he told Jay he wanted in a job? What is Kevin's B3 for the outcomes he was actually receiving? What was causing the difference in the two B3s?

Case 6-10 describes an employee, Kevin, who understood and could verbalize what he wanted in a job. He told Jay about the four most important ones, the ones he considered essential, the ones that above all the rest are the most satisfying. Kevin places the highest possible value on having this set of four things in a job (B3 = +10). What is Kevin's B3 for the set of outcomes he actually is receiving from Jay? Jay is focusing on one of the four, while completely ignoring the other three. Kevin's B3 would be very low, only as high as a low positive rating (in the +1, +2, +3 range) and perhaps a negative rating (in the −1, −2, −3 range or even lower). In any case, this definitely is a B3 problem. What is the cause? One thing: Kevin is not receiving valued outcomes.

Case 6-11—Interpreting B2 Information Obtained by Communication. Clare had had only limited experience conducting management training programs when she accepted a job conducting three eight-hour sessions per week. She was achievement oriented and worked hard to become the best. After several months she began consistently to get the highest ratings among the thirty trainers in the organization. Everyone recognized her as the best of the bunch. As she repeatedly conducted her five different one-day programs, she gradually lost enthusiasm. One morning when getting ready to go to a session, she said to herself, "I hate doing these stupid programs over and over, and I'm going to quit." Within days she was meeting with her boss to tell him she no longer enjoyed her work and was resigning. What was Clare's B3 early in her job? What was it toward the end? What caused it to change?

In the situation of Case 6-11, Clare no longer received personal satisfaction from the work she did. The work itself did not continue to be personally rewarding. That is, the intrinsic outcomes that once were rewarding (sense of accomplishment, meeting a challenge, learning to do something well, etc.) were no longer so. Initially she had a high B2 for the intrinsic rewards she wanted because simply doing the work insured getting them. As she continued in her job, she concluded that doing the work meant she would not get the sense of accomplishment, challenge, and growth and development she wanted. With this conclusion, her B3 dropped significantly. The low B3 was caused by work that was not intrinsically rewarding.

The eleven cases presented here have illustrated eight major causes of B3 problems. They are summarized as follows: Case 6-1—Nance was "undervaluing an outcome being received" (heading up the project), "overvaluing an outcome not received" (reserved parking space), and "overvaluing an outcome not received" to the point where it (a promotion) had become an obsession. Case 6-2—Frank's "changing values" (from career to family) and "conflicting values" (work itself versus time with family) were the problem. Case 6-3—George had "confused values" (couldn't decide if he wanted the outcomes from the new job) and was "undervaluing an outcome received" by placing less value on his pay raise because he mistakenly believed someone else unfairly got a bigger pay raise. Case 6-4—After the changes in Bert's job duties, the "work itself is not rewarding." Case 6-5—In the new job, David would be "receiving outcomes not valued" (being hassled by customers and his boss), "would not be receiving valued outcomes" (working alone, recognition), and "the work itself would not be rewarding"). Case 6-6—James was "not receiving valued outcomes" (opportunity to deal with people) and was "receiving outcomes not valued" (repetitive work that called for precision and attention to detail). Case 6-7—James was "not receiving valued outcomes" (acceptance, influence, recognition, etc.) and was "receiving outcomes not valued" (rejection, unpleasant meetings, etc.). Case 6-8—These employees were "not receiving valued outcomes" (nice pay raises, good promotions, opportunities for growth and development, and job security). Case 6-9—"Not receiving valued outcomes" (big pay raises) caused all faculty members to have low B3s and "undervaluing of outcomes received" because of inequity further diminished the already low B3s of the high performers. Case 6-10—Kevin was "not receiving valued outcomes" (frequent interaction with his manager, detailed feedback, and recognition). Case 6-11—The "work itself was not rewarding" to Clare.

OBTAINING B3 INFORMATION

Following the pattern established earlier for B1 and B2, obtaining B3 information has the dual focus of diagnosing both B3 levels and B3 causes. A third focus, however, is also relevant here, an emphasis on obtaining B3 information that will be instrumental in determining B3 solutions. Why this third focus? When employees are discussing outcomes, they tend to mention solutions as well as problems. For example, an employee may say, "You keep putting more and more work on me (a problem), and I think I deserve to be paid more for it (a solution)." As this frequently happens, it makes sense to capitalize on it.

With this in mind, the B3 information you ideally want to obtain from employees is listed following this paragraph. Realistically, you will not get all of it from each of your employees, but the list provides direction for your information-gathering process. If you could get all the information you wanted, it would include the following:

1. The full set of outcomes (both good and bad) that the employee sees as being available (i.e., within reach)
2. How satisfying the set of available outcomes is to the employee
3. How satisfying each available outcome is to the employee
4. Outcomes the employee wants that currently are not available
5. How satisfying the wanted but unavailable outcomes would be
6. The causes behind any B3 problems (not receiving valued outcomes, receiving outcomes not valued, work that is not itself rewarding, undervaluing/ overvaluing of outcomes, and changing/conflicting/confused values)

This information not only makes it possible to properly diagnose B3 levels and causes but also enables you to identify solutions that will work. Solutions derived this way will work because they represent what employees want.

How do you obtain this information? There are seven ways: communication, observation, skills analysis, job analysis, work environment analysis, organization analysis, and manager analysis. You will use all of them, though some more than others. It is not necessary to use each one for diagnosing the B3 for each employee, but more than one is advised to insure a solid information base on which to make your diagnosis. Getting information from more than one source fits in with the "guess and guess again" approach recommended here, as suggested earlier for B1 and B2. The idea is to make your best guess about an employee's B3 level and causes and to continue obtaining information and revising your guess until it becomes an accurate and verifiable diagnosis.

Communication

As with B1 and B2, communication with employees is the best way to obtain information for a B3 diagnosis. If you want to know what outcomes employees like and dislike, ask them. Most employees will tell you, if you ask in the right way. You will learn how to do this shortly. Some employees, however, are reluctant to reveal how satisfying outcomes are or will be to them. The biggest reason is that they are afraid you will use the information against them in some way. This fear comes about because of a distrust for you that stems either from something you have done or from a general distrust the employee has for everyone, particularly managers. The communication approach presented here, in combination with the other six ways of obtaining B3 information, will help you deal successfully with reluctant employees.

Communicating with employees to obtain B3 information follows the same pattern used for B1 and B2. It is the "ask, shut up, and listen" approach, with the asking including open, direct, and clarifying questions and the listening based on restating, summarizing, responding to nonverbal messages, and responding to feelings.

There are some standard open questions that work well for obtaining B3 information from employees. They are presented following this paragraph. You can use them verbatim or change the wording to make them more comfortable for you. All of these are questions that will get the ball rolling toward a B3 diagnosis.

To Diagnose B3 Levels—For Individual Outcomes
1. "What are the main things you look for in a job?"
2. "What do you like (dislike) about your job?"
3. "How do you feel about _____ (a specific outcome)?"
4. "What's your reaction to _____ (a specific outcome)?"
5. "What do you think about _____ (a specific outcome)?"

To Diagnose B3 Levels—For Sets of Outcomes
6. "How do you like your work?"
7. "What do you think about the way you are rewarded here?"
8. "All things considered, how do you feel about your job?"

9. "What's your overall reaction to the way things have turned out?"

10. "How does your job compare to the way you had hoped it would be?"

11. "How does your job compare to the best (worst) job you ever had?"

To Diagnose B3 Causes

12. "How do you feel about the things we are giving you here?"

13. "How could things be improved for you here?"

14. "What do you dislike about your job?"

15. "How does this job compare to the best (worst) job you ever had?"

16. "What is causing you to be unhappy with your job?"

17. "What caused your performance to change recently?"

18. "What do you want that you're not getting now?"

19. "What are you getting that you would rather not have?"

20. "Could undervaluing things (or overvaluing) be affecting the way you feel about your job?"

21. "Could changing (conflicting or confused) values be affecting the way you feel about your job?"

Three things should be noticed about these questions. First, many of them are so open that they may elicit B1 and B2 information rather than B3 information. This tends to happen when B1 or B2 are more problematic to the employee than B3. If you ask what is intended to be a B3 question and get a B1 or B2 response, do not be upset. Instead, realize you are getting valuable information, and pursue it. Then use other questions to go back to the B3 issue. Second, there are three categories of questions dealing with diagnosing the B3 level for sets of outcomes. The first category focuses on intrinsic (question 6) and extrinsic (question 7) outcomes. The second (questions 8 and 9) takes a direct look at the total set of outcomes. The third category (questions 10 and 11) is intended to obtain additional information by using comparative questions. Third, there also are three categories of questions for getting information to diagnose B3 causes. The first category (questions 12 through 15) normally elicits good information, but it must be carefully evaluated to identify the B3 causes accurately. The second category (questions 16 and 17), on the other hand, puts the burden on the employee to identify the causes. Sophisticated employees often can answer these questions. In the final category (questions 18 through 21), each question identifies possible causes and asks the employee to indicate if they apply.

When there is a need to guide employee responses in a particular direction, you will want to use direct rather than open questions. Some standard direct questions with proven effectiveness are as follows:

To Diagnose B3 Levels—For Individual Outcomes

1. "Do you want _____ (a specific outcome) or not?"
2. "How important is _____ (a specific outcome) to you?"
3. "Would you rather have _____ (a specific outcome) or _____ (another specific outcome)?"

To Diagnose B3 Levels—For Sets of Outcomes

4. "Do you enjoy the kind of work you are doing?"
5. "Is the work itself rewarding?"
6. "All things considered, are you happy with your job?"
7. "Overall, are you satisfied with your job?"

To Diagnose B3 Causes

8. "Is not getting something you wanted causing the problem?"
9. "Is getting something you don't want causing the problem?"
10. "Are you underestimating the value of some of the things you're getting?"
11. "Are you overestimating the value of some of the things you want but are not getting?"
12. "Are your values changing?"
13. "Is there a conflict in the things you want?"
14. "Is there any confusion about what you want?"
15. "Do you enjoy your work?"

Three comments are needed about these direct questions. First, some appear to be duplicates of the open questions in the previous list. They are similar, but not identical; the difference centers on the degree of openness and directness that distinguishes the two types of questions. Compare direct question 6 with open question 8 to see the difference. Second, questions 4 and 5 deal with intrinsic outcomes associated with the work itself, while questions 6 and 7 address all outcomes (intrinsic and extrinsic). Third, each of the questions that deal with diagnosing causes (questions 8 through 15) focuses on a different one of the eight causes of B3 problems.

Clarifying questions are particularly useful in diagnosing B3 levels and causes. This usefulness comes from the follow-up to employee responses to open and direct questions. When employees hint at B3 levels and causes, ask them clarifying questions (1) to get more information about B3 levels and (2) to get to the bottom of what may be causing the employee to have a B3 problem. Some standard clarifying questions are as follows:

To Diagnose B3 Levels—For Individual Outcomes

1. "Did you say you like or dislike that?"
2. "How important did you say that was to you?"

3. "Which one did you say is most important?"

4. "Of the several things you've mentioned, would you tell me again which one you'd most like to have?"

To Diagnose B3 Levels—For Sets of Outcomes

5. "Are you saying that overall things are pretty good (bad), but there are a couple of things that could be improved (that you're happy with)?"

6. "You've mentioned a lot of specifics, but could you tell me how you feel about your situation overall?"

To Diagnose B3 Causes

7. "What specifically would you like to have that you're not getting now?" (Low B3 is caused by not receiving valued outcomes.)

8. "What specifically are you getting that you didn't really want?" (Low B3 is caused by receiving outcomes not valued.)

9. "Can you help me better understand how much (how little) this means to you?" (Low B3 is caused by overvaluing or undervaluing outcomes.)

10. "Can you give me some examples of how the value you place on things at work has changed (is changing)?" (Low B3 is caused by changing values.)

11. "You say that in some ways you really want it, but in other ways you don't. Can you tell me more about what you're thinking?" (Low B3 is caused by conflicting values.)

12. "Can you tell me more about the confusion you're having about what's really important to you?" (Low B3 is caused by confused values.)

So much for asking. Now for the "shut up and listen" part. Give employees every possible opportunity to talk without interruption. Then use the active-listening techniques of restating, summarizing, responding to nonverbal messages, and responding to feelings. These are used in the same way as that discussed in relation to obtaining B1 and B2 information. Let's take a look at them as they apply to B3

Restating first. You'll remember that a restatement is putting into your own words what an employee tells you. It is a good way to encourage continued discussion on the same line of thought, thereby providing additional information that can be useful in your diagnosis. Some examples of restatements are as follows.

To Diagnose B3 Levels—For Individual Outcomes

1. "So what you're saying is that getting the promotion is more important to you than anything else." (B3 for the promotion.)

2. "Then doing work you enjoy is more important than getting more money doing something you wouldn't like." (B3 for the work itself, for money.)

3. "What I hear you saying is that if we do offer you this job, making it challenging is very important to you." (B3 for challenging work.)

4. "So having a corner office, reserved parking space, and that kind of thing isn't that important to you as long as you can accomplish a lot and make a contribution here." (B3 for status, achieving significant things.)

To Diagnose B3 Levels—For Sets of Outcomes

5. "So you love your work, but everything else about the job has been a big disappointment." (B3 for intrinsic versus extrinsic outcomes.)

6. "All things considered, it looks like you are unhappy with the way things have turned out for you here." (B3 for the full set of outcomes.)

7. "The way you see it, then, everything you were hoping to get out of this job is being made available to you." (B3 for the full set of outcomes.)

To Diagnose B3 Causes

8. "In other words, you're not getting everything out of your job that you want and need." (Low B3 is caused by not receiving valued outcomes.)

9. "The main reason you're discouraged about your job is that it's the same old boring thing every day." (Low B3 is caused by the work itself not being rewarding.)

10. "Basically you don't see why everybody thinks it's such a big deal to be selected to be in the manager trainee program." (Low B3 is caused by undervaluing outcomes.)

11. "What you're saying is that getting the promotion doesn't mean as much, considering some of the others who were promoted, too." (Low B3 is caused by undervaluing outcomes as a result of inequity.)

12. "You realize you may have jumped to conclusions about this, but the thought of somebody else getting a bigger pay raise upsets you anyway." (Low B3 is caused by undervaluing outcomes as the result of a misperception of inequity.)

13. "So you're saying the importance of this maybe has gotten distorted a little by losing sight of some other things that are important, too." (Low B3 is caused by overvaluing outcomes.)

14. "Looks like you are saying that even though it seems foolish, this has more or less become an obsession with you." (Low B3 is caused by overvaluing outcomes, in this case to the point of having an obsession for the outcome.)

15. "So you're at a point in your life where you are mixed up about what is really important." (Low B3 is caused by confused values.)

Next comes summarizing. A summary of key points lets the employee know you are listening and understanding, allows you to get employee verification of what you have heard, and gives the employee a chance to correct or add to your summary of the main issues. Here are some examples of summarizing:

To Diagnose B3 Levels—For Individual Outcomes

1. "You're saying you've seen situations where every time people do a good job they are given more responsibility, and for a while they see it as a

reward, but eventually they feel almost as if they are being punished for doing good work. If you're saying that's not fair to anybody, I'd have to agree with you." (B3 for too much responsibility.)

2. "You're saying several things. One, you really enjoy the work you are doing now. Two, a 5 percent pay raise to move into another position does have some appeal, but you don't think you would enjoy that kind of work. Three, your preference is to pass up that opportunity and stay where you are." (B3 for a specific amount of money, for the work itself in two positions.)

3. "Sounds like your career goals are really important to you, but that your family is, too, and that you want to strike a good balance between the two." (B3 for career, for family.)

To Diagnose B3 Levels—For Sets of Outcomes

4. "So, even though there are a few things you'd like to see changed, you're pretty much satisfied with everything else and overall are pleased with the way things are going here for you." (B3 for all outcomes.)

To Diagnose B3 Causes

5. "So, you like working here, and you have no complaints about money or anything, but you've been eager and ready to take on more responsibility for a long time." (Low B3 is caused by not receiving valued outcome.)

6. "You really feel constrained by having no flexibility in when you come to work and when you leave, especially when so many companies have adopted flexible work schedules, and it has become such an issue with you that you don't think you're willing to keep working under those conditions." (Low B3 is caused by overvaluing an outcome not received.)

7. "OK, so you were really happy with your pay raise, but then you heard what some other people got and that has taken all the glamour out of your increase." (Low B3 is caused by undervaluing outcomes due to inequity or a misperception of inequity.)

8. "So you feel as if you're going to survive your midlife crisis, but different things are becoming important to you and you'd like to discuss a few of them." (Low B3 is caused by changing values.)

9. "You've been sharing an office for two years, you enjoy the working relationship you have established, and now that you have a chance to have your own office, you are torn between taking it and staying where you are; and trying to deal with your feelings about it is interfering with your work." (Low B3 is caused by conflicting values.)

Employees often are discussing emotional issues—things they love and hate, difficulties with basic values, and concerns about matters of equitable treatment—when you are communicating with them about B3 issues. As a result, much of their communication is nonverbal, like a facial expression of joy or a posture that indicates stress. It is necessary to observe the things employees say with their bodies rather than with words. But more is required. You must interpret them. The best way to do this is with the help of the employee. This is where the active-listening technique of responding to nonverbal messages can be useful. Responding like this is a way of asking employees to tell you more about what they are thinking and feeling so that you can make a more complete, more accurate B3 diagnosis. Here are several examples of how to respond to nonverbal messages:

1. "I could see the hurt on your face yesterday when they were critical of the study you had worked so hard on." (B3 for criticism—low B3 caused by receiving an outcome not valued.)

2. "You looked upset when the announcement was made that someone else had been chosen as the project manager." (B3 for a promotion—B3 caused by not receiving valued outcome.)

3. "This is the happiest I've seen you. More responsibility seems to agree with you." (B3 for increased responsibility—high B3 from receiving valued outcome.)

4. "You look as if you've been having trouble concentrating since the meeting yesterday, when you learned that for the first time in nine quarters you were not the leading salesperson." (B3 for achievement—low B3 caused by not receiving valued outcome.)

5. "You never look more enthusiastic and energetic than when you're getting ready to make a big group presentation. This is the first one you've done for a while, isn't it? Is that why you've been down a little bit lately?" (B3 for a certain kind of work activity—low B3 caused by not receiving a valued outcome, followed by a high B3 from receiving it.)

6. "Judging from your actions, especially the way you're treating some of the people in the office, you are really upset that someone else is getting the new office." (B3 for the new office, for status, for recognition—low B3 caused by not receiving valued outcome.)

7. "I can tell by the tone of your voice that you are very concerned about not being treated fairly, especially relative to some of your coworkers." (Low B3 caused by undervaluing outcomes due to inequity or the perception of inequity.)

Employees often show their feelings when B3 matters are involved. This is normal and to be expected. You may see their feelings in nonverbal messages, in what they say and the way they say it, and in their behaviors, like throwing things and slamming doors. These feelings should not be ignored. Your responses to feelings usually are welcomed by employees because they make it easier for the employees to express what they feel and why and to suggest ways to make things better. This is the stuff a good diagnosis is made of and successful solutions are derived from. Here are some examples of how to respond to feelings:

1. "You seem to be having some pretty strong feelings about not being more involved in key decisions of the department." (B3 for participative style of management—low B3 caused by not receiving valued outcome.)

2. "What I hear you saying is that you are very disappointed that you were turned down for the promotion." (B3 for the promotion—low B3 caused by not receiving valued outcome.)

3. "I've never had anybody thank me so many times for changing job responsibilities. You must really be excited." (B3 for the work itself—high B3 from receiving valued outcome.)

4. "It seems that you are more than a little discouraged that things haven't turned out here the way you thought they would." (B3 for the full set of outcomes available—low B3 caused by not receiving valued outcomes and/or receiving outcomes not valued.)

5. "From what you are saying, it must have hurt you a lot not to be recognized for all the hard work you did on the project." (B3 for recognition—low B3 caused by not receiving a valued outcome.)

6. "What I hear you saying is that you are unsure about what you want in your career and as a result are unhappy with your job, and that the whole situation is very frustrating." (Low B3 caused by confused values.)

7. "You really seem unhappy since the nature of your work has changed." (B3 for the work itself—low B3 because the work itself is not rewarding.)

Observation

Observation is a valuable way to obtain B3 information. Although observation alone is insufficient to determine B3 levels and B3 causes, it forms the basis for doing so. Here is the three-step observation process that will yield the information you need: (1) observe changes in employee performance and behavior; (2) identify factors that may explain the changes; and (3) make a guess about B3 level and B3 causes. This process can be used to identify all the causes of B3 problems, especially not receiving valued outcomes, receiving outcomes not valued, and the work itself not being rewarding.

When observing changes in employee performance, focus on end results when possible and on less-direct measures, like work progress, amount of effort, and kind of effort, when necessary. Unsatisfactory changes likely signal a motivation problem. But what happens if there are no observed changes in these measures of performance? Can you safely assume everything is fine with the employee? Not really. Sometimes, especially when employees are in the early stages of a motivation problem, there may be no observable changes in performance, progress, and effort. If not, you can, however, expect other kinds of changes. Many of these can be observed, like changes in attitude, feelings, complaints, and satisfaction. When these change in an undesirable direction, motivation problems are suggested.

As you can see, observation is only a starting point for obtaining B3 information, because observation alone seldom provides enough information to determine B3 levels and B3 causes. Nevertheless, observation is important because it often provides the first indication that a B3 problem exists. If observation allows you to spot a potential problem several weeks, or even a few days, earlier than otherwise, the payoff will be worthwhile. Certainly it is worth the effort it takes to think about observations you probably are making already.

Once these changes are observed, the next step is to identify factors that may explain the changes. Look for events that happened shortly before the changes occurred. Decide if any of the events could be possible causes of the changes. Here are several examples of events that can explain performance declines and identify B3 causes.

—Having best performance (in sales volume, number of new clients, units produced, cost reduction, or profitability) but not receiving any recognition for it. (B3 cause—not receiving valued outcomes.)

—Being turned down on a request for a change in duties or a transfer. (B3 cause—not receiving valued outcomes.)

—Increased work load, more responsibility. (B3 cause—receiving outcomes not valued.)

—Employee with a fear of flying receiving a free trip for two to Hawaii instead of being able to choose between the trip and a cash bonus as in the past. (B3 cause—receiving outcomes not valued.)

—Recent selection, after year-end performance appraisals, to be in the company's fast-track management development program. (B3 cause—undervaluing outcome received or receiving outcome not valued.)

—Being told they'll have to continue waiting for the reserved parking space or an office with a window they've asked about "a hundred times." (B3 cause—overvaluing outcomes not received.)

—Terminal illness or death of a close family member or friend. (B3 cause—changing, conflicting, or confused values.)

—Separation or divorce. (B3 cause—changing, conflicting, or confused values.)

—Narrow escape from death, like a heart attack or an accident. (B3 cause—changing, conflicting, or confused values.)

—Major changes in job duties (B3 cause—work itself not rewarding.)

The third step in the observation process is to guess the employee's B3 level and, if there is a problem, the causes. Changes provide the basis for guessing the B3 level. The greater the changes, the lower the

B3 is likely to be. Linking events to changes is the basis for making guesses as to possible B3 causes.

Remember, obtaining information from one source, like observation, is sufficient to start making guesses but normally is not adequate for making a conclusive diagnosis about B3 levels and causes. But remember, you have to start somewhere. Observation is a frequent starting point.

Case 6-4 provides the basis for seeing how the observation process works. Read the case and the case analysis again, and determine how the three-step process can be applied. When you have done this, continue with the following paragraph and compare your results.

Observation as a way to obtain B3 information is applied to Case 6-4 as follows: Regarding step one in the observation process, observed changes included a decline in effort and performance, a negative change in attitude, an increase in complaining, and a decrease in satisfaction. With respect to step two, the only event that occurred prior to the changes was a significant shift in job duties. This event appears to be linked to the changes. In step three, it is guessed that the B3 probably has dropped considerably, from a high positive rating likely in the +7, +8, +9 range to a rating in the +1, +2, +3 range, maybe even falling to a negative rating. The most likely cause of this, given the new duties, is that the work itself is no longer rewarding.

Skills Analysis

Skills analysis, in the context of B3, is a way of determining the extent to which the skills used in a job are rewarding to a particular employee. By keeping three points in mind, you will be able to use skills analysis to identify two causes of B3 problems, namely, not receiving valued outcomes and receiving outcomes not valued. Here are the three points.

First, outcomes that are both satisfying and dissatisfying can be derived from the work itself (intrinsic outcomes). Satisfaction often comes from performing well, doing challenging things, accomplishing difficult tasks, enjoying the work, etc., whereas dissatisfaction frequently comes from doing boring work, engaging in meaningless activities, disliking the work itself, etc. Outcomes derived from employees themselves are called intrinsic outcomes.

Second, the use of one's skills may or may not be intrinsically rewarding. You will remember, from chapter 2 on obtaining B1 information, that a skills analysis compares the skills an employee has with the skills required for the job. In some cases, employees are fortunate and find themselves in jobs where the skills they possess are a good match with the skills required. In other cases, employees are faced with the problems of mismatches. When skills exceed those required for the job, employees tend to be bored and find it difficult to enjoy their work. When their skills are inadequate, they cannot perform well and tend to dislike their work.

Third, most employees (1) like to do what they do best, (2) don't like to do things they don't do very well, and (3) like work that makes them stretch their abilities a little. Employees find it more satisfying to use skills that lead to success than skills that result in failure. However, employees tend not to find work very satisfying if their skills always and easily lead to success. That is, most employees enjoy their work more when an element of challenge is present, where they must stretch their skills a little to perform well; otherwise, the work tends to become boring and not as satisfying.

What does all of this mean? It means that getting a good match between the employee's skills and the skills required for the job is important to each employee's B3. Specifically, if an employee does not have the skills to perform well in a job, the intrinsic outcomes associated with performing that work, like failure and self-doubt, will not be satisfying to the employee. This is a B3 problem. (It also is a B1 problem—"I can't do it.") Likewise, if an employee has more skills than are required in a job, the intrinsic outcomes related to the work itself, like boredom, lack of challenge, or no sense of accomplishment will not be satisfying. Again, a B3 problem.

Doing a skills analysis can provide valuable B3 information. The resulting information helps you recognize and solve existing B3 problems stemming from unwanted intrinsic outcomes. It also helps prevent these problems when skills analysis is used for decisions about whom to place into what positions. That is, hiring and placement decisions, decisions about employee transfers, and promotion decisions all could benefit from doing a skills analysis in the context of B3.

Case 6-5 shows how skills analysis can be used in this way. Read both the case and the case analysis again, noting the results of the skills analysis and the projections of outcomes that likely would accompany the job. When you have done this, continue here with the next paragraph.

The skills analysis in Case 6-5 revealed that David's technical skills were very strong, but his people skills were not. Knowing this made it possible to guess David's B3 for a job he was being considered for. As he did not have all the skills required for the job, it was projected that he would be receiving outcomes not valued (regarding customers—having to be nice and having to live with stupid questions, unrealistic demands, and complaints; and regarding his boss—listening to complaints and being hassled). Also, because he did not have all the skills, it was projected that he would not be getting several outcomes of value to him (doing work that is enjoyable, satisfaction from doing a good job, praise and recognition for good performance, and nice pay raises). Case 6-5 illustrates that skills analysis allows you to make projections, and to make them with considerable accuracy, as the basis for informed, though not conclusive, guesses about an employee's B3 for a job.

Job Analysis

Job analysis, in the context of B3, refers to analyzing a job to determine the extent to which the work itself is, or will be, intrinsically rewarding to a particular employee. This analysis enables you to identify one cause of B3 problems, namely, work that is not intrinsically rewarding. The job must be analyzed with specific employees in mind, because work that is intrinsically satisfying to one employee may not be so to another. There are seven main factors to look for when doing a job analysis.

It is interesting that three of the factors do not relate directly to the work itself. Instead, they focus on the results of the employee's efforts. One is identification with results. This refers to the extent to which employees identify with the output of their work. Employees who assemble one part of a product tend to identify less with it than if they assembled the entire unit by themselves. Another factor is knowledge of results. This refers to the feedback employees get regarding the effectiveness of their efforts. Employees who get feedback as part of the work itself, as in testing the products they produce to see if they work properly, have a better knowledge of results than employees who must depend on supervisors to evaluate their work. A third factor is the contribution of the results. This refers to the extent to which the results of the employee's efforts contribute to something worthwhile, like making a better product, offering a better service, saving lives, improving the environment, or helping other employees grow and develop. How do these three factors relate to intrinsic rewards? The more employees identify with the results of their efforts, the more knowledge they have of their results; the greater the contribution of their results, the more intrinsically rewarding the work tends to be.

The four remaining factors deal directly with the work itself. Three of them are the variety, freedom and independence, and challenge associated with the work. Employees tend to want (1) variety in the work they do and in the skills they use; (2) a certain amount of freedom and independence over what they do, when they do it, and how they do it; and (3) work that is challenging relative to their skills and abilities. Variety, freedom and independence, and challenge are intrinsically rewarding when the amount and type the job offers matches the employee's preferences. When too little of each is offered, the work is not intrinsically rewarding. However, too much of each is not intrinsically rewarding, either. Excessive variety can be frustrating. Too much freedom and independence does not meet the need for guidance, structure, and support. Work that is too challenging can be discouraging. Because the amount and type of variety, freedom and independence, and challenge that employees prefer varies from one employee to another, the amount and type a job offers must be compared to employee preferences to determine if the work itself is intrinsically rewarding to a particular employee.

Probably the most important of the seven factors to consider when doing a job analysis is appeal. The other six factors may contribute toward making the work intrinsically rewarding, but the work must appeal to the employee to be intrinsically rewarding. Employees simply do not like certain kinds of work, no matter how much variety, freedom and independence, and challenge it offers or what their identity with the results, their knowledge of results, or the contribution they are making to something worthwhile. Some employees like to work with numbers, some don't. Some like to interact with people, others don't. Some like technical work, others do not. The appeal that the work itself has for employees is a very personal matter. Work that appeals to one employee may not appeal to another at all. Consequently, when analyzing a job in terms of appeal, the focus of the analysis should be on the specific employee in question. The more the work itself appeals to the employee, the more intrinsically rewarding it will be.

Read Case 6-6 again, and do a job analysis. Specifically, analyze James's job in terms of the seven factors in the previous paragraph. Incorporate James's B3 for certain individual outcomes as mentioned in the case. Using the B3 rating scale, indicate how intrinsically rewarding you think this job would be to James. When you are ready, compare your results with the following:

Looking at James's job in terms of the seven factors indicates: (1) it is hard for James to identify with the final product because he is involved with only a small part of it; (2) he gets little, if any, feedback about the final product; (3) he has little reason to feel he is making a significant contribution to the final product because he is involved with only a small part of it and because he doesn't really know much about the final product; (4) there is little variety in the work James does and in the skills required because of the degree of specialization; (5) he does not have much freedom and independence regarding what to do and how to do it because his work must be done in accordance with job specifications given to him; (6) the work is not particularly challenging, except perhaps initially, because of its repetitious nature; and (7) the work itself is not appealing to James because he loves to deal with people but has little opportunity to do so and because the work involves doing the same thing over and over and requires precision and attention to detail, which he dislikes. Based on the B3 information obtained from this job analysis, you would conclude that this job yields little that is intrinsically rewarding and is loaded with intrinsic elements that are dissatisfying to James. The B3 rating for the work itself in this job probably would be in the −8, −9, −10 range.

Another motivation situation that focuses on intrinsic rewards of the work is described in Case 6-11. Reread this case and do a job analysis. Evaluate as many of the seven factors in the job analysis as you can. How intrinsically rewarding was the work itself to Clare when she was new in the job and later? What changed?

Let's look at each of the seven factors. It is likely that Clare could identify with the results of her work. She did the whole job as she conducted each eight-hour training session from beginning to end. Two kinds of feedback gave her a good knowledge of the results of her work. As a trainer, she was continually receiving feedback from the reaction of the group. In addition, her performance in each session was rated. Clare could see that she was making a contribution by helping the trainees grow and develop in the skills she was teaching them. Case 6-11 does not give any information about how much appeal the work itself had for Clare, but whatever it was would have remained essentially the same throughout the period she was doing the work. This sameness also would be true for each of the other four job factors mentioned thus far.

Two of the factors in Clare's job did change, however. One was the challenge the work offered. As an inexperienced trainer, the job must have been quite challenging initially. As Clare mastered her work and became recognized as the best of the trainers, the challenge naturally waned considerably. The variety factor has an interesting twist. Although the job had the same variety at the end as it did in the beginning, it was viewed differently. Initially the job would be viewed as having variety because it would be compared to the previous work that Clare had done. As time went on, Clare was simply repeating the same few training programs over and over, and the work became boring. A job that was intrinsically rewarding initially became less so over time because two of the factors changed, namely, the challenge and variety that the work itself offered.

Work Environment Analysis

Work environment analysis is a way to determine the extent to which a work environment is rewarding to employees. The focus is on selected extrinsic outcomes that can be provided by the work environment (like praise and recognition from coworkers), as opposed to outcomes derived from the organization (like safe working conditions and fringe benefits) and from the employee's manager (like more responsibility and attractive job assignments). Work environment analysis includes the following steps: (1) identify extrinsic outcomes each employee wants from the work environment, (2) analyze the environment to determine the extent to which these outcomes are made available, and (3) compare outcome availability with the value the employee places on the outcomes. An analysis of the work environment with this B3 focus can identify two causes of B3 problems, namely, not receiving valued outcomes and receiving outcomes not valued.

Regarding step one, employees typically want several kinds of extrinsic outcomes from the work environment. The most common relate to outcomes derived from employee interaction with others, including coworkers and others in the organization or persons outside the organization, like clients, customers, and vendors. All of these people hold numerous outcomes in their hands and can choose to give them to or withhold them from a particular employee. What are some of these outcomes? They include giving praise to the employee (recognition), socially interacting with the employee (affiliation), accepting the employee as a person (acceptance), being respectful of the employee (respect), showing confidence in the employee (self-esteem), and being influenced by the employee (power). These are some of the more common kinds of extrinsic outcomes that work environments may offer. As you identify others, be sure to add them to your list. This will help you with the first step in work environment analysis, namely, to identify outcomes in the work environment of interest to your analysis.

As you move ahead to step two and actually analyze the work environment, the emphasis is on determining the extent to which certain outcomes are being made available to employees. If employees are alone in the work environment, the outcomes mentioned in the previous paragraph would not be available. However, the fact that others are present in the work environment does not insure that the outcomes will be given. Although these people may give the outcomes to some employees, they may withhold them from others. The latter often happens if an employee is different from the others in personality, interests, values, age, education, social standing, cultural background, religion, or languages spoken. Because of these differences, the employee or the others or both parties may choose to limit interactions, in which case the employee would have little opportunity to receive outcomes from others. Determining the extent to which outcomes are being made available by the work environment ultimately requires observing interactions and asking the employee and others about the frequency and nature of the interactions.

The third step is comparing the availability of outcomes from the work environment with the value employees place on outcomes they want from the work environment. This is important because different employees place different values on the same outcomes. If a work environment does not allow for much interaction with other people, this may be a significant B3 problem for an employee who has a high need for affiliation with and acceptance of others, but not a problem at all for a person who prefers working alone. Looking at the work environment alone is insufficient. It is necessary to relate what you find in the environment to the likes and dislikes of the employee, that is, to the employee's B3 for the individual outcomes in question. When you do this, you will be able to determine adequately the extent to which selected extrinsic outcomes in the work environment will be viewed as rewarding to that employee. Case 6-7 deals with work environment analysis. Go back and reread this case and case analysis. Notice how the three steps in work environment analysis, as outlined here, are used to obtain valuable B3 information.

Organization Analysis

Organization analysis, with a B3 focus, is a way to determine the extent to which outcomes made available by the organization are rewarding to employees. There are three steps in organization analysis: (1) identify outcomes employees would like the organization to provide, (2) analyze the organization to determine the extent to which the outcomes are available, and (3) compare the availability of the outcomes with the value the employees place on the outcomes they want the organization to provide. This kind of organization analysis can identify two causes of B3 problems, namely, not receiving valued outcomes and receiving outcomes not valued.

Looking at step one first, what are some of the outcomes employees typically want organizations to offer? There are many. Some of the common ones are listed below. Because the outcomes made available are determined by what an organization is and does, the list presented here first includes an example of what an organization is or does and then indicates the outcome offered (in parentheses)—provides good training programs (opportunity for employee growth and development), offers a mentoring program (growth and development), allows job rotation (growth and development), has a policy of promoting from within (opportunity for advancement), maintains a low turnover rate (job security), is experiencing controlled growth (job security), has an above-average pay scale (money), provides good insurance and retirement programs (money), is a decentralized organization (responsibility), regularly upgrades physical facilities (working conditions), has a warm-caring-personal-informal organization culture (feeling of belonging), has adequate policies and procedures (job structure), and emphasizes placing workers into jobs they are best suited for (work itself). These are but a few of the outcomes organizations can offer their employees and a few of the ways to make them available. As this is not a comprehensive listing, you should feel free to add to it for a thorough analysis of your organization.

In step two, you may find it helpful to approach the analysis of your organization in two ways simultaneously. The first is to start with a list of outcomes you think are important to employees and analyze your organization to identify what it is and does that makes each outcome available. The second way is to start by listing the key things about your organization, that is, what it is and does, and then to identify the outcomes each makes available. Using both these approaches will yield a more comprehensive organization analysis.

The third step calls for a comparison of outcome availability in the organization with the value each employee places on the outcomes. This is a critical step because employees value outcomes differently. You already know how to determine the value employees place on outcomes. You have learned ways to obtain B3 information from employees and how to interpret it. When you apply this to step three, you can determine the extent to which outcomes made available by the organization are rewarding to each employee.

Cases 6-8 and 6-9 illustrate the application of the three-step process for organization analysis. Reread both cases and the case analysis of each, and identify how the three steps are applied. When you have done this, compare what you find with the two summaries below.

The application of the three steps is as follows in Case 6-8: (1) four outcomes the employees wanted the organization to provide were identified: money, advancement, growth and development, and job security; (2) analysis of the organization showed that pay increases have been small, opportunities for advancement and for growth and development have been limited, and job security is shaky; and (3) limited availability of highly valued outcomes suggests that the total set of outcomes being received is not very satisfying to these managers.

In Case 6-9, the three steps in organization analysis were applied as follows: (1) the outcome of interest to employees was pay raises; (2) the case showed that everyone got a 3 percent raise, with little difference in dollar amounts between high and low performers; and (3) the small raises were not very satisfying to any of the faculty members, especially the higher performers.

Manager Analysis

Manager analysis, with a B3 focus, is a way to determine the extent to which you make outcomes available that are rewarding to your employees. The same three basic steps suggested earlier for both work environment analysis and organization analysis also are recommended here: (1) identify outcomes each employee would like you to provide; (2) analyze yourself to determine the extent to which you make the outcomes available; and (3) compare the availability of the outcomes with the value each employee places on them. This kind of manager analysis can identify two causes of B3 problems, namely, not receiving valued outcomes and receiving outcomes not valued.

The first step is to identify outcomes your employees want you to provide. Even if you don't have control over promotions, raises, and other significant outcomes, employees typically want quite a few outcomes from you. Here are some of the things you can do, with the resulting outcome shown in parentheses—praise workers (recognition), expand the scope of an employee's job (responsibility), give assignments that stretch employee ability (challenging work), be clear about what to do and how to do it (job structure), be respectful (respect), show confidence in employees (self-esteem), give promotions (opportunity for advancement), focus on long-term employment relationships (job security), allow and encourage the employees to do their best (achievement), give pay raises (money), coach employees when they don't know how to do something (growth and development), provide training (growth and development), and show concern for employees (consideration). This list represents only a few of the many outcomes you can offer the employees you manage and of ways you can make them available. This is far from being a comprehensive list, and you should feel free to add to it for a more thorough self-analysis.

In step two, you will find the approach suggested for organization analysis to be quite helpful here. Do two things at the same time. One, start with a list of outcomes employees want from you, and analyze yourself to identify what you do to make each outcome available. Two, list the key things you do, and then identify the outcomes each makes available. Using these approaches together will result in a thorough manager analysis.

Step three is a comparison of the availability of outcomes with the value each employee places on the outcomes. Remembering that different employees often value the same outcomes differently, it is important to individualize this step for each employee. The focus is on determining how satisfying outcomes are or will be to each individual employee.

Case 6-10 illustrates the use of manager analysis to obtain B3 information. Reread the case and the case analysis, and identify how the three steps of manager analysis were applied. When you have done this, compare what you found with the summary below.

Manager analysis was applied as follows: (1) the outcomes Kevin wanted from Jay were opportunity for growth and development, frequent interaction, detailed feedback, and recognition; (2) analysis showed that Jay was making only one of the outcomes available, the opportunities for growth and development; and (3) the satisfaction Kevin received in total from the set of four desired outcomes fell far short of what he had hoped for.

SUMMARY

This concludes the discussion on interpreting B3 information and the seven ways to obtain it, which are communication, observation, skills analysis, job analysis, work environment analysis, organization analysis, and manager analysis. The information gathered is used in two ways, as discussed. One is to diagnose employee B3 levels, that is, to determine employee beliefs about outcomes leading to satisfaction. The other is to diagnose what is causing the problem if B3 levels are low. Identifying the causes is important, as they determine which solutions are most appropriate to use. If you have carefully read and understood this chapter, you should feel comfortable with and confident about obtaining and interpreting the B3 information needed to solve outcome-satisfaction problems.

7

Solving Outcome-Satisfaction Problems

Dealing with outcome-satisfaction problems, where employees do not see current outcomes as satisfying ("I don't like it") or do not believe future outcomes will be ("I won't like it"), can be easier than you think. Yet, many managers view these as the toughest problems they face. It seems that no matter what you do for employees, they always want more and are never satisfied. Everything you do seems to backfire. It is a frustrating, helpless feeling, and understandably so. The tendency is to give up and not even to try.

If you are hesitant about dealing with outcome-satisfaction (B3) problems, you can put your reluctance away. There are some very clever, yet simple and practical, ways to handle these problems. No, you will not be able to solve all of them the first time every time. However, approaching the problems as outlined here can make all the difference in the world. You will see this as the basic approaches and step-by-step methods unfold.

In this chapter, you will learn how to select and implement appropriate B3 solutions. Selection is based on the identification of B3 problems and their causes, as discussed in chapter 6. Eleven B3 solutions are presented here: giving valued outcomes, substitution, withholding outcomes not valued, offsets, job matching via job placement and job design, communication, values clarification, leveling, preference shifting, transfers, and terminations. Deciding which solution to use is simple because selection is tied directly to problem causes. Implementing solutions is straightforward when the guidelines presented in the chapter are followed. Some of the solutions are designed for employees with very difficult problems. Others are intended for situations where it is impossible to provide the outcomes employees want.

GIVING VALUED OUTCOMES

Giving valued outcomes to employees is a systematic process that, if followed, yields good results. Not following it spells trouble. As this process is explored, keep in mind that giving valued outcomes is the solution for B3 problems that are caused by employees not receiving valued outcomes. Also keep the distinction between B2 and B3 in mind. Whereas B2 is the employee's belief about the likelihood performance will lead to outcomes, B3 is the belief about how satisfying the outcomes will be.

OK, what is this first B3 solution all about? Giving valued outcomes, when seen in its broader context, is the culmination of a decision-making process. It actually is the implementation of a series of decisions that ends with giving the outcomes to the employee:

1. Deciding when to give valued outcomes
2. Deciding what outcomes to give
3. Deciding how much of each outcome to give
4. Deciding how to give the outcomes
5. Giving the outcomes

All of these steps were discussed and illustrated relative to B2 in chapter 5. The emphasis with step 5 was on giving valued outcomes in such a way that employees would see the relationship between outcomes and performance. This B2 focus was appropriate because the emphasis was on preventing and solving B2 problems. A B3 focus also is called for when giving outcomes. This insures that valued outcomes are given in a such way that employees receive full satisfaction from them. This B3 focus is appropriate not only for solving B3 problems but also for preventing them as well. OK, how do you achieve a B3 focus, and the resulting benefits, when giving employees valued outcomes?

Giving valued outcomes is a process that includes five important steps that are easy to apply but often ignored:

1. Prepare to give the outcome
2. Prepare the employee to receive the outcome
3. Give the outcome to the employee

4. Get employee's reaction and respond to it

5. Reinforce employee satisfaction

This five-step process can be used for giving most any type of outcome, including pay raises, promotions, more challenging work, more interesting work, growth and development opportunities, more responsibility, praise, recognition, participation in goal-setting/decisions/meetings/etc., a reserved parking space, executive dining room privileges, or a corner office. Let's take a look at each of the five steps.

The first step is to get yourself prepared. This includes (1) being clear on prior decisions about what outcome is to be given, how much of it is to be given, and the performance it is being given for and (2) determining the end results you want from giving the valued outcome. Here is an example of a desired end result.

You (to yourself): "I want her to realize that we are acknowledging the improvements she has made in the performance of her unit and that we appreciate all she is doing. I also would like her to make a commitment to continue working hard and get the unit completely turned around."

Preparing yourself also includes (3) deciding when to give the outcome, considering day, time, and circumstances; (4) deciding if others are to be present and, if so, who; (5) deciding whether to give the outcome in a formal or informal setting, whether in your office, the employee's work area, a meeting room, or some other place; (6) planning what you will say; (7) anticipating the employee's reaction and deciding in advance how to respond to it; and (8) deciding how you will conclude the discussion, including what you will say ("Congratulations," or "nice job," or "wish we could have done more," or "back to work," etc.) and what you will do (shake hands, give a pat on the back, walk them to the door, take them to lunch, etc.). Some of these things may seem trivial to you, but they may be important to the employee. They may be important enough that mishandling one of them might nullify the effect you are shooting for in giving the outcome.

Step two is to prepare the employee to receive the outcome. This often makes a big difference in how well it is received. Two approaches are especially effective when you are certain the employee will be pleased with the outcome. One, if employees want a certain outcome, but are convinced it is not forthcoming, it may be best to allow them to continue believing this and let it be a surprise. Two, if employees are hopeful about getting the outcome, they may respond best if you let them anticipate, worry, and fret for a while before receiving it. Preparing employees is even more important if the outcome to be given is different from and valued less than some other anticipated outcome. One approach in such a situation is to help employees develop a more realistic expectation of what is to come. This can be done by being truthful and saying something appropriate prior to giving the outcome to prepare the employees. Here are some examples:

—"Limits have been set on what I can do."
—"It's out of my control for the time being."
—"We're having to make cutbacks on everything."
—"All of our plans are out the window."
—"Maybe we'll be in a position to do more later."
—"Things are going to be tough for a while."

Lowering expectations like this eases the blow and gives employees time to deal with the disappointment. It may even cause them to place more value on the outcome when they receive it.

With the preparation complete, the third step is actually to give the outcome to the employee. Every move you make now is important, else all that you hope for and have planned for can slip away. So, what do you do? There are two key things. Doing them is not the hard part. The difficulty is that most managers simply don't give them enough attention. First, clearly communicate the outcome being given. Give the employee all of the relevant facts about the outcome.

You: "In you new position, your job title will be _____ . You will be responsible for _____ . You will have authority to _____ . The main duties of the job are _____ . The hours you are expected to work are _____ . Your new office will be _____ . The five people who will report to you are _____. Your salary will be _____ . The benefits include _____ ."

Indicating what the outcome is not is often helpful, too. For example, uncertainty is removed and clarity added by saying, "The new assignment does not mean you'll be moving to the old plant and working the second shift like some of the other guys who have been promoted recently."

Making employees feel good about receiving the outcome is the second key in giving valued outcomes. This is accomplished best by helping them see the full value of the outcome. You don't want employees to see outcomes as less than what they are. That is, you don't want undervaluing, thereby diminishing the satisfaction received. You don't want the outcomes to be overvalued either. This only leads to disappointment, and possibly even to blaming you, when the true value is realized. So, how do you help employees see outcomes for what they are? One way is to highlight associated outcomes. In the example of a new position, you could stress related outcomes.

You: "You will be part of a supportive team, the work will be challenging and meaningful, and you will have an excellent opportunity for pay increases, personal growth and development, and advancement."

Another way to help employees see the full value of outcomes is to indicate how you, the organization, and others interpret the outcome. Understanding how others view an outcome provides a more realistic and more complete picture of its true value.

You: "As far as I'm concerned, this promotion puts you in an elite group. The organization sees you as a high performer and views this new position as a stepping-stone to bigger and better things. Everybody sees this as a real opportunity for you. A lot of people would like to be in your shoes now."

Another thing you must do to make employees feel good about outcomes they receive is to withhold any negative feelings you may have. If you think the outcome is too much (more than deserved) and you were opposed to it, there is no need to let that show and diminish the positive impact the outcome will have. You may be tempted to let your true feelings come out, saying things like the following:

You: "Some others deserved this promotion more than you. I don't think you're ready for it. I got outvoted, so I guess it's going to be yours anyway."

This doesn't help anyone, including you. Likewise, if you think the outcome is too little, there is no need to say anything to make the situation worse than the employee will find it anyway:

You: "I know you're not going to be happy with this because it's not what you deserve. It isn't much of a promotion, but it's the best I could do under the circumstances with all of the politics that go on around here."

There is no need to highlight the inadequacy you feel about the outcome. If the employee is unhappy with it, you will have a chance to find out and address that feeling. That's the next step.

Once you have given the outcome to the employee, step four calls for getting the employee's reaction and responding to it. This allows you to determine how valued the outcome is to the employee. From this you can assess the impact of the outcome on employee motivation, effort, and performance. This gives you the opportunity to take any corrective action, if possible, in the event you were wrong in guessing how satisfying the outcome would be. How do you get an accurate reading of the employee's reaction? The key is to ask. After you give the outcome, ask questions that encourage an honest response. Here are some examples.

—"What do you think?"
—"How do you feel about this?"
—"What's your reaction to all of this?"
—"Tell me what you're thinking."
—"How does this sound to you?"

Then let the employee talk. Respond to feelings. Respond to nonverbal messages. Restate. Summarize. This will help you find out what the employee is thinking. How do you respond? If the employee is not as pleased as you had hoped, find out why and discuss what has to happen for the employee to get outcomes of greater value. If the employee is pleased, reinforce the satisfaction shown.

Reinforcing the employee's satisfaction with the outcome is the fifth and final step in the process of giving valued outcomes. This can be accomplished by (1) restating the outcome given, (2) summarizing the employee's reaction, and (3) confirming that the satisfaction expressed by the employee is justified.

You: "I'm glad you're pleased with the promotion. You have a right to be. It opens the door to a lot of the things you want in your career."

This five-step process of giving valued outcomes to employees is an essential B3 solution. It is one of only two ways to solve B3 problems caused when employees are not getting valued outcomes. Not getting valued outcomes is one of the two most common causes of B3 problems, the other being getting outcomes not valued. With this in mind, you will want to make this way of giving valued outcomes an integral part of the way you manage. Start using this process at your first opportunity and continue using it until it becomes second nature to you. That will not take long. Using it will be worthwhile. You will see a difference, a big difference, in the way employees respond.

SUBSTITUTION

There is another solution to B3 problems caused when employees are not receiving valued outcomes. The need for this second option arises when it is not possible to give employees the outcomes they want. This happens often. Employees want something, and you can not give it to them. Money is not available for raises. There are no promotion opportunities. Jobs cannot be redesigned. These are only a few examples of the many situations where you cannot give the outcomes employees want. What can you do?

The solution is to provide substitute outcomes. When you can't give the outcomes employees want, give them the next best thing. This may not generate the same level of employee satisfaction, but it is better than nothing and may be much better. It shows that you care, that you are sensitive to their needs, that you are making an extra effort for them. Often "it's the thought that counts." Most employees view this as an outcome of considerable value.

Here is an example of using substitution as a B3 solution. Let's say an employee has been working hard in hopes of getting a promotion, but there are no promotion opportunities available now or in the immediate future. This is discouraging and tends to have a negative impact on employee motivation, effort, and performance. What can be done to prevent this reaction? Are there any outcomes that would be acceptable substitutes, at least in the short run, to a promotion? Only the employee can answer this question. You might say, "Tell me why you want a promotion." The employee's response usually will indicate some outcome substitutes that you can provide. The employee may say, "Because it offers more money, added status, additional responsibility, more challenging work, opportunity to grow and develop, and more authority." In this example, you may not be able to offer more money, authority, or status, but you may be able to give the employee more responsibility, work that is more challenging, and opportunities for growth and development. When you have identified substitutes you can give, simply follow the five-step process discussed in the previous section for giving values outcomes.

So, when you can't give employees outcomes they want, identify some substitutes that will be valued and provide them. Saying "no" to a promotion is harsh and typically results in problems in motivation, effort, and performance. Substitute outcomes can go a long way in preventing these problems from getting out of hand. Remember, giving something is better than nothing, and may be much better.

WITHHOLDING OUTCOMES NOT VALUED

Another B3 solution is withholding outcomes not valued. This is the best way to solve B3 problems caused when employees are getting outcomes they do not want. A simple process can be used, one that is easy to apply. The biggest danger in applying it is failing to see the need for it. Here is the bottom line: To stop giving employees unwanted outcomes is not enough. Doing it the right way matters. Taking something away from employees, even when they do not want it,

196 / Performance and Motivation Strategies

can be interpreted numerous ways, many of them negative. The way you withhold outcomes does matter to employees. You will get the results you are looking for by following these steps:

1. Prepare to withhold unwanted outcomes
2. Prepare the employee for outcomes to be withheld
3. Determine the employee's withholding preferences
4. Agree on what and how to withhold
5. Get and give commitment to the withholding plan
6. Withhold outcomes as planned

This six-step process is applicable to withholding most outcomes not valued by employees, including boring work, difficult work, stressful work, too much work, too much responsibility, too much criticism, too much pressure, too much travel, too many meetings, too many rules, forced participation, obnoxious work partner, and perfectionist clients.

Let's look at the six-step process in detail, doing so by applying it to a situation where an employee has become very vocal about being given too much responsibility that is accompanied by long hours, not enough sleep, eating on the run, meetings all the time, problem after problem, not enough time to get everything done, enormous pressure and stress, and declining performance in view of all this.

If you are going to withhold an outcome an employee does not want, you have to get prepared to do it. This is step one. It includes clarifying prior decisions about which outcomes are to be withheld and how much of each one to withhold.

You (to yourself): "I've talked with the employee and we tentatively agreed on two things. One, that her responsibilities should be narrowed. Two, that they should be reduced by having someone else take charge of _____."

Preparing yourself also means determining the end results you want from the withholding. Here are some examples.

—"I want her to realize we are responsive to problems and needs."
—"I want her to have a more positive attitude."
—"I'm expecting to see a more-motivated, higher-performing worker."

In addition, the preparation includes developing a plan for withholding the outcomes, planning what you will say to the employee, anticipating the employee's reaction and deciding in advance how to respond to it, deciding how you will conclude the discussion, and including what you will say ("glad we're taking this step," or "thanks for bringing this to my attention," or "we should have done this sooner," etc.) and what you will do (shake hands, give a pat on the back, walk the employee to the door, go to lunch together, etc.). It also means deciding when to discuss the withholding with the employee, including day, time, and circumstances and, and deciding where to discuss it, whether in your office, the employee's work area, a meeting room, or some other place. These are not trivial matters to employees. Planning to handle each of them properly is important, especially if you want the full impact of improving the employee's motivation, effort, and performance.

The second step is to prepare the employee. But why is this necessary? Aren't employees going to be anxious to give up unwanted outcomes? Not necessarily, for two reasons. First, most unwanted outcomes have positive features the employee does not want to give up. Here are some examples of ways employees may react.

—"The responsibilities are just too much, but I do like the power that comes with the job."

—"The stress is almost unbearable, but I enjoy the prestige of the job."

—"I hate all of the travel, but I love the freedom that goes along with it."

—"I don't like all of the meetings, but I like having the opportunity to participate in decisions."

—"I don't like working with a difficult client, but in a way it is a welcome challenge."

—"My boss is really demanding, but I enjoy working with someone so intelligent and powerful."

Second, even when employees want to give up unwanted outcomes, they are left wondering what others will think. If others interpret the giving up or the taking away of unwanted outcomes in a negative way, their respect for and acceptance of the employee may diminish. From the employees' point of view, giving up one unwanted outcome is replaced by another unwanted outcome.

Employee: "I have too much to do, and it's showing up in my performance. But if I give up some of my responsibilities, I don't want everybody to start questioning my ability and lose respect for me."

Why is it necessary to prepare employees before withholding an unwanted outcome? They may not want to give up certain things and may be concerned about what others will think. In view of this, how do you prepare employees?

Preparing employees to give up unwanted outcomes is basically a process of letting them come to terms with it themselves. In doing so, employees may reach one of three conclusions. One, they may confirm their preference to give up the outcomes. Two, they may decide, when all things are considered, that they would rather keep them. Three, employees may want to keep certain elements of an outcome while giving up other elements. For example, an employee who has been complaining about having too much responsibility may prefer to keep all of it if someone can be assigned to help do some of the work. Your focus should be on finding out which of these conclusions the employee reaches. This will be useful in deciding how you should proceed. So, how do you prepare employees to give up unwanted outcomes?

Several things can be done to prepare employees for withholding outcomes not valued. One, encourage employees to rethink the satisfaction being derived from the outcomes, which allows you to reassess your earlier diagnosis of the employee's B3 level. Two, indicate your willingness to explore making some changes. Three, ask the employee to think about how things could be changed. Plan a time to discuss this with the employee. This approach gives employees time to get mentally prepared for outcomes to be withheld. It also prepares them to influence the way unwanted outcomes ultimately will be withheld.

The third step in the withholding process is to determine the employee's withholding preferences. This includes preferences about what to withhold and how the withholding should be done. It may be difficult for the employee to make a decision about what to withhold. The decision is complicated by the uncertainty of how the outcome would be withheld. Employees may prefer to keep an unwanted outcome rather than to give it up in a way that has the appearance of reducing authority, stripping away important job functions, or in any other way embarrassing, degrading, or reflecting negatively on them. Withholding unwanted outcomes can be a very sensitive matter, and getting the employee's suggestions about how to do it is very important. This can be done by asking questions and helping the employee think through the situation carefully. Keep asking questions until the employee's suggestions seem to be well thought out. Here are some examples:

—"What do you want changed?"

—"How will that make things better for you?"

—"Are you sure that's what you want?"

—"How should we do this?"

—"Is there another way that would work better?"

—"What do you want me to do?"

—"How should we explain this to others?"

—"Anything else?"

Step four is to reach agreement on what to do and how to do it. The employee's ideas can be the basis for this. You need to come up with a fully developed plan for the what and how. The plan should include a clear understanding of the expected results of withholding the unwanted outcomes and who is to do what by when. Contribute your own ideas only if the employee needs help. The aim here is for the withholding plan to be developed as much as possible by the employee. This is the best way to solve a B3 problem without causing another one that may be bigger.

The fifth step is to get and give commitment. Getting the employee's commitment is important. As you are basically allowing the employee to determine what will be withheld and how it will be done, you want to be sure the employee is committed to the plan. This is essential for the successful withholding of unwanted outcomes. Getting the commitment should be easy because your approach has caused the employee carefully to think through the implications of withholding the outcome and because the withholding plan is based on the employee's preferences. The only thing left is for you to get the employee to make a verbal commitment. This can be done by asking if the employee is committed and summarizing the response. Here are some ways to ask:

—"Are you fully committed to this?"

—"Are you in full support of this?"

—"Are you in total agreement with this?"

Success in withholding unwanted outcomes depends on your commitment as well. It is important that the employee knows you are committed. Make it clear that you will do your part to withhold unwanted outcomes in a way that will solve the B3 problem. You can accomplish this in several ways, including the following:

—"I'll do everything I can to make this work."

—"You have my full support on this."

—"I think you've come up with a good plan. I fully agree on doing it this way."

Step six is to withhold unwanted outcomes as planned. This should be easy, if the plan includes desired end results, a list of things to accomplish, who is to do each one, and time frames for completion. A plan that includes these four elements also makes it easy to follow up and be sure things turn out as planned, namely, that unwanted outcomes are in fact withheld.

OFFSETS

There is another solution to B3 problems caused when employees are receiving outcomes they do not want. The need for this option arises when it is difficult, if not impossible, to withhold the unwanted outcomes. This happens often. Here are some examples: The more successful the salesperson, the more she has to travel. The better the work done for a client, the more demanding he becomes. The more valuable an employee's input, the more meetings she must attend. The greater the fluctuations in demand, the more employees must work overtime. There are many situations where employees are receiving unwanted outcomes and it is difficult to do anything about it. When there isn't much you can do, what can you do?

The solution may be to give additional outcomes to offset the unwanted outcomes. This is an alternative to giving up and saying, "There isn't anything I can do," or struggling to withhold outcomes you really don't have much control over. The idea is to give enough additional outcomes to outweigh the unwanted outcomes. Employees can live with outcomes they don't want, at least for a while, if the good outweighs the bad. This will not have as much positive impact on motivation, effort, and performance as removing the unwanted outcome, but it is better than doing nothing. Giving something to offset unwanted outcomes shows that you are aware of the problem and are doing the best you can to resolve it. While offsetting may not completely solve the problem, it shows you are trying and "the thought counts." For some employees, it counts a lot.

What are some good offsetting outcomes? It depends on the individual. Each employee views both wanted and unwanted outcomes differently. What it takes to offset an unwanted outcome varies from one individual to another. However, if you want to know what it takes, you can ask. For example, you might say, "Mary, I know that as a supervisor your hours are long and hard. Is there anything I can do to make it easier to live with?" She may say, "It's lonely not having anybody to discuss things with, I hate all the administrative work, and I feel stressed out all the time." Rather than interpreting these comments as employee complaints, view them as suggested ways to offset the long, hard hours she is working. Here are some offsets she probably would welcome: (1) regular interaction with other supervisors to share concerns, frustrations, and ideas; (2) more interaction with you for the same purpose; (3) advice on how she can shift part of the administrative work load onto one of her employees who may enjoy that kind of work; and (4) the opportunity to attend a stress management workshop. When you have identified offsets you can give, follow the five-step process presented earlier in the chapter for giving valued outcomes.

So, when you can't withhold unwanted outcomes from employees, identify some desired outcomes that will offset the negative ones and then provide them. Saying "there is nothing I can do" is hard for employees to accept and typically results in motivation, effort, and performance problems. Offsetting outcomes can do a lot to minimize these problems. Remember, giving something is better than nothing, and may be much better.

JOB MATCHING

Now comes job matching as the solution. It is used for B2 problems caused by work that itself is not rewarding to employees. The goal of job matching is to get employees into jobs where the work itself is rewarding. In such jobs, satisfaction comes from doing the work. This is entirely different from the satisfaction employees get from receiving things, like a pay raise, after they have completed the work. Satisfaction derived from the work itself comes from accomplishing things, learning new skills, doing challenging work, using talents to the fullest, and doing something worthwhile and fulfilling, to name some sources.

To understand why, let's think back to the earlier discussion on intrinsic and extrinsic outcomes. Extrinsic outcomes, such as pay raises, bonuses, promotions, praise, a company car, etc., have two main characteristics. One, employees get these outcomes after the work is performed. Two, they are given to employees by somebody else. Now consider intrinsic outcomes, like the satisfaction that comes from making progress when doing challenging work. First, intrinsic outcomes are received during, not after, the performance. Second, they are not given by someone else, but instead are derived from employees themselves.

The importance of job matching is not to be underestimated. Here's why. When the work itself is rewarding, employees have a positive net preference for the set of outcomes associated with the work itself, that is, they have a high B3 for the outcomes. When the work itself is rewarding, doing the work is a guarantee of getting the rewards. The employee knows with certainty that performing leads to these rewards. Consequently, the employee's B2 automatically is high.

Here is the point. When employees are matched into jobs where the work itself is rewarding, many motivation problems are prevented. Yes, prevented. So, invest whatever time is necessary to get good job matching. It's a sound investment. There are two ways to achieve job matching, namely, job placement and job design. Let's look at both of them.

Job Placement

Getting good job matches may be easier than you think. Consider job placement. It is the process of finding people, from within the organization (transfers) or from outside (hiring), and placing them into jobs where there is a match between the individual and the job. Using job placement to achieve job matching is easy because it only means going about the finding and placing process in a slightly different way. The main concern when finding and placing employees into jobs often centers on the question, "Can they do the work?" If they can't do it, motivation and performance problems will follow. This "can they do it" focus, while necessary, is not enough. Another question also must be answered, "Will the work itself be rewarding?" If it isn't, B3 problems will result. Using a hiring process with this dual focus can be an easy and effective way to achieve good job matches.

Two things can be done to insure good matches. One is to get information from applicants, and the other is to give information to them. The first calls for getting enough information from applicants to make a judgment about how rewarding the work itself would be to them. The second is to give applicants enough information so that they can decide for themselves if the work itself would be rewarding.

The first route has two steps, namely, finding out how applicants value outcomes associated with work and, based on this, judging whether or not the work itself will be rewarding to them. Applicants normally will give you the information needed, if you ask. Any number of questions can be used. What are you looking for in a job? What kind of work do you like best (least)? What gives you the most (least) satisfaction in a job? If they are not giving relevant information, it probably isn't intentional, so rephrase your question and ask it again. When applicants mention only one or two things at first, encourage them to continue and they will. This can be accomplished with more questions. What else? Anything else? Any other thoughts? End by summarizing what you've heard. Now you are ready for the second step. Take what you have heard and compare it to the work itself. Will it be rewarding to the applicant? That is, is there a job match?

The second route involves giving applicants information about the work itself and then finding out how rewarding they consider the job. Giving them information can be done in several ways, some better than others. You can describe the job to them, particularly in terms of outcomes related to the work itself. Mention things like how much task variety is involved, how challenging the work is, how much creativity is involved, how meaningful the work is in the overall scheme of things, how fulfilling the work can be, etc. In addition to yourself, have a couple of employees do some of the describing. Choose employees who are doing the same work the applicant would do and prepare them to describe the job in terms of outcomes from the work itself.

Describing the job is helpful, but seeing it is better. Give applicants a firsthand view of the job. Let them walk around the work area and watch, touch, feel, smell, and hear what is going on. Spending time like this gives applicants more insight than describing the work to them. Accomplishing this doesn't have to be time-consuming, but it does mean doing more than giving a quick tour of the work area.

Observing is better than describing, but experiencing is best. Experiencing the job gives information not only to the applicant but to you as well, because it provides an opportunity for you to evaluate their performance. There are several ways for applicants to experience the job. Some organizations include assessments in which applicants actually perform samples of work. These assessments could be extended or refocused to allow applicants to experience the work itself more fully. Other organizations use employment tryouts to evaluate employees. This is the best way to let applicants experience the work itself, to let them see how rewarding the work can be for them. Many organizations that use temporary employment agencies eventually hire employees assigned to them for temporary work. This is a type of employment tryout. Other organizations ask applicants to complete training successfully before being hired, with the training designed, in part, as an employment tryout. Others include employment tryouts in which applicants work for up to one week on a trial basis before final job offers are extended.

Whether the work is described, observed, or experienced, applicants are in a better position to decide if the work itself will be rewarding to them. Most applicants, once they make this decision, will self-select themselves out of the hiring process if they conclude the work itself will not be rewarding. They will either take the initiative to tell you or readily let you know if you ask. So ask. Do you think this job is what you've looking for? Is this the type of work you want to do? Would you be satisfied doing this kind of work every day? You can expect an honest answer most of the time. Applicants usually don't want a job they wouldn't like. This is especially true when applicants have other job opportunities. Honest answers also are encouraged by a hiring process that stresses the importance of job matching to the organization and to applicants as well.

How open should you be with applicants about the job-matching process, particularly their role in helping determine whether or not a match exists? The answer is simple. Be very open. There are several things to point out. One, you are looking for high-performing and long-term employees. Two, experience shows that both these aims are accomplished best when employees like their work. Three, getting a good match between employees and jobs is important. Four, your organization corrects any mismatches that do occur. Five, correcting mismatches is a difficult and costly process for everyone involved. Six, it is best for the organization and applicants to do everything possible during the hiring process to determine if a match exists. Seven, the hiring process is designed to enable the organization, and especially applicants, to make well-informed employment decisions. With this seven-point introduction, applicants usually see the need for making a good job-match decision.

Job Design

Even when applicants and employees work toward job matching, in many jobs applicants or employees see the work itself as not rewarding. This raises a question. Is it always possible to have good job matches? Probably not. However, there may be something you can do. Technically speaking, your choices are either to change the job or to change the person. In reality, changing the job is the only feasible option. Although this is not always possible, many jobs can be designed differently to give the work itself greater appeal.

Several things must be considered when trying to make the work itself more rewarding. Most employees want (1) enough variety to prevent boredom but not so much as to go beyond their interests and capabilities; (2) identification with the product or service their work relates to; (3) meaningful work, work that in some way is important and makes a contribution in the overall scheme of things; (4) a degree of freedom in deciding what they do, how they do it, and when they do it; and (5) interaction with other employees. When jobs are designed to provide these, the work itself will be more rewarding, making job matching easier and more successful because the job offers more of what more people are looking for.

Job design combined with job placement will yield good job matches when both are carried out with a focus on job matching. Let's take a further look at how to do this by considering the situation described in Case 7-1. Read the case and decide two things. First, how should Gary go about finding the employees he needs (job placement)? Second, how should their jobs be designed (job design)?

Case 7-1—Job Matching. Gary had been an independent consultant for about ten years. Most of his work had been conducting management training programs. He had developed five one-day programs and specialized in conducting them. In most cases he was hired to do one or two days of a one or two-week training program a client was conducting. It was rare for a trainer to have more days on a program. Eventually Gary decided to go beyond his one-man operation. He wanted to design and sell training programs, and to hire and train trainers to conduct them. This newfound desire came about because he no longer got the same satisfaction from doing training as he once did. It had become boring doing the same thing over and over. Gary designed two one-week programs that he sold with unusual success, in large part because of very competitive pricing. Most clients who contracted with him did so for the two full weeks of training. With the contracts secured and with a couple of months to hire and prepare trainers, Gary started to think seriously about how to find three trainers who would do a good job and stay with him for a long time. To do this Gary knew he had to have good job matches. How can he accomplish this? That is, how should he go about finding the trainers he needs (job placement) and how should their jobs be designed (job design)?

Let's consider the job placement issue in Case 7-1 first. Finding the right trainers is critical to Gary's success in his new business. With this in mind, perhaps it would be best for Gary not to take the risk of trying anything new and different. He could make a list of trainers he knows or has heard about. In addition, he could get the names of good trainers from clients as well as from some of the people he has trained. With such a list, he could find out who would be interested, interview them, check references, and make hiring decisions. This wouldn't take too long or be too costly. He already knows several good trainers, and he could recognize the necessary qualities in others by talking with them. After all, he'd been in this business for a long time and knew it well. This kind of thinking and this hiring process will insure one thing. Gary will have problems. He will make little, if any, money, and he will be consumed with trainer-related problems. This definitely is not the way to make good job placement decisions, although it is the traditional way of doing it. So what should Gary do?

Gary should realize several things. First, his preconceived notions about trainers he already knows likely will lead to nothing but trouble. That is, Gary should realize that better trainers will be hired if everybody goes through the same rigorous hiring process. Second, as repeat business is essential for success, each trainer must perform well from day one, or the opportunity for repeat business may be lost. Third, with Gary's pricing, there is little room for error in hiring even one trainer who has to be replaced, either because of performance problems or because the job isn't what it was thought to be. Replacing trainers is a time-consuming and costly proposition that Gary cannot afford. His efforts may fail unless every job placement decision is a good one.

Four, the bottom line is that Gary has everything to lose by hiring wrong and everything to gain by hiring right. He should throw tradition out the window. He should hire only people who (1) demonstrate (not just claim) they can do the job, and demonstrate it before hiring decisions are made, and (2) prefer the work itself that constitutes the trainer's job in Gary's new organization.

Gary should use the job placement approach described earlier of getting and giving information, especially information related to the work itself. A major part of each job interview should focus on the issue of satisfaction from the work itself. Applicants also could look over the training materials Gary has developed. Gary could describe the job of the trainer in considerable detail. Applicants could observe Gary conducting a training session using his materials, with Gary doing a session for a client or conducting a special session solely for the applicants. Applicants who were still interested at this point could be asked to conduct part of a session using Gary's materials, with other applicants and/or Gary serving as trainees. This gives applicants a firsthand experience and at the same time allows Gary to evaluate their performance. All this gives each applicant, and Gary, ample information to make good hiring decisions. Job placement will be more effective and less risky using this approach. If the cost seems greater, it is greater only on the front end, but certainly not in the long run.

Let's look beyond job placement in Case 7-1 and consider job design. There are two main issues here. The first is whether trainers should do any selling in addition to conducting training sessions. For most trainers, selling would make the work itself less appealing. It would be appealing primarily to a trainer who wanted to eventually leave Gary to start his own company and take Gary's clients with him. This is a simple job-design question. Do not include selling as part of the job. The other major issue is whether to have each trainer specialize in three or four of the ten one-day training sessions, or to have each person prepared to do all ten days. Gary may want to start out by having them specialize and then move away from specialization soon. This would ease the initial workload of the trainers in preparing for the first few sessions. Quickly moving away from the specialization should be done to reduce the likelihood that the work itself would become boring and less satisfying and to give Gary more flexibility in scheduling trainers for the sessions. To make the work itself more appealing, Gary also could design the job to allow trainers (1) some freedom in deciding how to conduct the training sessions and (2) an opportunity to meet frequently to interact with each other.

Every job may not lend itself to the full range of job placement and job design opportunities, some of which are shown in Case 7-1. Even so, taking one or two small steps toward better job matching can pay off handsomely. The less well a job lends itself to job placement and job design, as recommended here, the more likely it is that one or two small steps will make a big difference. With other jobs, your success will be more pronounced. If you go after better job matches, you will get them. If you understand what you've read here, you should be ready to use it. The problem most managers face is not in doing it, but rather in seeing the need to do it. And you have both. You see the benefits. You see the need. And you know how. You're ready!

COMMUNICATION

Several B3 problems can be solved simply by communicating with employees. The solution is found in either giving information to or receiving information from employees. Communication is the preferred solution when B3 problems are caused from (1) undervaluing outcomes received, (2) overvaluing outcomes not received, and (3) changing values. Solving B3 problems through communication has two steps. One is to determine which of the three causes is creating the problem. The other is either to provide information to the employee (for causes 1 and 2) or to obtain information from the employee (for cause 3). Let's look at each of the causes and how to deal with them.

Employees undervalue outcomes received because (1) they are not fully aware of what has been received (as when an employee knows that a memo documenting his outstanding performance on a project was placed in his personnel file but is not aware that it was distributed to key executives as well), (2) they don't see all the positive elements of the outcome (as when they don't see the advancement potential of a new position or don't realize the value of the experience that comes with increased responsibility), and (3) others who are less deserving have been given the same outcome (inequity) or seem to have been (perceived inequity). When undervaluing is causing a B3 problem, the solution is simply to provide the employee with information as appropriate to create a more complete awareness of (1) what has been received, (2) the positive elements associated with it, and (3) the absolute value of the outcome as opposed to its value relative to other recipients (in view of inequity or perceived inequity).

Employees overvalue outcomes not received because they don't see all of the negative elements associated with the outcomes. An example is the employee who badly wants a promotion without being aware of some of its undesirable elements, such as the pressure and stress of the job. Sometimes employees even become obsessed with getting a certain outcome. This is a special case of overvaluing outcomes not received. The employees place such an exaggerated value on an outcome that receiving it becomes an obsession. The solution here is to help employees see a more complete and realistic picture of the outcome. This is accomplished by providing information about the negative aspects of the outcome.

The value employees place on outcomes changes over time. When employees are young they often place a premium on growth and development, responsibility, money, and advancement, for example. As they get older, these same employees tend to place more value on job security, insurance programs, and retirement plans. The value for some outcomes changes far more rapidly. The realization that a certain outcome is much different than originally believed can cause a dramatic, overnight change in the way the employee values it. What is the implication of changing values? It means that employees' B3s for outcomes being received and for those not received can and do change. With these changes often come B3 problems. When B3 problems stem from changing values, the solution is to get information frequently from employees about the changes and take action accordingly.

VALUES CLARIFICATION

Two kinds of B3 problems are solved by helping employees clarify the value they place on outcomes. Values clarification is called for when B3 problems are caused by (1) conflicting values and (2) confused values. Let's first look at these two causes, then see how to deal with them.

Conflicting values refers to the situation where employees want two outcomes that are mutually exclusive. That is, they want two things, even though having one means they can't have the other. Conflicting values often stem from (1) wanting opposing outcomes, like wanting a promotion that requires a transfer, yet not wanting to relocate;(2) differences between what the employee wants for himself and what significant others want for him; and (3) what the employee wants to do and what he knows is the right thing to do.

Employee: "I really want that promotion, but I don't want to relocate."

Employee: "I'm looking for advancement, power, money, and travel, but my family wants me to spend more time with them."

Employee: "I want the promotion at any cost, but to get it will require playing hard ball in a way that wouldn't be morally and ethically right."

Confused values refers to situations where employees simply are confused about what they want. They may (1) want a certain outcome and at the same time not want it or (2) be unable to make up their minds. The employee is in a state of confusion about what is wanted.

Employee: "In one way I want the promotion, but in another way I don't."

Employee: "One minute I want to head up the project, the next minute I don't. I just can't make up my mind."

B3 problems caused by conflicting and confused values can only be solved when employees clarify their values for the outcomes in question. Employees must do this for themselves, but you can help by following a simple three-step process. The first step is to help them recognize what is happening. Employees often do not realize, especially in the early stages, that they have conflicting values or that they are confused about their values. Helping them realize this is an important first step. Here are some ways to do this.

—"Do you think it's possible for both of those things to work out at the same time?"

—"It looks like getting one means you can't get the other one."

—"You seem like you're confused about what you really want."

—"I get the feeling you can't decide what is most important to you."

The second step is to help employees see the need to resolve the conflict or erase the confusion. This normally can be done by helping them see the consequences, including such things as indecisiveness, wasted time, and frustration, all of which negatively affect their performance. This step includes helping employees (1) realize and accept the fact that, in the case of conflicting outcomes, some outcomes are mutually exclusive and are going to stay that way and (2) recognize that the problem of confused values does not improve unless they take steps to deal with it. Here some ways to address this:

—"What happens if you keep wanting both of them when it's only possible to have one of them?"

—"How is the confusion affecting you?"

—"Sometimes you can't have everything you want, and I think this is one of them."

—"Being confused about what you really want is hard, but you're the only one who can get it straightened out."

Step three is to encourage employees to clarify the value they place on the outcomes in question. This means deciding how much each outcome means to them and being able to put the outcomes in an order of priority. Here are some examples:

—"Just how important is that to you?"
—"How much does that mean to you compared to ———— ?"
—"If you had to choose one or the other, which would you take?"
—"Considering all the possibilities, which three are the most important to you?"
—"Can you rank them in order of importance?"

This simple three-step process will go a long way to help employees clarify the values they place on the many outcomes available to them. It is impossible for you to give employees what they want unless you know what they want, and it is impossible for you to know that if they have conflicting or confused values.

OTHER B3 SOLUTIONS

Four of the performance-outcome (B2) solutions presented in chapter 5 also can be used to solve outcome-satisfaction (B3) problems. The four are leveling, preference shifting, transfers, and terminations. Each can be used when outcome-satisfaction (B3) problems stem from any one of the following three causes: (1) not receiving valued outcomes, (2) receiving outcomes not valued, and (3) the work itself not being rewarding. Let's quickly review how each of the four solutions can be applied when employees believe outcomes do not or will not lead to satisfaction (B3).

Leveling

The idea of leveling, as discussed in chapter 5, is to put the cards on the table with employees, letting them know that certain outcomes of importance cannot and will not change. Leveling is being honest with employees, letting them know that desired outcomes are not forthcoming and that undesired outcomes will continue. This removes any false hope employees may have and enables them to make better and more timely decisions about what to do. Leveling will lead some employees to seek employment elsewhere in hopes of getting the outcomes they want. For others it may be preliminary step that leads to preference shifting and thereby an increase in motivation, effort, and performance. In some cases, it stimulates employees to come up with creative ideas that give them the outcomes they want. The bottom line is that leveling with employees can be an effective solution to outcome-satisfaction (B3) problems.

Leveling can be accomplished with eight steps, as outlined in chapter 5: (1) indicate performance is not acceptable and why; (2) indicate you are unwilling to tolerate unacceptable performance any longer; (3)

point out that the situation regarding outcomes is not going to improve; (4) present the options, including quitting, getting fired, or improving performance; (5) point out that it is the employee's decision; (6) establish a deadline for the employee to decide; (7) be sure employees understand you have the authority to decide if they don't; (8) offer your help in making and implementing the decision. Leveling allows employees to accept the situation, to come up with their own solutions, or to look for other opportunities.

Preference Shifting

You will remember from chapter 5 that preference shifting refers to shifts in employee preferences for outcomes. Employees shift preferences when they change how much they like or dislike an outcome. Downshifting occurs when the preference for an outcome declines. For example, the preference for a promotion may lessen when employees become more aware that the new job requires longer hours, intense pressure to perform, high risk of failure, greater stress, etc. Upshifting is when the preference for an outcome becomes stronger. Employees, for example, who are dissatisfied with their job because the work itself is not rewarding may become happier with it when they stop and think about their job security compared to friends who have lost jobs because of the economy, plant closings, downsizing, etc. Upshifting is used when employees are receiving outcomes they don't want, whereas downshifting is called for when employees want an outcome they are not getting. Managers can initiate preference shifting, either downshifting or upshifting, by following the five-step process outlined in chapter 5, namely, (1) leveling with employees so that they realize they cannot have a desired outcome or cannot stop receiving one that is undesired, (2) helping employees understand that by not quitting their jobs they are choosing to stay in the situation, (3) convincing employees they will be happier by shifting preferences, (4) showing employees that no on has everything desired, and (5) persuading employees they can get out of the dissatisfaction rut by focusing on the positive rather than on the negative. This is a B3 solution that will work effectively with many employees.

Transfers and Terminations

Sometimes outcome-satisfaction (B3) problems simply cannot be resolved with employees remaining in their current positions. When all options have been considered and the appropriate ones tried, but nothing seems to work, only two possibilities remain. One is to transfer the employee to another position in the organization. The other is to terminate the employee. If a position is available elsewhere in the organization that offers (B2) what the employee wants (B3), and the employee can handle (B1) the job, all three of the conditions required for the employee to be motivated to perform well are met, and a transfer makes sense. Otherwise, terminating the employee is the best decision. Keep in mind that termination is recommended as the last resort, when nothing can be done to bring employee performance to an acceptable level.

SUMMARY

In this chapter you have seen the following eleven solutions for B3 problems: giving valued outcomes, substitution, withholding outcomes not valued, offsets, job matching via job placement and job design, communication, values clarification, leveling, preference shifting, transfers and terminations. The solution appropriate to use depends on what is causing the problem. You learned how to diagnose B3 causes in the previous chapter. In this chapter you have learned (1) how to pick the right solution according to the cause of the problem and (2) how to implement each of the solutions. Following the guidelines presented in these two chapters will enable you to diagnose and solve most of the B3 problems you will be facing. Give it a try and you will see how successful you will be.

8 —————————————————————————

Putting It All Together

The power of the expectancy theory of motivation comes not only from the theory (chapter 1) and not only from the components of the application model (chapters 2 through 7), but from putting it all together in a practical application format. Four things are important in doing this. The first is being able to sit down with employees to conduct a diagnostic interview and come up with solutions that are acceptable to both of you. The second is being able to handle the really difficult motivation and performance problems. The third is knowing what to do when your hands are tied with regard to some of the solutions you want to use. The fourth is knowing what to do when nothing seems to work. Each of these situations will be discussed in this chapter.

As you finalize your own assessment of the approach to motivation and performance presented in this book, you may be wondering how your opinion compares to others'. Such a comparison is possible, as the final section of this chapter summarizes the reactions of some of the highest level of human resource executives in several of the largest corporations in America. You will find this interesting.

ONE-ON-ONE WITH EMPLOYEES

How do you handle one-on-one discussions with employees to resolve performance problems? There is a simple and effective way to do this. It calls for applying much of what you have learned in the earlier chapters. The starting point is (1) to document the employee's performance, then meet with the employee and (2) state your performance concern; (3) agree that performance is a problem; (4) diagnose B1, B2, and B3; (5) ask the employee for solutions; (6) agree on a solution; (7) get and give a commitment; (8) establish follow-up; and (9) give positive reinforcement.

The overall approach is to get the employee to do two things: to provide the information you need to diagnose the problem and to come up with solutions that are acceptable to both of you. This approach works for three reasons. One, it recognizes that employees tend to know more about the problem than anyone else. It is their problem, and they have been living with it. Two, this approach recognizes that employees tend to know the best way to solve the problem. Because they have been living with the problem, they have been thinking about how to solve it. They tend to know what will work. Three, the approach recognizes that employees have preferred ways of solving problems they face. Remember, a second-best solution that employees will accept is better than the best solution, if they resist it.

The role of the manager with this approach is to let the employee do most of the talking, usually 80 percent or more, or the process will not work. The manager guides the discussion by asking questions and using active-listening techniques. Let's see how this is done by looking at each step in the approach.

Document Employee Performance

Before meeting with the employee, gather specific information to document the employee's performance level. Be prepared to show the employee that actual performance is not meeting performance standards. Get specific performance data whenever possible. Examples of instances where performance has been a problem are helpful. Learn as much as possible about the symptoms and causes of the problem. It is impossible to resolve employee performance problems if you do not know exactly what performance levels are. Do you homework.

State Your Performance Concern

Meet with the employee and indicate your concern about performance. Point out why you are concerned. Be direct and to the point. When doing this, show concern rather than being accusing or threatening. Come across as wanting to help rather than punish. Here are some ways you can do this.

—"I've noticed lately that your performance seems to have dropped off some. I wanted to talk about it with you and see if there is anything I can do to help."

—"You've looked a little 'down and out' lately. I was wondering what's going on and whether there is anything I can do to help."

—"Your progress hasn't been moving along as I expected, and I wanted to see if I can do anything to help."

After stating the purpose of the meeting, stop and wait for the employee to respond. This is the first step in getting the employee involved in solving the performance problem. The employee may be hesitant the first time you approach a problem this way. Be patient. Offer encouragement. Do not let the employees get by with comments like, "Oh, golly gee, I didn't know anything was wrong." Responses like this usually are a sign of reluctance to talk. Try to remove the reluctance by saying something that shows you sincerely want to help.

Agree That Performance Is a Problem

Progress is impossible unless both you and the employee agree that there is a performance problem. There should also be agreement as to the nature of it. This is where your documentation of the employee's performance comes in handy. It is fine to say, "Your performance hasn't been up to par," but you must have solid evidence to back it up. Employees often challenge vague statements about performance. It is very important that you have indisputable evidence to support your contention that performance is a problem.

Diagnose B1, B2, and B3

Once you and the employee are on the same wavelength regarding the existence and nature of the problem, it is time to diagnose B1, B2, and B3 levels and causes. As recommended in earlier chapters, ask open questions followed by direct and clarifying questions and use active-listening techniques. Here is an example:

Manager: "Is there anything I can do to help?" (This is a direct question, but it normally has the same effect as an open question.)

Employee: "I don't know. With all the recent changes in procedures, I've really gotten confused about things." (Bingo. Sounds like a low B1 caused by not knowing what to do and/or how to do it.)

Manager: "Can you give me an example of what you mean?" (clarifying question)

Employee: "We got all these new procedures written up by engineering. A lot of us had trouble understanding them. The meeting didn't help much and we didn't get any training." (Solutions are implied here.)

Manager: "Anything else?"

Employee: "Not really. Everything was smooth sailing until all the changes. I was doing a good job. Now I'm having trouble getting my work done right and on time. I don't like that."

When the diagnosis is completed, summarize your understanding of the problem. This gives the employee a chance to confirm the diagnosis or to make corrections or additions. The summary should be a brief restatement of B1, B2, and B3 levels and causes mentioned by the employee. Nothing else is necessary or desirable. There is no need for explanation or justification, criticism or sympathy, lectures or finger pointing, or being defensive or offensive, or offering suggestions or solutions. Just summarize. Then wait for employee feedback to be sure you have summarized the problem correctly. Here is an example.

Manager: "So what you're saying is that even if you work hard, you can't do the kind of job you want to do because you don't fully understand all the new procedures we've gone to." (The employee is saying, "I can't do it because of the new procedures.")

Employee: "You've hit it right on the head." (Now you know both the B1 level and the B1 cause.)

Ask the Employee for Solutions

Now comes the hard part for many managers. Hold any ideas you have for solving the problem. Instead, ask the employee for solutions. Some employees will be eager to tell you. Others will not. If they seem reluctant, encourage them. They are sure to have some ideas. Ask again. Do not give your ideas first. This is tempting, very tempting when the employee is hesitant. Here is an example of how to do it.

Manager: "What's the best way to handle this?"

Employee: "I'm not sure. What do you think?" (Do not fall for the employee's turning the question back on you.)

Manager: "You're good at figuring out things like this. What do you think we should do?"

Employee: "I just need sombody to go over a few things with me. I know where I'm confused, so I know the questions to ask."

Manager: "Do you have anybody in mind to help you?"

Employee: "I hit it off pretty good with one of the engineers that helped develop the new procedures. You know Bob. I'd feel comfortable working with him."

Manager: "How much time are we talking about?"

Employee: "Probably just a couple of hours the first time, and half an hour or so one or two more times."

Manager: "Anything other than the time with Bob?"

Employee: "No, that should do it."

End this part of the discussion by summarizing the employee's suggestions. The purpose is to be sure you understand the key points the employee is making. It is a fatal mistake to ask for solutions and move ahead with a misunderstanding of what the employee has said. Summarizing is the way to check yourself out.

Agree on a Solution

Sometimes the solution recommended by the employee will meet with your approval. In this case, indicate your agreement and move on to the next step. When the solution isn't acceptable, what can you do? If your concern centers on minor points, you can handle it in several ways. One, asking questions about your points of concern often will make the employee aware that an alternative would be better. Then ask for some options and settle on one that suits both of you. Two, point out what you are concerned about and why, suggest an alternative, and ask for the employee's opinion. If you build a good case for your preference, the employee probably will go along with you.

What if the employee's solution simply is too far off base? This will happen sometimes. What should you do? The first option is ask the employee for any other ideas for dealing with the problem. If an acceptable approach surfaces, pursue it until agreement is reached. If not, the second option is to ask questions to help the employee come to the conclusion that the preferred solution is not a good one. For example, "How would you go about implementing this?" Or, "How do you think our customers (other employees, management, etc.) will react to this?" Or, "Can we do this given our time, cost, and manpower constraints?" If this doesn't work, the third option is to point out the flaws in the solution, as tactfully as possible, offer suggestions for overcoming them, and ask for the employee's reaction to the new solution you are recommending. One of these three normally will work. Try all of them if necessary.

Get and Give a Commitment

Once agreement is reached on how to solve an employee's performance problem, it is vital to get the employee's commitment to solve the problem and to give your commitment to help. How should you do this? First, summarize the solution both of you have agreed to. Get the employee to accept the responsibility for its success and make a commitment to implement the solution. State what the employee is to do and indicate what you are making a commitment to. Here is an example.

Manager: "Let me see if I've got this right. You want to meet with Bob for about two hours, then a couple more times for half an hour or so."

Employee: "That should do it."

Manager: "Do you think this will get your performance up where it should be?"

Employee: "Yes sir, I do." (This is the employee's commitment.)

Manager: "OK, I'll talk with Bob and have him get in touch with you to set up a time for the first meeting." (This is the manager's commitment.)

Establish Follow-Up

A commitment from both sides to take action is not the end of the process. It is necessary to indicate how the solution will be monitored. That is, what kind of follow-up will be done by both you and the employee? Here is an example.

Manager: "A couple of things I want you to do. First, as soon as you and Bob set a time to get together, let me know. Second, after you meet with him—the same day—I want you to let me know how the meeting went and if you still think this approach is going to get your performance back up to where it used to be."

Give Positive Reinforcement

End your one-on-one discussion by thanking the employee and giving positive reinforcement for being willing to talk, for helping figure out what to do, for being concerned about doing better, etc. Anything and everything the employee did in the meeting that you would like to see repeated in future discussions should be praised.

Manager: "One more thing. Thanks. I'm glad to have you working here. You're always concerned about doing a good job, and I appreciate your help in working this thing out."

Employee: "Hey, I'm the one who needs to thank you. Most managers would have chewed me out and not really helped get me back on track. So thank you. And I'll let you know as soon as Bob and I get a time set. Can I expect him to contact me today?"

The key to diagnosing and solving performance problems quickly is to put the ball in the employee's court. Rely on employees to help diagnose problems and to come up with solutions. It takes information to solve problems. When it comes to performance problems, employees have information you need to make good decisions. Using the employee-centered approach recommended here will work. You can make it work for you.

HANDLING DIFFICULT PROBLEMS

Although some motivation and performance problems can be solved quickly and easily, others are more difficult. Sometimes you simply don't know what to do. Or you know what to do, but you don't have the resources or authority to do it. A different strategy is needed to handle difficult problems. An approach that goes beyond the usual is important.

What are some examples of difficult problems that must be treated differently? There are many, including the following: (1) an employee wants a promotion, but there are no opportunities available now or in the immediate future; (2) an employee wants a promotion now and feels ready for it, but isn't; (3) an employee wants more money, but the organization is strapped and doesn't have it to give; (4) an employee wants more money and thinks it's deserved, but it isn't; (5) a top performer is not being rewarded fairly, and you can do nothing about it; (6) an average performer honestly believes greater rewards are deserved, but they aren't; (7) an employee doesn't like the work and wants to do something else, but no other opportunities are available in the company; (8) an employee was hired several years ago at low pay compared to others, the inequity continues, the person's motivation is a problem, and the manager can do nothing to correct the pay situation because upper management will not let him or because the company does not have the resources to do it now; (9) while other employees are responding to the need for higher productivity, an employee who has gotten by with marginal work for a long time refuses to change; (10) a manager has inherited a low-producing employee who is trying to hold on for a few more years until retirement; and (11) an employee who simply can't do the job has no other options in the company or outside.

Difficult problems like these can be handled best by facing them head on. They do not get solved by ignoring or sidestepping them. You have to look difficult problems squarely in the eye, confront them, and deal directly with them. This means being open and honest with employees about what can and cannot be done to solve the problem. Managers sometimes are reluctant to do this. They are afraid employees will react negatively. This is an unfounded fear. Employees prefer managers who care enough about them to be open and honest in dealing with difficult problems. Employees respect and appreciate managers who are willing to tackle tough problems. Trying to solve difficult problems is much better than dodging them.

You can handle difficult problems more often than not, if you try, and especially if you use the three-step process presented here. The process takes selected solutions presented in previous chapters and combines them into an approach designed specifically for handling difficult problems. Let's see how it works by looking at each step. This process assumes that you have followed steps 1 through 5 of the one-on-one discussion format as outlined in the previous section (document employee performance, state your performance concern, agree that performance is a problem, diagnose B1-B2-B3, and ask the employee for solutions), but got stalled on step 6, agreeing on a solution. With this in mind, here are the three steps in handling difficult problems.

The first step is leveling. This is telling it like it is, telling employees exactly how things are, as discussed in chapter 5 as a solution to performance-outcome (B2) problems. It means being on the level with employees, which requires being open and honest about the situation. Sometimes it means saying things employees may not want to hear. There are at least six difficult situations that call for leveling. Here they are. Each is accompanied by an example of leveling.

1. When employees want something you cannot give them. This is a B3 problem.

   Leveling: "I know you are interested in advancing in the company as soon as possible. We have reached the point where there simply are not any promotion opportunities available. I want to talk with you about why this has happened and discuss some things we can do in the meantime."

2. When employees dislike something and you can do nothing about it. This is a B3 problem, too.

   Leveling: "I want to thank you for making me aware that you do not like the kind of work you are doing now. At the same time I want to level with you and point out that I don't see any opportunity for that to change in the near future. Let me tell you why, and then we can discuss what this all means."

3. When employees are not getting outcomes their performance deserves and you can not do anything about it. This is a B2 problem.

   Leveling: "I know you are concerned about being one of the top performers and not being rewarded for it. To be honest with you, this isn't likely to change any time soon due to the new leadership at the top and our current financial situation. With all this said, I would like to get your thinking on it and explore any ideas you have."

4. When employees think they deserve more but their performance does not merit it. This is a B2 problem.

    Leveling: "You recently indicated a concern about the way you are rewarded here. I will be glad to show you the performance data on everybody in the department, as well as the guidelines used for determining rewards. If you have been treated unfairly, I'll do what I can to straighten it out."

5. When employees have been getting by with poor performance and think they can continue to do so. This is a B2 problem.

    Leveling: "This isn't the first time we have discussed your performance. I've made a mistake in the past by not working with you more closely to get it up where it should be. My plan now is to work with you in whatever way I can to get this situation back on track. I think that by working together we can come up with some ways that will be acceptable to both of us."

6. When employees simply are not qualified for the job. This is B1 problem.

    Leveling: "We have been discussing this situation for a long time now, and I think it has become apparent to both of us that the position you are in is not a good match for you. If we are in agreement on this, I would like to discuss some options with you that I hope will make sense to both of us."

You can see from these examples that leveling is a way of facing difficult problems head on in an open, honest, and direct way. It can be done tactfully and without being critical and threatening. This is important. Otherwise employees will not cooperate, and progress toward an acceptable solution is not likely.

The second step in handling difficult problems is to probe/check. This is the step of probing, checking, and verifying your understanding of the employee's motivation problem, based on prior discussions and other sources of information. It means being sure you know exactly what the problem is (B1, B2, B3) and what is causing it. This includes knowing whether employees believe they can do the job (B1), believe they will get certain outcomes if they perform (B2), and knowing what outcomes employees want and don't want (B3). Here is an example:

Probe/Check: "Can you tell me what there is about a promotion that is attractive to you?"

A probe/check often opens the door for information to surface that may lead to a solution to difficult problems. With the probe/check shown prior to this paragraph, for example, employees often will say they want a certain outcome when they really want something else. They may say they want an outcome (a first-level outcome) they believe will lead them to other outcomes (second-level outcomes) they really want. Employees who push for promotions, for example, may really be saying they want more money, more prestige, increased responsibility, a greater challenge, more recognition, etc. Knowing what employees really want is important. Although a manager may not be able to give the promotion, he may be able to give some of the other outcomes. Here are some additional examples of how to probe/check. They are tied to leveling examples 2 through 6 presented earlier.

—"What is there about your work that you don't like?"

—"Can you give me some specific examples of how rewards have not been tied to your performance?"

—"Is there anything you want to say about your performance?"

—"How do you feel about being able to handle this job?"

The third step in handling difficult problems is to give the problem to the employee. When you have done everything you can do and the problem still remains, give it to the employee and see what happens. Some solutions rest more in their hands than in yours anyway. Employees, however, are not aware of this, and you must help them. Specifically, you must make employees aware of their options and encourage the selection and use of one or more of them. There are three options. They were discussed at length in chapter 7 as solutions for managers to use. In the discussion that follows, they are refocused and intended as solution approaches for employees to apply. You may or may not have tried them with the employee who is at the center of a difficult motivation and performance problem. It doesn't matter. At this point, it makes sense to give employees a shot at them, with your help, of course. Here are the three options.

1. Preference shifting. The idea here is for employees to shift preferences away from outcomes that are unavailable (downshifting) and toward outcomes that are available (upshifting).

2. Substitution. This is where available outcomes acceptable to the employee take the place of desired outcomes that are not available. The employee still has a strong preference for the desired outcome but is willing to accept substitutes for it.

3. Offsets. This is where available outcomes that are acceptable to the employee offset an undesired outcome that cannot be eliminated. The employee still has a negative preference for the undesired outcome, but enough desirable outcomes may offset it.

With these options in mind, how do you apply step three, that is, how do you give the problem to employees? You have already set the stage for this by leveling (step one) and doing a probe/check (step two). By leveling, you basically said, "There is a problem, and I don't know a good solution for it." After the probe/check, where you are trying to better understand the employee's view of the problem, it is time to give the problem to the employee. Here are two ways to do it. The first is for the employee who cannot have a desired outcome. The second is used when an undesired outcome cannot be removed.

Manager: "We have a dilemma. There are two options as I see it. The first is to rethink the importance of the different things in your job (this refers to preference shifting). The second is to come up with some alternatives to the things that are unavailable to you (this refers to substitution). Let me explain what I mean here and give you a couple of examples. . . . It's your decision. Are you willing to consider either, or both, of these options?"

Manager: ". . . The second option is to come up with something that will make up for the things you don't like about your job (this refers to offsets). . . ."

The direction you take from here depends on the employee's response. It may be to help work through preference shifting or help come up with outcome substitutes or offsetting outcomes.

There are other ways to give the problem to employees. Here is another example:

Manager: "Having the door closed on something you really want is disappointing. There are a lot of ways you can react. I can't tell you what to do or where to go from here. That's your decision, but I'll help in any way I can."

This leaves the door open for either substitution or preference shifting. Suppose it makes sense for the employee to consider preference shifting. What could you say? Here is one way:

Manager: "You may be lucky that there are no promotion opportunities available now. I used to think getting a promotion every six months was important. Then I realized a lot of promotions put you in dead-end jobs, or jobs that are not very satisfying, or positions with very little job security. And promotions always mean more responsibility, longer hours, added stress, and less time with the family. I wasn't seeing my children grow up and wasn't at home when they needed me. I didn't have a balance in my work life and personal life. It takes a toll. This is something you may want to think about."

This encourages downshifting relative to a promotion and upshifting toward outcomes associated with the current position, including job security, satisfying work, and family.

Here is an example of giving the problem to the employee in a way that focuses on the substitution option:

Manager: "As I said, there are no promotion opportunities available now. There may be some other goals you would want to shoot for. I can't tell you what they are. That is a personal decision only you can make, but I'll help in any way I can. Have you thought about other things that might be attractive?"

Encouraging the employee to look at other goals sets the stage for the substitution option. It is another way of saying, "Is there anything that will substitute for a promotion and motivate you to work hard and perform well?" You may want to go a step further by giving the employee suggestions regarding outcome substitutes and a way to obtain them. Here is an example:

Manager: "Some of the things you are looking for in a promotion coincide with several of the changing needs in our department. I'm looking for someone to head up a special project that will be challenging and have a lot of visibility with top management. It would not involve a pay increase, but it would give you a chance to show a lot of people what you can do."

Helping employees with the offsetting option, where desirable outcomes are used to offset undesirable ones, can be just as easy. Here is an example of one way to do it:

Manager: "Even though you are going to have to continue doing the one part of your job that you really dislike, maybe something could be done to make it easier to live with. Is there anything good that might offset the bad? I can't give you a big pay raise or anything like that, but if you can come up with something that makes sense, maybe we can work it out. Do you have any ideas?"

Notice that in all of these examples, the manager gives the problem to the employee and leaves it there. While the manager is being supportive and is helping the employee work through the options, the manager does not take the problem back from the employee. This is important. Difficult problems are more likely to be solved when employees are forced to be major players in the process.

WHEN YOUR HANDS ARE TIED

No matter how creative you and your employees are, your hands often are tied when it comes to solving motivation and performance problems. Many solutions simply are not available to you. Every manager must work within these constraints. Let's explore the kinds of constraints managers must live with, then take a look at the resulting consequences, and finally see what can be done when your hands are tied.

Constraints and Consequences

What do managers need to influence the B1, B2, and B3 of employees positively? For B1, they need (1) money for employee training; (2) authority to redesign jobs to match employee skills; (3) resources to provide needed tools, such as equipment, materials, staff, etc.; (4) time to manage the employees (communication, setting goals, training employees, giving instructions, and confidence building, all of which influence employee B1s); (5) authority to lower performance standards and expectations; and (6) authority to influence hiring decisions. For B2, managers need (1) availability of outcomes (money for raises, openings for promotions, bonus money, choice assignments, company cars, awards, etc.); (2) authority to give the outcomes; (3) authority to give the outcomes based on performance (rather than across-the-board raises, promotions based on seniority, etc.); and (4) budget and staff to set up a system to measure employee performance to know who deserves what. For B3, managers need (1) sufficient amounts of the valued outcomes (like money for pay raises, bonuses, travel expenses, etc.) and (2) authority to give valued outcomes, including work that in itself is rewarding, and to remove outcomes that are not valued.

When the things managers need in order to influence the B1, B2, and B3 of employees are inadequate, they become constraints that tie the manager's hands. The consequences are considerable. First, employees will not be nearly as motivated as they could be. Second, the lack of motivation shows up in the form of inadequate effort to get the job done. Third, performance falls below what it should be. Fourth, this means quality and service suffer, and so does profit. All these consequences will be present, every day, as long as the manager's ability to influence B1, B2, and B3 is limited.

Dealing with Constraints

What can you do when constraints make it impossible to do your job? Many managers become frustrated, eventually conclude that "I can't do it," and then give up. This is understandable. Just don't give up too soon. There are two options to consider before throwing in the towel. One is to focus on getting around the constraints. The other is to remove them. When the circumstances are right, both options can work. Let's see how.

What about getting around constraints? This doesn't always work, but it never will if you don't try. Remember, "There is more than one way to skin a cat." When you can't use the solution you want, look for an alternative. This is the idea behind preference shifting, substitution, and offsets and is the reason they are popular and effective solutions. They are designed to search for alternative ways to solve problems when preferred solutions cannot be used. When you can't give an employee a certain desired outcome, find a substitute that will be satisfying. When you can't remove an undesired outcome, find something to offset it. Get employees to shift preferences away from outcomes you don't control toward those you do. Constraints make it difficult to solve motivation problems, but not impossible. Focus on getting around constraints. You may be surprised at how often you can do it. Give it a try.

When you can't get around constraints, you may be able to remove them. This may be easier than you think. Here is an approach that often works. First, isolate the constraints that must be removed for you to solve the employee's motivation and performance problem. Second, find the person nearest you in the organization who can remove the constraints. Third, identify outcomes that are both satisfying to that person and within your control. Normally, improving performance in your unit will be a desirable outcome to that person, who typically is a person above you. If performance and improvement isn't enough, find something else. Fourth, go to that person and make your pitch.

When making your sales pitch, include the following: (1) describe the employee's motivation and performance problem; (2) give evidence to document the nature and magnitude of the problem; (3) explain all you have done to solve it and why that hasn't worked; (4) itemize the negative consequences if the problem isn't solved, doing so in a way that touches on outcomes the person hearing you would want to avoid; (5) indicate what needs to be done and why this approach will work; (6) point out the specific constraints that need to be removed for you to solve the problem; (7) state the end results of this approach, stressing the outcomes to be derived personally by the person you are talking to; and (8) ask for what you want. Focus on, and be convincing about, the fact that the person will get (B2) desired outcomes (B3) by removing the constraints as you request. If you can give the person a high B2 and B3, the person will be motivated to give you what you need.

Managers face many constraints when trying to solve motivation and performance problems. This is a reality of managing. The way you deal with these constraints determines how successful you will be as a manager. Keep in mind that constraints often can be handled effectively, either by getting around them or by removing them. The key is believing you can do it. That is, you must believe, "I can." If you can deal with your own B1 problems here, the door will be opened to deal effectively with the constraints you face. You know enough about the expectancy theory of motivation to apply it successfully to yourself in this way.

WHEN NOTHING WORKS

The strategies presented in this book for dealing with employee motivation and performance problems do not always work. Nothing works in every situation. Some employees simply will not perform under any circumstances. No matter what you do, they will not get the job done. They want something for nothing, a free ride. They get their satisfaction from causing problems. They may have personal goals that are inconsistent with the goals of the organization. They may have a lot of energy, but their motivation is directed outside the job.

Leveling Bold

What should be done when nothing works? The approach that gives the best results is called leveling bold. This is similar to leveling, as discussed earlier in this chapter, in which the basic message to the employee is, "You have a performance problem, I do not know what the solution is, maybe you can come up with some final suggestions, and I am willing to help you via preference shifting, substitution, and offsets." Leveling bold takes this a step further. The bolder message is, "You have a performance problem, neither of us has come up with a workable solution, and I am not willing to live with the problem any longer."

This is a bold type of leveling in which you objectively and tactfully convey that the employee must either "shape up or ship out." Is this a cruel way to treat employees? Not at all. At least it doesn't have to be. It is not a message to be shouted with anger, bitterness, or vengeance. Rather, this kind of leveling is done with kindness and concern for the employee. After all, it is based on the belief that employees should be given a final opportunity to take control of the situation and preserve their job if they want to do so. What more could employees expect than a chance to control their own destiny?

How can you level bold with an employee and come across in a positive way? First, there is a prerequisite. Leveling bold should not come until you have already worked with the employee to explore every possible opportunity to solve the problem. If you have done this, and done it in good faith, leveling bold is a logical next step and should not come as a surprise to the employee. Second, the key is what you say and how you say it. Here is an example:

Manager: "Given what you want, and my knowledge of the situation here, I honestly don't believe we will ever be able to meet your needs, certainly not in the forseeable future. You have a lot of capabilities. Have you considered any other opportunities that might suit you better?"

From this point forward, leveling bold follows the process outlined in chapter 5 for transferring and terminating employees. As mentioned in that discussion, this process does not have to be traumatic for either the manager or the employee. Far from it. As you will recall, the approach puts the decision squarely in the hands of employees. It gives them control in a situation where typically they are helpless. They clearly know the alternative is either to improve performance or to face a transfer or termination. It is their choice. Employees appreciate managers who level with them, and they welcome the opportunity to choose. Most employees are not this fortunate.

What should you do when employees choose not to improve performance? The answer is simple. The employee should be replaced. This is not an easy and pleasant solution, but it is the only option under the circumstances. In the life of every manager, there always comes a time when it is necessary to bite the bullet and move ahead. When you have exhausted all options and nothing has worked, the time has come.

CORPORATE REACTION

By now you have formed your own opinion about the expectancy theory of motivation, but what about the reactions of others? The author conducted in-depth interviews with over thirty vice presidents of human resources and corporate directors of management training and development in approximately twenty corporations, including AT&T, BellSouth, Coca-Cola, Delta, Equifax, Georgia Pacific, Home Depot, IBM, Lanier Worldwide, and Lockheed. Each was presented a detailed description of the content of this book. The following is a summary of the reaction of the executives interviewed:

—None of the executives had ever used the expectancy theory of motivation. Only three had ever heard of it.

—Everyone agreed that the theoretical model (chapter 1) was simple and easy to understand.

—They all believed the application model (chapters 2 through 8) was straightforward and practical.

—They all agreed it was the most comprehensive approach to motivation they had ever seen.

—Everyone said it was logical and made sense.

—They all believed it would be relatively easy to learn and use.

—All said they would expect significant increases in performance if the managers in their organizations used the approach.

—More than half showed immediate interest in training their managers in this approach to handling motivation and performance problems.

There was another reaction worth mentioning, too. Everyone viewed the approach in the context of what was going on in their own organizations. As a result, expectancy theory was seen as an important ingredient in managing diversity, improving quality, team building, managing change, performance management, and corporate culture. Let's take a brief look at each of these.

Managing Diversity

The approach to motivation presented in this book focuses on the individual. It doesn't assume all employees are motivated the same way. It does not call for global approaches to motivation. Instead, it recognizes that people are different and maintains that the best way to get people to perform is to focus on their individuality. Several of the executives put it another way. They said the approach recognizes that there is diversity in the workforce and presents helpful strategies for managing diversity. This is true.

Total Quality

The quality movement today is based largely on the belief that empowering employees is the key to quality improvement. There are two assumptions here. The first is that all employees want to be empowered. The second is that all employees can handle everything that comes with empowerment. Some of the executives interviewed pointed out the danger of these assumptions. They see quality improvement as coming only when employees are motivated to improve quality, and they view the expectancy theory of motivation as a better way to achieve quality than empowering everyone regardless of whether he or she wants it (B3) or can handle it (B1). Good point.

Team Building

Some of the executives who were interviewed focused on the use of expectancy theory in team building. They said a common problem was that team members often had difficulty getting members of their own team and members of other teams to cooperate with them, to attend meetings, to complete key tasks on time, etc. Because team members have no authority over each other, they frequently feel helpless when their success depends on others. They wanted to know if it was possible to teach team members how to motivate each other using expectancy theory. The answer is yes.

Managing Change

Many organizations are undergoing tremendous change today. Managing change can be overwhelming, especially in view of the wide-ranging reactions of employees. For this reason, several of the executives interviewed indicated an interest in using the expectancy theory of motivation as part of the change process. Their thinking is that it would enable managers better to address the individual needs and concerns of employees and consequently would make it easier to motivate employees to perform better in changing environments. It would.

Performance Management

Some organizations are putting performance management systems in place. The idea is to improve organization performance by placing more emphasis on individual performance. Several of the executives interviewed expressed concern about the results of such efforts in their own organizations. They said that other companies were equally concerned. This stems from the realization that the performance management approaches being used are little more than the combining of several popular management techniques that do not fit together well. The executives who saw expectancy theory in the context of performance management believed it to be a superior method of improving individual performance. This is an interesting possibility.

Corporate Culture

Three executives were interviewed in a major company that prides itself on having a corporate culture that places great emphasis on the needs and concerns of its employees. This focus on the employee is accomplished primarily by having large group meetings with employees around the world to identify ways to meet their needs better. It is a method that has worked very well. The three executives believe that training their managers to use the approach outlined in this book is a way both to maintain and to enhance their corporate culture. That is, they believe that by using the one-on-one approach with employees, as called for by the expectancy theory of motivation, managers would be able better to address employee needs and concerns. They would.

SUMMARY

This chapter has focused on some of the most important issues in dealing with motivation and performance problems. You have learned how to do many things that few managers know how to do. All are vitally important to managerial success. Specifically, you have learned (1) how to sit down with an employee and figure out what the problem is and how to solve it, (2) how to handle difficult problems, (3) what to do when your hands are tied, and (4) what to do when nothing works. Finally, you have seen the reaction of key executives to this approach.

Overall, this book has presented a thorough and detailed approach for dealing with motivation and performance problems of employees. It is a practical approach that works. You should feel comfortable with it and confident in it. You also should be confident in your ability to obtain and interpret B1, B2, and B3 information and to select and implement appropriate solutions. The next step is to practice. Reading and understanding take you only so far. Experience will take you the rest of the way. Give it your best try, and you can make it work. Be realistic. Do not expect your first attempts to be perfect. The idea is to improve each time you use the method. You will, if you stick with it. With practice, you will find a level of management capability you never imagined. You will become the kind of manager you always wanted to be.

Selected Bibliography

Green, Thad B., and Hayes, Merwyn A. *Closing the Motivation Gap.* Winston-Salem, N.C.: HRD Consulting, 1992.

Green, Thad B., and Sutton, Kurt H. *InSync Management.* Atlanta: Sutton & Associates, 1991.

Lawler, Edward E. III. *Motivation in Work Organizations.* Monterey, Calif.: Brooks/Cole Publishing Company, 1973.

Michigan Organizational Assessment Package: Progress Report II. Ann Arbor, Mich.: Survey Research Center, Institute for Social Research, University of Michigan, 1975.

Nadler, David, and Lawler, Edward E. III. "Motivation: A Diagnostic Approach." In J. Richard Hackman, Edward E. Lawler III, and Lyman W. Porter, eds., *Perspectives on Behavior in Organizations.* 2d ed. New York: McGraw-Hill, 1983.

Vroom, Victor H. *Work and Motivation.* New York: John Wiley & Sons, 1964.

Index

About the Author

THAD B. GREEN is a writer and management consultant in Atlanta, Georgia. He has been on the management faculty at the University of Georgia, Auburn University, Mississippi State University, and Emory University. Dr. Green has been a consultant for many major corporations including AT&T, Delta Airlines, The Coca-Cola Company, Georgia-Pacific, Holiday Inns, Outboard Marine Corporation, and many government agencies including the Department of Labor and the Department of Agriculture. His specialty is in the areas of motivation, performance, training, and development.